Medieval Women's Writing

D1566324

Medieval Women's Writing

Works by and for Women in England, 1100–1500

DIANE WATT

polity

First published in 2007 by Polity Press

Polity Press
65 Bridge Street
Cambridge CB2 1UR, UK

Polity Press
350 Main Street
Malden, MA 02148, USA

ISBN-13: 978-07456-3255-1
ISBN-13: 978-07456-3256-8 (pb)

A catalogue record for this book is available from the British Library.

Typeset in 11.25 on 13 pt Dante
by SNP Best-set Typesetter Ltd., Hong Kong
Printed and bound in Great Britain by MPG Books Ltd, Bodmin, Cornwall

The publisher has used its best endeavours to ensure that the URLs for external websites referred to in this book are correct and active at the time of going to press. However, the publisher has no responsibility for the websites and can make no guarantee that a site will remain live or that the content is or will remain appropriate.

Every effort has been made to trace all copyright holders, but if any have been inadvertently overlooked the publishers will be pleased to include any necessary credits in any subsequent reprint or edition.

For further information on Polity, visit our website: www.polity.co.uk

Contents

Acknowledgements

Medieval Women's Writing is a book that I have wanted to write for a long time. Years of studying, learning, teaching, listening and conversing lie behind it; the writing was, of course, just the final stage. The debts I have accumulated are so many that it is not possible to acknowledge all of them here. Nevertheless, it is a pleasure to identify some individuals and organizations that have made this book possible. I would like to thank Jocelyn Wogan-Browne for her generous support and encouragement, and Karen Cherewatuk for the help she gave me in the project's earlier stages. Amy Appleford, Ruth Evans and Nicholas Watson shared work with me prior to publication, from which I benefited greatly. For the opportunity to present research that went into this book, I would like to thank Raluca Radulescu, Bob Hasenfratz, Glenn Burger and Steve Kruger, Emma Campbell, Anke Bernau and David Matthews, and Liz Herbert McAvoy and Colman O'Clabaigh. In Fall 2005, I had the good fortune to be awarded the Charles A. Owen, Jr Distinguished Visiting Professorship in Medieval Studies at the University of Connecticut. The graduate class I taught there enabled me to explore some of the ideas in this book with exceptionally motivated and lively students. Special mention must be made of Josh Eyler, Erin Lien, Nadia Pawelchak, Becky Perry and Britt Rothauser. Thanks also to Bob Hasenfratz for inviting me to Connecticut, and for doing so much to make me feel welcome. I should also mention my doctoral students working on medieval literature at Aberystwyth University, past and present, especially Liz Herbert McAvoy, Malte Urban, Robin Gilbank and Janet Gunning. I extend a general thanks to all the Masters and undergraduate students over the years who have shared my love of medieval women's writing, for our lively discussions and for their perceptive and sometimes hilarious observations, which often enabled me to see old texts in a completely new light. I am grateful to the Department of English Literature at Aberystwyth University and the Arts and Humanities Research Council for enabling me to take a year's study leave in 2006, thus making possible the timely completion of this book. I would also like to thank Sally-Ann Spencer, formerly commissioning editor for literary studies at Polity, for inviting me to write the book in the first place, and especially her successor, Andrea Drugan, for seeing it through to realization with such enthusiasm, patience and professionalism. The anonymous readers for Polity and assessors for the Arts and Humanities Research Council offered engaged, thoughtful and constructive criticism at various stages of this project, from inception to completion. Heike Bauer has been here throughout to discuss ideas, to read and to comment upon my writing, to suggest new perspectives and to offer me much needed reassurance. I can never thank her enough. Patricia Watt has, once again, been a careful reader of my work. Clare A. Lees also read the draft manuscript, made many useful suggestions and was incredibly compassionate in her criticisms. In the final stages of the writing of this book, Clare and I shared many ideas, and, indeed, the afterword arose directly out of one of our conversations. It is through knowing her that I have gained new insights into how collaboration and feminism work, and work together. This book is, therefore, dedicated to Clare.

A Note on the Texts

In this book, accessibility has been one of my primary concerns. My target audience includes undergraduate students as well as postgraduates and scholars working in the field of medieval English literature, as well as those interested in women's writing in later periods, and in literary history, and specifically feminist literary history. The medieval works I discuss here are written in Latin and French as well as Old and Middle English. I have therefore decided, wherever possible, to quote from my sources in modern English, either using readily available published translations, or providing my own translations or modernizations. However, in order to preserve some sense of the original languages, and to enable some attention to linguistic detail, wherever I quote at length I also provide the original text following the translation. In addition, I quote and discuss the original language in the text of my argument where it is crucial to a specific point that I am making. I have followed these practices whatever the language of the original text because I do not want to imply a linguistic hierarchy or to make any assumptions about the linguistic training of my readers. Only limitations of space have prevented me from quoting in translation *and* in the original languages throughout.

Introduction

When did women writers first enter the English literary tradition? This apparently straightforward question is impossible to answer simply because it is the wrong one to ask. Women's writing in the Middle Ages, especially prior to the fourteenth century, remains peripheral not only to conventional masculinist accounts of the literary canon but also to feminist (re-)constructions of *women's* literary history. The relative dearth of texts identifiable as by women and the lack of biographical information about medieval women writers have contributed to this tendency. Other factors include the often religious (and thus 'non-literary') content of surviving works, the problem of writing not in the medium of English, and the question of authorial agency in medieval culture's different models of the relationship between composition and writing. This study, which examines women's writing produced in England, primarily in the period between 1100 and 1500, and written in the three literary languages of the period, Latin, French and English, aims to stand as a corrective. The very existence of a 'tradition' of women's writing in the Middle Ages is still in fact widely contested. This applies especially to the marginalized Anglo-Saxon period, which, although chronologically outside the scope of this study as a whole, is considered in terms of the continuity of influence of the Old English saints' lives and in relation to questions of their reception. Most medieval women's writing was religious in content and so the primary focus here is on devotional texts – specifically saints' lives and visionary and mystical treatises – although more overtly literary works, as well as personal letters, are included. Atypically of studies of women's literary history, women's writing is here interpreted broadly to include both writing *by* women ('women-authored'), such as Marie de France, Clemence of Barking, Julian of Norwich, Margery Kempe and the Paston women, and writing *for* and *about* women ('women-oriented'), such as *The Life of Christina of Markyate*, the St Albans Psalter and the legends of women saints by Osbern Bokenham. A central argument of this book is that the drawing of a firm distinction between these types of texts does not necessarily stand up to scrutiny:

that female patrons, audiences, readers and even subjects can contribute to the production of texts and their meanings, whether they be written by men or by women. In other words, only an understanding of medieval textual production as *collaborative* enables us to grasp the nature and extent of women's engagement with and contribution to literary culture.

This introduction addresses two central questions. The first is: What can studies of medieval women's writing contribute to our understanding of women's literary history more broadly; in other words, in what ways can they challenge pre-existing exclusionary paradigms and help to construct new enabling ones? The second question is to what extent medieval notions of 'authorship' are useful when considering women's writing. As we will see in the next section, feminist scholars have made the case for extending the definition of women's writing to include a range of texts not typically considered women-authored. The scope of this book differs somewhat in emphasis in its inclusion of women-oriented texts alongside original compositions by women, translations, compilations and a range of texts that are the product of collaboration between a female 'author' and male secretaries. Furthermore, at the end of the final chapter on the letters of the Paston women, I specifically examine the problems with trying to identify the 'gender' of a narrative voice. Underpinning my selection of authors and texts is the conviction that writing cannot be understood in isolation from its intended and/or actual readership or audience, an audience that for some of these texts may be not exclusively female but male or mixed. In addressing the question of authorship, I explore the ways authors and readers/audience work together to produce meaning. Ultimately the blurring of the distinction between women-authored and women-oriented texts that I trace could be extended to other medieval texts, from conduct books to romances, and to a broader range of devotional material produced for and read by women, including manuscripts and miscellanies known to have been owned by women. Importantly, the insights that emerge from this study might usefully be extended to women's writings of other (earlier and later) periods.

Women's literary history

Women's literary history, and more specifically the tracing of an *English* tradition of women's writing, has its own history and politics. The starting point for the search for a women's literary history is usually taken to be the publication of Virginia Woolf's *A Room of One's Own* in 1928.[1] In this extended essay, Woolf lamented what she perceived to be the absence of

women writers throughout literary history. The recovery and recupera-
tion of texts authored by women and the controversial attempts to establish an alternative women's canon of English literature are closely associated
with Anglo-American feminist writers and critics. Key formative works
were (to name only a few): Kate Millett's *Sexual Politics*, Ellen Moers's *Literary Women*, Elaine Showalter's *A Literature of their Own* and Sandra M.
Gilbert and Susan Gubar's *The Madwoman in the Attic*.[2] More recent articulations and reformulations of the debate include Janet Todd's *Feminist Literary History*, Margaret J. M. Ezell's *Writing Women's Literary History*, Joan
M. Ferrante's *To the Glory of her Sex*, Laurie A. Finke's *Women's Writing in
English* and Jennifer Summit's *Lost Property*.[3] Numerous anthologies make
available some of the primary texts discussed in these studies: one of the
most influential being Gilbert and Gubar's *The Norton Anthology of Literature
by Women*.[4] The first edition of *The Norton Anthology of Literature by Women*
famously characterizes the medieval and Early Modern period as the 'Dark
Ages' of 'the female imagination'.[5] Although the earliest of these feminist
literary histories do not address women's writing in the early and pre-
modern periods, some of the more recent publications make this lacuna
the specific focus of attention.

In recent years, a great deal of research has been undertaken successfully
to identify female authors and their works and to explore the extent of
their impact and influence in their own time. An increasing number of
surveys of women's writing extend back to at least the high Middle Ages.[6]
Yet as Jennifer Summit has also shown, the notion of the lost female author
was, *from the beginning*, an integral part of the conceptualization of the
English literature: that at the very point it was first formulated in the later
Middle Ages and the Early Modern period, the woman writer, even when
highly visible to contemporaries, was already always constructed as absent
from the literary tradition. According to Summit:

> The idea of the 'lost' woman writer can be traced to the medieval and
> Early Modern periods, in which 'the woman writer' emerged as a unified
> cultural category through her perceived opposition to literary tradition.
> This is not to argue that women writers were thereby removed from liter-
> ary history – to the contrary, they are present to a surprising degree at the
> key sites at which 'English literature' is first invented. But they enter these
> sites as emblems of loss and figures of a literature that tradition fails to
> enshrine.[7]

Yet Summit's conclusions cannot simply be transported back to even
earlier periods where the absence of women writers is even more

pronounced. In a key essay first published before *Lost Property*, Clare A. Lees and Gillian R. Overing argue that both Anglo-Saxon religious historian Bede and twentieth-century Anglo-Saxonists have conspired in their representation of Cædmon's *Hymn* as the 'birth' of English poetry, to exclude completely his patron, Abbess Hild, from this originary narrative.[8] Here the omission of women's involvement in cultural production is the product of 'forgetting' rather than a more symbolic negation, but it is as a result possibly more destructive in its consequences. The 'problem' of women's writing in the earliest eras of the history of writing in England is a very real one, even if here, as in later periods, it is partly a matter of (mis-)perception.

Summit's study, which cuts across the medieval/Early Modern divide, takes as its starting point the latter part of the chronological range covered in this book. The most important aspect of Summit's contribution is that she adds a gendered dimension to our awareness that the construction of the literary canon emerged from a growing sense of a national and linguistic identity. My primary focus here is not, however, on the early construction of the literary canon itself and how women fit into it, but rather on what sort of women's writing and women's engagement in textual production existed in the later medieval period. That is, I am interested in what sort of tradition of women's writing can be traced. My approach is then perhaps pragmatic rather than highly conceptual, but I am also interested in why this tradition is often overlooked, and what an understanding of it might contribute to our understanding of feminist literary history per se. Ezell's ground-breaking work, *Writing Women's Literary History*, offers a nuanced analysis of the ways pre-existing, evolutionary models of women's literary history exclude writing by women produced before the eighteenth century. Ezell makes the case for prioritizing archival research over theorization; in other words, for allowing the theories to arise out of the empirical evidence. She also argues for less restrictive preconceptions about the trajectory of women's literary history and indeed about what counts as women's writing and about the reality of early and pre-modern women's lives, education, levels of literacy, and social isolation and integration. As Ezell points out, we should not assume that women's literary history mirrors that of men, and that the same period and genre boundaries apply. It is crucial that, for the earlier periods, we have more enabling and elastic definitions of authorship (to include pseudonymous, anonymous and collaborative texts), and of literary production (to include privately circulated and uncirculated manuscripts and domestic or household texts as well as more widely disseminated or professionally published works). It is equally crucial that, while we may legitimately look for an articulation of women's interests, we do not approach women's texts with the expectation or requirement that they will be proto-feminist, politically radical and alienated. In other words, we have to be attuned not solely to similarities and consanguinity but also to differences and discontinuities.

Critics working specifically within the field of medieval women's writing have made parallel claims and constructed similar arguments to those working with material from later periods. In an influential essay entitled ' "Mothers to Think Back Through": Who are They?' Sheila Delaney launches an attack on a strand of criticism that seeks to resurrect Christine de Pizan's reputation as a champion of women and women's rights, rather than to offer an impartial assessment of her privilege and conservatism within her own social and historical context.[9] Disabling stereotypes, not only about the disempowering potential of medieval antifeminist images of women, but also about women's illiteracy, lack of education and cultural isolation – stereotypes that misrepresent those women writers whose existence is acknowledged as necessarily exceptional rather than representative – have been successfully challenged and refuted.[10] Notably, the greater awareness of the need to represent writing in languages other than English for the early period has enabled a better understanding of the range of female-authored texts. A vivid illustration of this is the inclusion of Marie de France in the third edition of the *Norton Anthology of Literature by Women* (2007). Critics such as Alexandra Barratt, Julia Boffey and Laurie A. Finke have debated questions such as whether certain anonymous texts should be (re-)considered as female-authored, and also whether definitions of what constitutes women's writings in medieval England should extend to translations and compilations by women, and even translations by men of texts authored by women in other languages and cultures.[11] Such approaches can seem essentialist and it is equally crucial that we have a more developed understanding of literary communities and networks and that we acknowledge that women can be involved in literary production in a range of other ways, as scribes and annotators, for example, or as patrons and book-owners. Extending our definitions of women's writing further, as did Carol M. Meale in the early 1990s, to include writing that is produced for and read by women enables a more subtle understanding of women's engagement with medieval literary culture.[12]

This book does not act upon all the recommendations put forward by feminist critics theorizing the early periods of women's literary history, but it does accept their validity. In concentrating primarily on the period 1100–1500, I apply this thinking to an already well-known body of work and do not challenge accepted definitions of the late medieval period. I do not extend my range of reference into the English Renaissance, even though the applicability of the medieval / Early Modern divide to women's history is one that I have questioned elsewhere.[13] Equally, although reference is made in this book to Anglo-Saxon work, I do not attempt to address fully the specific problems for women's literary history raised by writing in Old English. Indeed it is perhaps a particular limitation of this study that it only partially engages with the already marginalized Anglo-Saxon period. This is an area that has already been considered by Lees and Overing in *Double Agents*, but it is important to see this work as only a starting point. Whereas, according to the *Norton Anthology of Literature by Women*, there are 'no texts in the Old English period that have been definitively identified as composed by women', Lees and Overing are more circumspect, observing that 'texts written by women are few and far between'.[14] Their analysis, which looks at Latin texts, including letters, historical records and legal documents, alongside Old English texts such as saints' lives and riddles, is theoretically and methodologically distinct from but nevertheless broadly complementary to my own. Due to the scale of the project undertaken, this study does not attempt to offer a fully comprehensive survey of the entire range of writing by and for women in Middle English, or in the late medieval period, or of women's engagement with manuscript and book cultures more generally. Notable omissions from this book are anonymous texts for which an argument of female authorship can be made, and translations by men of works of Continental women writers – specifically Christine de Pizan (*c*.1364–*c*.1431), who was popular in England in the century after her death, but from the evidence seems to have been particularly widely read by men.[15] Also excluded is Joan of Arc (1412–31), who certainly has strong connections with English culture. Indeed this book as a whole is largely and self-consciously insular in its scope. While it is crucial, for example, that we should not ignore the debts the English women visionaries owe to Continental European mystics, these have hitherto been emphasized at the expense of exploring specifically English traditions. But a focus on the English tradition has its casualties. Two English women translators who are not discussed, but whose existence and works must be acknowledged, are Eleanor Hull (*c*.1394–1460) and Lady Margaret Beaufort, countess of Richmond and Derby (1443–1509). The former was a pious gentlewoman who served in the household of Henry IV before retiring to a religious community. She translated two French devotional works (a meditation on the days of the week and a commentary on the Psalms) into English prose. The latter was mother to the future Henry VII. She translated part of Thomas à Kempis's *The Imitation of Christ* and the *Speculum Aureum* or *Mirror of Gold*. Margaret Beaufort was deeply engaged in humanist scholarship and extended her patronage to John Fisher, bishop of Rochester, and the two early printers, William Caxton and Wynkyn de Worde.

Constraints of space have meant that I have also not been able to include one of the most well-known and widely studied Middle English texts written for women, *Ancrene Wisse* or 'The Guide for Anchoresses'. Also excluded from consideration are the works (*Hali Meiðhad* or 'Holy Virginity', and *Sawles Warde* or 'The Custody of the Soul') which, together with the legends of Katherine, Margaret and Juliana, make up the 'Katherine Group', and a related set of texts known as the 'Wooing Group'. *Ancrene Wisse*, for example, vividly illustrates the importance audience plays in the composition and revision of a text. Originally written for three female recluses, it clearly addresses them and their situation (although it is fascinating to consider what it misses out, as well as what it includes). Subsequently the work was altered for a larger community, and versions of the text exist which are aimed at readerships quite different from that originally inscribed or implied. *Hali Meiðhad* ('Holy Virginity'), and *Sawles Warde* ('The Custody of the Soul') share the spiritual concerns of *Ancrene Wisse*, especially its advocacy of almost complete withdrawal from the world, self-discipline and moderation. Questions that emerge are to what extent these texts actually would have appealed to and catered for real women, and to what extent they might be constrained by their inherent antifeminism (for which they are indebted to their Latin sources and models). The lyrical treatises on the love of God that make up the 'Wooing Group' provide us with further and rather different examples of the sort of devotional works that female recluses would have read, and that would have provided inspiration for their contemplative practices. Discussion of texts such as these would strengthen rather than undermine the arguments I put forward here. But while this study makes no claims to be definitive or exhaustive, what it does is offer a broader understanding of women's writing of the period in general and a detailed analysis of the specific (already widely studied and thus in some sense canonical) writers and texts under discussion.

Medieval women as authors?

The biographical and personal nature of, for example *The Life of Christina of Markyate*, *The Book of Margery Kempe* and the Paston letters, provides us with a wealth of information about the lives of some of the women in this book. This information is sometimes, although not always, supported and supplemented by surviving historical records. Yet many of the women in this study, including Clemence of Barking and Julian of Norwich, remain elusive figures. Marie de France is another case in point, and it is useful to examine the arguments surrounding this figure in order to explore more fully the issue of female authorship. The only evidence external to the manuscripts of 'Marie's' poems that supports her existence comes from her contemporary Denis Piramus. Writing around 1180 in the court of Henry II and Eleanor of Aquitaine, Piramus talks about the popularity of the lais of 'Lady Marie' amongst its men and women, which cause great praise to be heaped on her.[16] Various theories about Marie's identity have been proposed: one popular one is that Marie was the illegitimate daughter of Geoffrey Plantagenet, count of Anjou, and thus Henry II's half-sister. This Marie was born in France and was abbess of Shaftesbury between 1181 and 1216, and her life seems compatible with Marie de France's writings and vice versa. Three works are generally attributed to Marie de France: the *Lais*, the *Fables* and *Saint Patrick's Purgatory*. Her authorship of a fourth, an early thirteenth-century French translation of the Latin *Life of St Audrey* is widely contested.[17] However, it is important to remember that doubt remains not only over Marie's identity but also about whether even the first three works were all written by the same woman.

This enduring doubt is a key point: Marie de France might usefully be thought of in terms of what Michel Foucault has called an *author-function*. According to Foucault, the author is a function of discourse which 'permits one to group together a certain number of texts, define them, differentiate them from and contrast them to others'.[18] Certainly, the 'discovery' of Marie de France coincides with the emergence of the idea of the 'literary' author that Foucault traces back to the Early Modern period.[19] It is as if Marie de France were *invented* to fulfil a need for a specifically female author at this transitional moment in literary history; certainly, her 'discovery' seems rather fortuitous. But to think about Marie de France in terms of the author-function rather than as an author is not necessarily any more constructive than to dwell on doubts about her authenticity without any firm evidence to support the case against it. In an important response to Roland Barthes's 1968 essay 'The Death of the Author', in which Barthes famously called for a focus on the reader rather than the author, Nancy Miller makes the following claim:

The postmodern decision that the Author is Dead and the subject with him does not, I will argue, necessarily hold for women, and prematurely forecloses the question of agency for them.[20]

Miller goes on to observe that because 'women have not had the same historical relation of identity to origin, institution, production, that men have had' their relationship to textuality and authority is itself necessarily distinct.[21] From the perspectives of current feminist criticism and of women's literary history as it is constructed today, with its dearth of early women writers, the need for the *named* female author – whether Marie de France, Clemence of Barking, Julian of Norwich or Margery Kempe – necessarily remains very much alive. Yet, as Summit puts it, 'the modern idea of the author as a single, creative individual holds limited relevance for medieval textual culture . . . and limited application to the writings of medieval women'.[22] I will argue below that our definitions of women authors and women writers needs to be flexible enough to embrace a whole range of possibilities in terms of textual production, including translation, compilation, collaboration (especially in relation to visionary and devotional writing and hagiography) and patronage. In this respect our definitions need to extend far beyond the author-function described by Foucault. Thus, for example, while Foucault suggests that letters do not have an author, in the sense of an author-function, it is imperative that any study of medieval women's writing should be wide-ranging enough to include correspondence such as that of the Paston women.[23] Furthermore, in all of these cases, the role of the reader remains crucial.

If the idea of the author also has a history and a politics, then understanding what the author and authority meant in the Middle Ages and how these concepts related to women is essential. The criteria of originality that is so central to post-Romantic definitions had no relevance to medieval definitions of authorship, quite the contrary. God was considered the ultimate *author* or *auctor*, and the Bible was the source of all written authority or *auctoritas*. Author could also mean 'writer' but it was associated with the classical writers and the patriarchs of the Church, in other words with writers and thinkers of long ago, who were inevitably male.[24] Anonymous medieval texts were often ascribed (and those by known writers were often re-ascribed) to such august figures from the often distant past. Similarly medieval writers gained credibility for their own work by positioning it in relation to ancient authorities. Paradoxically women writers, such as Julian of Norwich or Margery Kempe in the book of her life, who were excluded

from authority because of their sex were, as visionaries, also able to appropriate authority for their work by claiming that it was the product of divine
inspiration. Julian of Norwich declared in her *Vision*: 'But because I am a
woman must I therefore believe that I must not tell you of the goodness
of God, when I saw at the same time that it is His will that it should be
known?'[25] Indeed, writers of other kinds of religious and devotional texts,
such as Clemence of Barking in her translation of the *Life of St Catherine* or
Marie de France in *Saint Patrick's Purgatory* defer to God in order to justify
their texts.

Even male medieval scholars, poets and writers did not see themselves
as authors but described themselves as lesser figures, as scribes, compilers
and commentators.[26] One named late medieval male writer whose work is
examined in this book, Osbern Bokenham, introduces his *Legends of Holy
Women* in the conventional terms of the academic prologue tradition. At
the same time he situates himself in relation to other medieval writers (in
Latin and in English), including most famously, Geoffrey Chaucer, and also,
I argue, John Gower. Nevertheless, Bokenham's collection of female saints'
lives is of course a work of compilation. Clearly this does not mean that
Bokenham's work lacks what we would now call originality. Indeed, it is
exactly because the hagiographic genre is so formulaic that the innovations
made by an individual writer become noteworthy. Bokenham's input is
evidenced not only in his prologues but also in the choice of lives (some of
which reflect the choice of his patrons) and the retelling of the lives themselves. The medieval definition of the writer as compiler was one that could
be fairly readily appropriated by women (more so than that of the role of
commentator, with its explicit or implicit assumption of clerical learning).
Marie de France, for example, represents her *Lais* and *Fables* as compilations,
at least in part. As such, Marie's poems are the articulation of the memories,
words and texts of others. Tellingly, the *Lais* are described by Marie in her
Prologue to the Harley manuscript as based on her recollection of lais she
had heard, which were themselves 'composed' by others 'to perpetuate the
memory of adventures they had heard';[27] in other words they are memories
of memories. The *Purgatory* even incorporates the voices and memories of
the dead. Yet this does not necessarily make Marie's poems derivative and
lacking innovation or what we would now think of as originality. Julian of
Norwich, in her earlier *Vision Showed to a Devout Woman*, depicts her role
as that of compiler, bringing together the revelations that God had granted
her. However, in her later *Revelation of Love* she is far more assertive, offering her own extended commentaries on and interpretations of her showings, although these also she ascribes to divine grace.

In addition to scribes, compilers and commentators, another category of writer whose role was acknowledged in the Middle Ages, albeit as a subordinate and derivative one, was the translator, who transformed a text from one language to another. Bokenham, for example, describes himself as such, as does Clemence of Barking in her *Life of St Catherine*. Marie de France's poems are also presented as either direct (the *Fables*, *Saint Patrick's Purgatory*) or indirect (the *Lais*) translations. No matter how self-effacing, translators, like compilers, make choices (about which text they will translate, about what to include and what to omit, about register and language) which allow them to augment and to change their sources. Even a translation that stays close to its 'original' is in its deference making some sort of statement about its understanding of the authority of that original. When a translation does not, but makes substantial innovations, the translator effectively elevates her or his own status. Bokenham, Clemence of Barking and Marie de France all reflect in the prologues and introductions to their 'translations' about their relationship to patristic, classical, and Latin and vernacular traditions. Bokenham sees himself in terms of clerical authority; Marie de France and Clemence of Barking, as women, have no entitlement to it, although Clemence and also Marie, especially in the *Purgatory*, usurp it. All three writers also make use of the opportunity to articulate their reasons for writing. These include the preservation of texts that might be forgotten or that have become corrupted and fallen out of favour and the defence of their own reputation and fame. But they are also driven by, variously, personal devotion, the moral imperative to share knowledge, to teach others and thus to preserve their spiritual welfare, and ultimately by a concern with individual and communal salvation. At the same time these writers express awareness of the aesthetic value of eloquence and of the recreational uses of poetry. Such articulations of authorial self-consciousness offer us important insights into medieval theories of writing and reception. What is striking however is that Marie de France situates herself within a range of hitherto exclusively male traditions and that neither Clemence of Barking nor Marie de France *explicitly* addresses the problems and difficulties of writing as a woman.

It is nevertheless the consideration of the role of scribe that exposes a major faultline in any discussion of female authorship in the Middle Ages. However, to understand why this is the case it is imperative that some consideration be given to questions of literacy. Earlier I mentioned the stereotype of the illiterate medieval woman, and like most stereotypes, there is of course some grain of truth behind it. Although Marie de France was multilingual, well versed in reading and writing in the full range of languages of late twelfth-century England (including, apparently, Old English, Welsh, French and Latin), as well as Breton, she must have been exceptionally privileged. Indeed medieval definitions of literacy as the ability to read Latin would have excluded almost all women and the vast majority of laymen, and even knowledge of the vernaculars (French and English) would have been restricted to an elite few. Furthermore levels of literacy vary not only across social classes but also between the sexes. In the early period, if Latin was the language of the clergy, French was that of the convents. Vocation is also a key factor. Nuns and recluses like Clemence of Barking, and almost certainly also Julian of Norwich would have had greater literacy in the Latin and/or their vernaculars than many laywomen. The question of literacy was clearly complex. At the early end of our period, Christina of Markyate may not have been able to write but she probably had some reading skills, possibly in Latin and French as well as English. But there was no straightforward teleology of literacy, with levels simply improving across all sectors of society as time progressed. Nevertheless, for laywomen in particular, the widespread use of scribes means that it is easy to miss the evidence of literacy. Furthermore, research in the last two decades has shown that many women as well as men would have been part of reading and writing communities and networks and thus had greater access to literate and literary cultures than has previously been acknowledged.[28] Extending our understanding of literate practices to include activities and processes such as communal reading, dictation, memorization and recitation provides a fuller picture of women's engagement with textuality. Margery Kempe and Margaret Paston clearly had some functional literacy that enabled their entry into the world of manuscripts and letters. Indeed, Margery Kempe's *Book* records an incident that occurred while she was kneeling in church with a book in her hand.[29] As Summit states, 'women who did not compose texts in their own hands nonetheless had a variety of means at their disposal to register their creative influence on textual culture.'[30]

A number of the women considered in this study then either did or may have relied on others to read and write for them. Throughout this book, I prefer the term *secretary* to that of *scribe*. As I explain in the chapter on *The Book of Margery Kempe*, the term *secretary* carries with it connotations of confidentiality, trust and intimacy not present in the term *scribe*, with its connotations of professional disinterest. Margery Kempe's first secretary was her own son, and her principal secretary was a priest to whom she was willing to confess her life story and religious experiences, including times of doubt and temptation. These secretaries were in a privileged position, but their position was also a subordinate one: they fully acknowledged the authority of Kempe herself. Margaret Paston likewise, as the most prolific correspondent in a prolific family, relied on secretaries to write for her, and chose men in whom she could confide and on whom she felt she could rely. These included the family chaplain, and again her own offspring, and she sometimes both asked them to and apparently allowed them to write letters in her own name. Dame Elizabeth Brews and her daughter Margery Brews, John Paston III's fiancée, clearly regarded their household servant Thomas Kela extremely highly. They not only entrusted him with writing down and writing out apparently private letters (including Margery's love letters) but also suffered, or encouraged, him to enter directly into the exchange of correspondence. The relations between secretaries and women's textual production could be extremely complex, and, in the case of Margery Kempe and possibly also Julian of Norwich, the secretaries played editorial roles and even, as clerics, lent the texts validation. Nevertheless, ultimately, in all of the examples just cited, the male secretary, whether writing a letter or a devotional text, remains deferential to his female authority. Thus, if Kempe relied on secretaries to write for her, she is in turn described as one of 'Our Lord's own secretaries', entrusted with divine revelations kept from ordinary men and women, including her own confidants.[31]

Collaborative writing: an alternative model

It is clear, then, that neither modern nor medieval definitions of authorship and literacy are adequate to describe the complex processes by which women contributed to and engaged in textual production. As noted already, the central argument of this book is that in thinking about women's writing in the Middle Ages we have to remember that medieval textual production was primarily collaborative – that texts were not simply composed by a single person, male or female. Women writers are often characterized as alienated from patriarchal culture and tradition, but this is not necessarily the case; or at any rate it is not the whole story. For religious women in particular, the necessity of forming strong associations with confessors and spiritual directors who not only guide but also legitimize their acts of devotion and visionary experiences is reflected in the way the textual testaments to their piety are produced. Books of revelation, attributed to the mystic herself but often written with the help of a secretary, and lives of devout women written by a hagiographer who may be his subject's close associate, or even confessor, are often produced in parallel ways. *The Life of Christina of Markyate* was written by an anonymous monk who knew her personally and who was able to elicit information about her experiences and visions from interviews and conversations with her immediate associates (in particular her close male supporter, Geoffrey of St Albans), even if she did not confide in him personally. *The Book of Margery Kempe* was largely dictated directly by Kempe to her secretaries. Discussing texts of this kind, Summit asks rhetorically, 'Who is the author: scribe or visionary, hagiographer or saint?' and provides the answer that 'all position themselves not as originators but as recorders of divinely inspired text that originates elsewhere'.[32] But in all such religious texts the woman as subject is still granted greater authority below God himself than her secretary or hagiographer.

Furthermore, it is useful to consider here the question of the woman's voice and its relationship to women's writing. Feminist discussions of women's writing, whether medieval, Early Modern, modern or contemporary, have often focused on women's voice, speech and silence.[33] Yet any consideration of women's voice, be it absent or present, mediated or muted, is problematic when the nature of the evidence is only textual. It can seem an impossible task to excavate the oral because it involves removing the 'layers of textual mediation that intervene between the moment of composition and that of reception'.[34] Nevertheless the question of retrieving the female voice is one that is addressed in the first and last chapters of this book, and this sometimes involves going back to a point that is prior even to that of composition. In the discussion of *The Life of Christina of Markyate* in Chapter 1, I look for where Christina's own voice, revered and respected as it is, might be located within her hagiography, and the extent to which it is (un)recoverable. In my examination of the Paston letters in Chapter 6 I address the question of the 'lost' voices of the rebellious daughters Margery and Elizabeth Paston and the deliberate attempts at their silencing and suppression. In my discussion of the collaborative processes of letter composition, I also specifically address the problem of defining the female voice. If the signature on a letter is no guarantee of authorship in a period where secretaries are widely used and illiteracy is common, the inclusion of a writer's name is certainly no testimony to composition. What happens when a male letter writer imitates or inhabits the voice of a female letter writer, when a man seems to masquerade as a woman, either on her behalf or at any rate with her consent? Whose voice do we hear, and who is the writer? Again, only a collaborative understanding of authorship, writing and, in this case, even voice can take account of such modes of composition.[35]

An understanding of women's writing as the product of collaboration enables us to pay greater attention to the role of readers and audience in the production of meaning.[36] Again, Marie de France provides a useful starting point to think about this issue. As we have seen, Marie's poems are presented as the products of different kinds of collaboration: both as compilations and as translations. On the one hand, the roles of the translator and compiler are potentially extremely creative – and Marie, more than most, makes these roles her own. On the other hand, as Mary Carruthers has convincingly argued, medieval identities or selves might better be thought of in terms of the 'subject-who-remembers' whereby subjectivity is expressed not through the expression of difference but with recourse to recollection of a 'chorus of voices' of commonplaces and textual authorities from the past.[37] As we will see in Chapter 2, Marie takes the oral and written texts of others and transforms them into her own poetry. Furthermore, Marie's poems (with their ellipses and open-ended conclusions) are also collaborative in so far as they not only invite, but actually require the participation of an active reader, who has to bring her or his own meaning to them in order to make sense of them. Marie's preoccupation with the problems of reader reception further reflects her awareness of the importance of interpretation as well as her fear of misprision. In Chapter 4 we see that Julian of Norwich was also concerned about controlling the ways her showings were understood. Thus in thinking about texts as collaborative products we have to give full consideration to questions of audience and readership, examining evidence of patronage, literary and religious networks and communities, circulation and reception.

Any attempt to identify or to reconstruct medieval audiences has to be approached with caution. Throughout this book, following and adapting Paul Strohm, I distinguish where possible between inscribed, implied, ideal, intended, and primary and secondary audiences, drawing on evidence that is textual, paratextual (dedications and addresses), contextual or extra-textual.[38] Sometimes the evidence about an audience is concrete, as is the case with the Paston letters, where there is often a specified addressee and where annotations by the recipients can be revealing about readers and their responses. At other times it is potentially unreliable (for example, when claims about patronage may be dependent on literary convention), or even hypothetical. However, cautious reconstruction is a necessary and invaluable part of any discussion of medieval audiences and textual communities.

The exchange between letter writers and their recipients, examined in some detail in Chapter 6, is one clear example of the mutual intellectual interdependency of writer and reader and of the blurring of the two roles. Furthermore, even if they did not write themselves, women could profoundly influence literary compositions through acts of commissioning.

The importance of the patron, both as the instigator behind the production of the medieval text and as its intended and ideal audience, illustrates further the symbiotic relationship between writing and reading. The clearest example of this is Bokenham's *Legends of Holy Women*: as we will see in Chapter 3, two of these were written at the explicit request of aristocratic women, while four others are dedicated to women. However, patrons could have books produced not for their own use but as gifts. In Chapter 1 we see that the St Albans Psalter was evidently presented to Christina of Markyate by her spiritual director and it reflects her interests and those of her community, at least in part. At the same time the Psalter illustrates the close interdependency of patron, author and scribe and recipient, reader and subject. Other texts considered in this study – the Old English lives of women saints, *The Life of Christina of Markyate* and Marie de France's *Fables* and *Lais* – were written, it would appear, for male patrons. Nevertheless, these also imply a wider audience that includes women. They are women-oriented texts that address issues that would have had particular significance for women and examine, variously, female relationships (for example, between mothers, fathers and their daughters); female vocations (in the household, court or convent); female experiences (childbirth, motherhood, childlessness, virginity); and the treatment of women more generally. Sometimes connections between texts can indicate how earlier texts were received by later generations of readers: thus, in Chapters 1 and 3, I examine the influence of the Old English saints' lives on Christina of Markyate. Even texts that do not specify patronage nevertheless indicate something of the community of readers (religious or secular, aristocratic or gentry) for which they were intended. Clemence of Barking, for example, seems to have written her *Life of St Catherine* for her own convent, although again this is not exclusively its intended audience and in fact this work seems to have been widely read and disseminated and very well respected. The audiences of Julian of Norwich's showings and of *The Book of Margery Kempe* are less self-evident and in both cases their circulation seems to have been restricted, possibly deliberately. Nevertheless it is clear that all these texts, from the St Albans Psalter and *The Life of Christina of Markyate* to Bokenham's legends and the Paston letters, arise out of their larger textual, spiritual and social communities.

Medieval women's writing

This book engages with a range of current issues in research in medieval women's writing. These include women's literacy and access to education and culture; notions of authority and theories of writing; sites of writing, whether they are the court, religious institutions or the domestic sphere; patronage; textual communities, and literary and religious networks. Given the focus, the methodological approach adopted to address these matters is necessarily feminist and materialist, and is indebted to and builds on research into literary cultures and cultures of literacy and textual criticism. It engages with arguments about women's authorship and writing and reading practices. It takes into account cultural, social, religious and linguistic contexts (especially issues of multilingualism). However the approach is primarily textual and intertextual rather than historicist. To provide an accurate and nuanced account of such a broad chronological period and range of different types of texts, special attention is given to form and genre, medieval ideas about language and literary theories, and evidence of reception.

The first chapter is an examination of the eleventh-century *Life of Christina of Markyate* (a Latin biography of a putative saint) and the famous illustrated St Albans Psalter, which provides a material as well as a visual, literary and devotional context for the *Life*. This is followed by a consideration of one of the first 'English' women writers, the twelfth-century Anglo-Norman poet Marie de France. The book then moves away from an author-based analysis in order to foreground questions of form, genre and function in relation to saints' legends and lives, while focusing on issues of reception and communities and networks in relation to textual production and readership. Deliberately disrupting by extending and cutting across the book's chronological range and across female- and male-authored and oriented texts, the third chapter focuses on the Anglo-Saxon lives of women saints, the late twelfth-century French work of Clemence of Barking, and Osbern Bokenham's mid-fifteenth-century English legends of women saints. This chapter also maps broad linguistic transformations from Old English to French to Middle English. The chapters then return to questions of authorship and readership in relation to late fourteenth- and early fifteenth-century vernacular English texts. In examining the work of Julian of Norwich and Margery Kempe particular attention is paid to authorial self-representation and implied audience, and to what the texts and their manuscript and print histories suggest about their reception and the uses to which they were put. To emphasize the collaboration across the sexes, the final chapter focuses on the fifteenth-century Paston letters rather than solely on the correspondence of the women. These letters offer a unique insight into the composition of medieval texts. In addition to discussing matters of voice, it considers the role of the secretary in the production of women's letters, and what multiple drafts illustrate about the process of composition. Here scrutiny of the original letters also enables exploration of what surviving replies and annotations made by the recipients reveal about readership and reception.

With the exception of Marie de France (a French aristocrat writing, it seems, in the English court), most of the texts examined here are not overtly literary. These texts were written primarily for devotional – or, in the case of the letters, domestic – purposes; they are texts for which their aesthetic qualities are to some extent incidental. While much anonymous and male-authored work is similarly religious or functional, the notion that literariness *evolved* during this period is widely accepted. This survey of women's writing suggests that the trajectory of women's literary history differs from the dominant aesthetic model associated with men's writing. It also crucially suggests that current models of women's literary history have to be rethought in order to take into account the full range of women's engagements with medieval textual culture. It is imperative that women's literary history should take into consideration, alongside the figure of the woman writer, the female patron or book commissioner, the female beneficiary of book patronage, the female subject and, crucially, the woman as audience and as reader.

1

Christina of Markyate
(*c*.1096–after 1155)

Introduction

The Life of Christina of Markyate is an appropriate starting point for this study of writing by and for women, raising as it does questions of patronage, authorship, collaboration, and readership.[1] The Latin biography of a sometime recluse and putative saint, it was written before her death, and reveals an intimate knowledge of its subject. Its anonymous writer was a monk of St Albans who knew Christina. The *Life* provides vivid insights into the difficulties and hardships Christina endured and sometimes overcame in her pursuit of spiritual chastity and a life dedicated to God. An understanding of the political, social and religious tensions of the period is crucial to any interpretation of this work. As an Anglo-Saxon noblewoman devoted to God in post-Conquest England, Christina's position – both privileged and subordinate – was complex, as the descriptions of her fraught relationships with both kin and the wider community reveal. Ultimately, Christina inspired a number of followers, men as well as women, French as well as English, and having taken her vows in *c*.1131, became prioress and foundress of Markyate in 1145.

The famous illustrated St Albans Psalter, which was produced or adapted for Christina and her priory, provides us with a material as well as a visual, literary, devotional and cultural context for reading the *Life*.[2] It also provides us with a pre-text for reading the *Life* because it was produced first, and because the *Life* may have grown out of and responded to it. The Psalter was probably commissioned by the Frenchman Geoffrey de Gorran (abbot of St Albans between 1119 and 1146), which means it would have been produced some time after 1119, and it was almost certainly presented to Christina around the early to mid-1130s. However one distinct section, the Alexis quire, seems to have been written in part and copied by Geoffrey himself and added to the Psalter between the mid-1130s and 1139–40. Geoffrey may subsequently also have commissioned *The Life of Christina of Markyate*, probably in the early to mid-1140s, in other words in his final years. It might have been continued in the short period following his death, but it was certainly concluded abruptly. While one part of the Psalter directly addresses Christina herself and includes very personal reflections on the relationship between Geoffrey and Christina, the *Life* is aimed at Geoffrey as well as at the religious communities at St Albans and Markyate. In this chapter I examine the complex relationship between the St Albans Psalter and *The Life of Christina of Markyate*, paying attention to the implications of the notion that Christina's early eremitic life offered Anglo-Saxon resistance to Norman and French colonialism. This resistance may have been countered by her profession as a nun and by the production of the St Albans Psalter, but is nevertheless partially articulated in the hybrid text of Christina's *Life*.

The chapter is made up of three parts. The first, 'Viewing and reading the St Albans Psalter', focuses in detail on one short text, the 'Discourse on Good and Evil', that appears in the Alexis quire and that is arguably composed by Geoffrey. I am particularly interested here not only in what this text reveals about the spiritual friendship between Geoffrey and Christina, but also in what it tells us about the clearly symbiotic relationship between author and reader, patron and recipient, writer and subject. The second part is entitled 'The *Life* and death of Prioress Christina'. Taking as a starting point an entry relating to St Hilda or Hild, abbess of Whitby, in the St Albans Psalter calendar, it argues that the beginning of *The Life of Christina of Markyate* suggestively echoes Bede's life of Hild. Although Hild's story ends very differently to Christina's, these resonances draw our attention to the *Life*'s debts to the hagiographic genre generally and to the Anglo-Saxon tradition in particular. The final part, ' "My Sunday daughter": reading Christina's *Life*', looks at the degree and nature of collaboration in the writing of the *Life* and develops the idea that the *Life*, despite being commissioned by Geoffrey, fleetingly articulates a repressed Anglo-Saxon voice. This is done, partly through foregrounding insular traditions as well as Christina's links with the indigenous community, partly through veiled anti-French sentiment, but more strikingly through recording the words of her fellow hermit Roger. In summary, the Alexis quire of the St Albans Psalter defines Christina's piety in terms of Continental and specifically French models. Its production supports the theory that Geoffrey tried to redirect Christina's life and learning along lines more familiar to him. The *Life*, even as it defends Geoffrey and celebrates St Albans Abbey, nevertheless offers some resistance to this process.

Viewing and reading the St Albans Psalter

The St Albans Psalter comprises, in addition to a liturgical calendar, a series of miniatures depicting scenes from the Life of Christ, the Alexis quire, the Psalms themselves alongside canticles and collects, and a diptych of St Alban and the psalmist David. The manuscript was produced at St Albans Abbey on the instructions of Geoffrey, abbot of St Albans. It is principally the calendar entries and manuscript illustrations that reveal that it was either designed from its conception for Christina herself, or adapted at some point – perhaps around the time of or in the years following her profession in 1131 – for presentation to her. Two of the illustrations provide the strongest evidence that the Psalter was dedicated to Christina, both emphasizing her intercessory role. In the first, a historiated initial, Christina is represented pleading for the St Albans monks (Psalter, 285). In the second she is depicted praying with her nuns for Geoffrey (Psalter, 403). Yet if Geoffrey was responsible for the Psalter, others contributed to it. Christina's sister Margaret, 'a virgin of admirable simplicity and uprightness' (*Life*, 141), joined the growing community of recluses around Christina at Markyate and subsequently entered the Priory. Margaret may have been responsible for the obits added to the calendar for Christina and members of her family. Tellingly, Margaret's own death is not commemorated, confirming that she was at any rate still alive when these additions were made.[3]

Equally noteworthy is the fact that stitch marks reveal that fabric coverings or curtains were added at an early stage to protect a number of the miniatures in the Psalter (although none in the Alexis quire), often at the expense of the surrounding text. It is feasible that Christina, a talented seamstress, may have been responsible for this innovation.[4] As the existence of the St Albans Psalter indicates, Christina and her companions would still have placed great value on books. We do know that a copy of Christina's *Life*, now lost, was owned by the Priory at Markyate, and thus must certainly have been familiar to the nuns there in the centuries after Christina's death. Nevertheless, the evidence indicates that Christina's own preferred form of cultural production was not the writing of books but weaving, sewing and embroidery. The *Life* recounts that Christina once made woven undergarments for Geoffrey of St Albans, at his request, when he was commanded to travel to Rome on official business (*Life*, 161–3). Other records reveal that a gift of Christina's embroidery – mitres and sandals – was presented to Pope Adrian IV by a successor of Geoffrey, Ralph of St Albans, in 1155.[5]

From this brief summary alone it becomes apparent that the genesis of the Psalter was complex, and that Christina may have made material additions to it. Likewise, even if the Psalter was presented to and adapted for Christina, it must have been intended for the use of others as well. Bella Millett has argued that the Psalter was designed for a larger audience or a range of readers with varying levels of literacy rather than for just one individual.[6] The canticles, collects or prayers, and litany in the St Albans Psalter are appropriate for use in a religious community of women such as that at Markyate.[7] Some aspects of the Psalter, such as the miniatures of the Life of Christ, which include an usually large number of female figures, suggest a general 'feminine bias' and indicate that it was, in part, a woman-oriented text.[8]

At the heart of the St Albans Psalter lies the Alexis quire itself. This seems to have been compiled as an independent project and at some later stage integrated into the Psalter. The Alexis quire is made up of a series of items. It takes its name from the most extended piece, the French *Chanson of St Alexis*. It also includes a letter of Pope Gregory, copied in both Latin and French; three illustrations of Christ at Emmaus; and a Latin psychomachia or conflict of the soul. Geoffrey of St Albans could well have been or overseen the scribe who copied out the quire.[9] He may also have translated and composed parts of it. Yet if we accept that Geoffrey produced the quire for Christina it presents us with a linguistic problem. French was the language of the Norman aristocracy, but, although Christina's mother, Beatrix, may have been an incomer (given her Latinate name), it is reasonable to assume that Christina would have been brought up speaking English. It is possible that the letter of St Gregory, copied as it is in French as well as Latin, was intended for instructive purposes. Geoffrey may well have been trying to teach Christina or improve her knowledge of the language of the Church and of his own mother tongue, which was also the language of the convents. Female literacy was limited in this period, but according to her *Life* from at least the point when she first fled her family Christina studied the Psalms (*Life*, 93, 99). She might have read and recited or sung them either in a version translated into or glossed in English or in Latin. In summary, the evidence indicates that Christina had some ability to read, possibly in all three languages. At the same time, it is feasible that the quire, like the Psalter as a whole, was intended for collective consumption. The *chanson*, for example, is introduced in its prologue as a narrative familiar to author or scribe and reader from recitations where both have been present:

Here begins the pleasant song and pious account of that noble lord named Eufemien and of the life of his blessed son about whom we have heard readings and song.

[Ici cumencet amiable cancun e spiritel raisun d'iceol noble barun eufemien par num e de la vie de sum filz boneuret del quel nus avum oit lire e canter.][10]

Furthermore, the quire was also designed to be viewed both by Christina and by her companions, who may have been less educated. The letter of Gregory explicitly (and famously) advocates the use of images to encourage the piety of those who cannot read:

For the thing that writing conveys to those who read, that is what a picture shows to the illiterate; in the picture itself those who are ignorant see what they ought to follow.

[Nam quod legentibus scriptura hoc ignotis prestat pictura, qua in ipsa ignorantes vident quid sequi debeant.][11]

The images are there not only as adornments but also to teach and instruct. While the relationship between image and text is not always so straightforward within the Psalter, the illustrations in the quire are key to the meaning of the quire and of the 'Discourse on Good and Evil' in particular.

A great deal of recent critical attention has focused on the special significance the *Chanson of St Alexis* gains when considered alongside Christina's *Life*. Nonetheless, as Jane Geddes suggests, the two pages (Psalter, 71–2) containing the Latin psychomachia 'are probably the most important and impenetrable in the whole book'.[12] Certainly they offer a useful starting point for my analysis and evaluation of the manuscript as a whole. The text of this discourse runs around the margins of two large illustrations. The first illustration is a depiction of the resurrected Christ vanishing from the table where he had broken bread with his disciples (Luke 24. 30–1). Two of the disciples look on in astonishment as Christ disappears upwards through the ceiling of the room. This picture would no doubt have held a particular meaning for Christina. One of the last miracles described in her *Life* concerns a series of encounters with a mysterious pilgrim, identified in the text as either Christ or an angel (*Life*, 183–9). On his second appearance the pilgrim joined Christina and her sister Margaret for a meal, but only tasted the food prepared for him. On the next occasion he vanished from the church in which Christina and her fellow nuns had been attending the Christmas mass. The second illustration is an illuminated initial B (for *Beatus* or Blessed). This serves as a frontispiece for the Psalms, the next item in the manuscript. It depicts David holding his harp and a book of Psalms, with a giant dove whispering in his ear. Above this initial is a smaller illustration of two knights on horseback locked in combat.

The text of this discourse itself seems to be original to Geoffrey. It begins with an abstract account of the battle that goes on between the 'heavenly athletes'[13] and the devil and his followers. In developing the metaphor of the chivalric Christian warrior, direct reference is made to the picture of the fighting chevaliers on the next page. It is noteworthy that this part of the text uses gendered metaphors of a sort also found in Christina's *Life*: the good Christian is 'armed in a manly spirit'[14] and 'must be manly and perfect in the constancy of . . . steadfastness'.[15] As the narrative proceeds the contest develops to an apocalyptic scale: it will end, we are told 'in great toil and a hundred thousand bucketfuls of blood'.[16] As the text progresses the narration shifts from the third to the first and then to the second person; from 'he' and 'they' to 'we' and 'us' and then to 'me' and 'you' in the singular. It becomes increasingly urgent and more intimate as the author addresses and engages with a reader, whom he portrays as a spiritual comrade-in-arms: 'we likewise . . . must always keep watch with all virtue . . .'.[17] At the same time, the author introduces the figure of 'wisdom, the queen, who leads the way to good counsel',[18] but who rides a warhorse and destroys her enemies. Here he mingles the Wisdom of the Old Testament, who is personified as a woman (Proverbs 1. 20), with the violent imagery of the Book of Revelation. This woman will be supported by the meditation of 'good people of the cloister and manly hearts that are temperate and chaste, and every faithful disciple'.

It becomes increasingly clear that the text is written to support Christina in her times of trial; it is, as Geddes puts it, a 'coded message'.[19] Christina's *Life* describes a period of diabolic temptations and torments when the Psalms themselves provided her with consolation and protection: 'Her peaceful existence irritated the devil: her reading and singing of the Psalms by day and night were a torment to him' (*Life*, 99). Furthermore, the author is inscribing within it Geoffrey in his dual roles as author and spiritual adviser and Christina as reader and spiritual support and co-fighter. The text builds up to its climax, an explanation of the B initial and the depiction of David, with a somewhat allusive reference to the circumstances underlying its composition:

> You [singular] recently heard our word and that verse which shall be written in the name of heavenly love, and honour of the spiritual war, lest any one of those talkers, who investigate, should rebuke us.
>
> [Modo audisti nostrum dictum & illum versum qui erit scriptus in nomine celestis amoris & in honore spiritualis belli ne aliquis illorum locutorum que scrutantur nos reprehendant.][20]

This suggests an extraordinarily close connection between male author and female readership or audience. It may be that Geoffrey had spoken with Christina about the discourse ('our word') before he began writing the text and that he also produced it partly as an act of self-justification.

Here we find reference to the problems at the heart of the relationship between Geoffrey and Christina. The writer of Christina's later *Life* writes in considerable detail about the malicious gossip the two endured. Christina was defamed as calculating and self-seeking and 'the abbot was slandered as a seducer and the maiden as a loose woman' (*Life*, 175). The *Gesta Abbatum*, which chronicles the history of the monastery of St Albans, provides corroboration that Christina and Geoffrey were not immune from rumours:

> So great was the affection of mutual charity between them that, unless the whole multitude had known how holy both were, it may be that evil suspicion would have arisen from so great a love.
>
> [Tantaque fuit inter eos mutuae caritatis affectio, ut nisi notissima fuisset toti vulgo sanctitas utriusque, fortassis orta fuisset de tanta dilectione mala suscipio.][21]

As the author of the 'Discourse' ponders the illustration that he envisages on the second page of this text (the illustration was clearly designed according to specific instructions embedded into the text), he reflects on the psalmist's prophecies concerning Christ's life ('that verse which shall be written'). He then offers his own justification of his controversial spiritual friendship:

> It has seemed to me that the sound of his [David's] harp signifies the voice of holy church, and his book, which he held in great affection, signifies the wisdom of prophecy, and that divine prediction, and for that reason spiritual people love the psalter and desire its own divine teaching, because it sows sweetness in their hearts.

[Michi visum est quod sonus sue cythare significat vocem sancte ecclesie
& suus liber quem habuit in magna dilectione significat sapientam prophe-
tie & illam divinam predictionem, & ideo spirituales amant psalterium &
cupiunt suam divinam doctrinam, ideo quia dulcedinem inserit cordibus
eorum.][22]

Here David's harp and book, standing for ecclesiastical teaching as well as
divine prophecy, point to the foundations of the bond between Geoffrey
and Christina, and provide it with a God-given sanction. The wisdom of
prophecy, while directly alluding to David inspired by the Holy Spirit,
refers back to the female personification of Wisdom and beyond the text
to Christina's roles as prophet and visionary, which also figure largely in
her *Life*. The dove, which stands on the head of David in the initial B, connects both Christina and Geoffrey with David, as well as, of course, with
Christ. As the *Life* relates, a dove figured in a vision in which Christina
received assurance of Geoffrey's salvation. Christina saw herself in a room
with two figures and a dove, while Geoffrey was shut outside. In response
to his pleading and her prayers the dove flew towards him, and 'she understood clearly that the dove meant the grace of the Holy Spirit, and the
abbot, once filled with it, would be able to aspire only to things above'
(*Life*, 157). This very vision is illustrated in the second visual depiction of
Christina to appear in the Psalter (Psalter, 403). As we will see, according
to the *Life*, a dove also appeared to Christina's mother when she was pregnant, and was understood as a sign of Christina's great holiness.

What is so remarkable about this section of the Alexis quire is what it
tells us about why, for whom and how it was initially written, and also,
by implication, about why and for whom the *Life* was written. All the evidence suggests that the 'Discourse on Good and Evil' was composed as
well as copied by Geoffrey in his role as spiritual confidant and friend of
the holy woman whom he venerated and supported and to whom he frequently turned for advice and help. But it grew out of devout conversations between author and recipient, and was directed not only towards
Christina and her immediate associates, but also at those detractors who
defamed the two of them. If Geoffrey originally intended the Psalter to be
a gift honouring Christina's decision to become a nun, of devotional use
to her and to her community, he subsequently adapted it for another
purpose. The Alexis quire was included to offer Christina consolation and
encouragement in her hour of need and to justify the patronage and
support Geoffrey continued to offer in the face of opposition even from
his own monastery. The *Life* was intended to serve a similar purpose.

The *Life* and death of Prioress Christina

The first section of the St Albans Psalter, as it has come down to us (the manuscript seems to have been subject to reordering during the course of its compilation) is a liturgical calendar. This calendar, which clearly originates from the area where Christina lived and has connections with the monastery of St Albans, is of some significance because of the later additions that link it explicitly to Christina. These include a reference to the dedication of Markyate Priory in 1145, and the entries recording the deaths of Christina and her family, including her parents, brothers and possibly her aunt, and that of the hermit Roger (with whom Christina had shared a cell for many years). They also include the feasts of a number of women saints who would have had particular significance to Christina, such as her own namesake St Cristina (possibly fourth century), and virgin martyrs who include her sister's namesake, St Margaret, and the early Christian Juliana (early fourth century). One female saint whose inclusion on the calendar has not been widely commented upon is Hild (614–80).

Hild's is not the most obvious choice of feast to celebrate. The only surviving medieval hagiography of Hild is that found in *Bede's Ecclesiastical History of the English People*.[23] The calendar in the St Albans Psalter is not the only post-Conquest calendar to mention Hild, but she did not enjoy a widespread cult.[24] According to Geddes, Hild's inclusion in Christina's calendar is explained by the fact that she was 'the earliest English abbess, a powerful leader of women'.[25] Hild, founder and abbess of Streonæshalch or Whitby, which hosted the Synod of Whitby in 663/4, was a politically important figure in seventh-century England. As an Anglo-Saxon, a noblewoman, the founder of a religious institution and patroness of hermits, Hild may well have been an inspirational role model for Christina. Other women saints included in the St Albans Psalter calendar whose experiences anticipated Christina's were also Anglo-Saxon.[26] Æthelthryth or Etheldreda (*d.*679) remained a virgin throughout her first marriage and fled from her second husband to live in a remote location with her female companions before she, like Hild, became the founding abbess of a monastery (Ely). Frideswide (*c.*680–727), like Christina, withstood pressure to marry in order to fulfil her vow to Christ, and, again like Christina, she escaped from a suitor and lived as a hermit. Frideswide was the first abbess of a monastery (Oxford) founded by her father.

There are some similarities between the lives of Hild and Christina. Bede's life includes an account of a marvellous dream Hild's mother had when her daughter was still only a young child.

This was bound to happen in fulfilment of a dream which her mother Breguswith had during the child's infancy. While her husband Hereric was living in exile under the British king Cerdic, where he was poisoned, Breguswith had a dream that he was suddenly taken away, and though she searched most earnestly for him, no trace of him could be found anywhere. But suddenly, in the midst of her search, she found a most precious necklace under her garment and, as she gazed closely at it, it seemed to spread such a blaze of light that it filled all Britain with its gracious splendour. This dream was truly fulfilled in her daughter Hild; for her life was an example of the works of light, blessed not only to herself but to many who desired to live uprightly.

[Oportebat namque inpleri somnium, quod mater eius Bregusuid in infantia eius uidit. Quae cum uir eius Heriric exularet sub rege Brettonum Cerdice, ubi ut ueneno periit, uidit per somnium, quasi subito sublatum eum quaesierit cum omni diligentia, nullumque eius uspiam uestigium apparuerit. Verum cum sollertissime illum quaesierit, extimplo se repperire sub ueste sua monile pretiosissimum, quod, dum attentius consideraret, tanti fulgore luminis refulgere uidebatur, ut omnes Brittaniae fines illius gratia splendoris impleret. Quod nimirum somnium ueraciter in filia eius, de qua loquimur, expletum est, cuius uita non sibi solummodo sed multis bene uiuere uolentibus exempla operum lucis praebuit.][27]

At the start of Christina of Markyate's *Life* occurs a description of a prophetic miracle that occurred during the pregnancy of Christina's mother, Beatrix. Here we are told that one day Beatrix was looking from a window towards St Mary's Priory in Huntingdon, when she saw a white dove fly out from that building towards her. The dove, which was entirely tame, settled in her sleeve, and stayed with her for a week 'nestling comfortably and with evident pleasure first in her lap and then in her bosom' (*Life*, 35). This miracle is cited as evidence that Christina was God's chosen servant, inspired by the Holy Spirit, and, in choosing to spend her life as a virgin devoted to contemplation, following in the footsteps of Mary. Both the life of Hild and *The Life of Christina of Markyate* begin then with maternal visions, of a type popular in the Anglo-Saxon tradition.[28] Both make use of traditional motifs: the brilliant light and the dove signifying the Holy Spirit frequently appear in representations of the Annunciation, although only Christina's *Life* explicitly mentions the Mother of God, whose cult developed strongly in the twelfth century but had already begun to flourish in pre-Conquest England.[29] The *Life* further underlines this connection by spelling out that Beatrix's miracle occurred between the feasts of the Virgin's Assumption (15 August) and of her Nativity (8 September), on a

Saturday, 'a day specially set aside by the faithful for the devotion to the Mother of God'.

As marked as the similarities are, there are also significant points of contrast between the openings of the two lives. Bede's story of Breguswith's dream has been expertly analysed by Clare Lees and Gillian Overing.[30] Lees and Overing reject a Freudian interpretation (whereby the necklace stands for the child who becomes the object of the mother's desire on the death of her husband) and instead draw our attention to the marginalization and silencing of Breguswith. Lees and Overing argue that 'this dream underscores the spiritual relation between Hild and Breguswith at the cost of obscuring any other relation between the two as mother and daughter'.[31] At the same time, Bede's narrative offers 'no evidence at all of Breguswith's own agency, her subjectivity or consciousness'.[32] The opening lines of *The Life of Christina of Markyate* also prioritize the 'spiritual relation' between Christina and Beatrix over the maternal, but, in contrast to the life of Hild, this is not at the expense of Beatrix's independent presence or voice. Indeed the writer of the *Life* specifies that he has heard the story at first hand, directly from Beatrix. Even the interpretation of the miracle appears to be that of Beatrix rather than the writer's own. The *Life* goes on to explain that Beatrix was convinced that these signs indicated that her child was blessed and that she rejoiced in this. It then proceeds to describe the events surrounding the child's birth. Beatrix is thus specified as the originator of the narrative. Furthermore, the initial prioritization of the spiritual relationship between Christina and Beatrix is soon undercut in the ensuing account of Christina's conflict with her parents over the subject of her marriage. The *Life* describes in unusually realistic detail the often bloody abuse to which Beatrix in particular subjected the young Christina. Far from remaining passive and silent, Beatrix the mother, in her anger, frustration and violence, as well as in her initial joy, is at times all too present.

There are two explanations for the contrasting representations of Beatrix within the first part of Christina's *Life*. One is that, despite the necessity for Christina's narrative that her rejection by her family be graphically depicted, Christina was eventually reconciled with her family before the *Life* was written, and that her mother contributed to the stories of her precocious piety. Certainly evidence within the *Life* itself (references to two of Christina's siblings who followed her into religion) and in the St Albans Psalter (the inclusion of family deaths in her calendar) support this argument. The second explanation is that this Annunciation-inspired scene is a conventional hagiographic episode of doubtful veracity grafted onto a narrative which otherwise often seems closer to a biography than a saint's life. The two explanations do not have to be incompatible. The *Life* writer and the eyewitnesses whom he consulted would have looked for similarities between Christina's experiences and the histories of her pious predecessors. Returning to Hild, for example, further parallels can be drawn with Christina's life. Bede records that, having turned her back on her previous existence, Hild initially wanted to dwell with her sister in exile in a monastery near Paris, but was persuaded by Bishop Aidan to return to Northumbria. There she initially lived 'with a small band of companions'[33] before embarking on her career as religious leader. Christina sought the life of a recluse, and was eventually joined by her sister Margaret, but, despite rejecting overtures to enter more powerful convents in England and France, with the encouragement of Abbot Geoffrey, she was professed in St Albans (*Life*, 127) and remained in Markyate. Indeed it is striking that both Bede and the writer of Christina's *Life* emphasize the association between the holy women and their influential male supporters. Furthermore, like many pious women in the Middle Ages, both Hild and Christina endured prolonged and debilitating illnesses; Hild's eventually resulted in her death,[34] Christina's was finally cured (*Life*, 121–9). Strikingly, both Hild's death and Christina's recovery from one illness are accompanied by nocturnal visions experienced by women in their own or neighbouring communities.

Yet there is one further particularly significant difference between *The Life of Christina of Markyate* and Bede's memoir of Hild, and indeed any of the legends and lives of the saints mentioned in the St Albans Psalter calendar. This is that Christina's *Life* was evidently written while its subject was still alive. While Bede recounts the demise of Hild and the circumstances surrounding it in considerable detail, the only allusion to Christina's death is her obit in the calendar (Psalter, 14) and we know nothing of the events surrounding her end. Rachel M. Koopmans has argued that the abrupt ending of the manuscript of Christina's *Life* is not accidental.[35] She believes that, as a result of factionalism within St Albans Abbey, and in particular of resistance to the late Abbot Geoffrey's patronage of Christina (Geoffrey died in 1146), the writing of the *Life* was suddenly aborted and any cult of Christina that may have been emerging was quite deliberately suppressed. St Albans, in other words, began a process of actively distancing itself from and then forgetting Christina.

It is impossible to say who was responsible for Hild's inclusion in the St Albans Psalter calendar. Although the entry was inserted after his own death (and, indeed, after Christina's), it is possible that, albeit indirectly,

Hild's addition was due to Geoffrey of St Albans. In urging Christina to give up her life as recluse and to become a nun, Geoffrey effectively directed her towards more 'organized and disciplined forms of religious asceticism'.[36] As C. H. Talbot illustrates, Christina initially escaped her family with the assistance of a network of monks, recluses and devout individuals, many of whose names reveal them to have been of Anglo-Saxon origin, and whose very existence may indicate a 'spiritual movement . . . particularly strong among the natives of the country'.[37] Geoffrey subsequently guided Christina down an alternative religious path that was more familiar to him, as an incomer from France, than that which Christina originally followed. In so doing, he may have recognized the usefulness of suggesting Hild as a different model of Anglo-Saxon female piety for Christina to emulate, at the same time identifying resemblances between Hild's relationship with Aidan and his own with Christina. In other words, the story of Hild may have figured in Geoffrey's attempts to direct or even control Christina. Yet another explanation also presents itself. It is equally plausible that the calendar entry and the parallels with Hild's history in Christina's *Life* emerge from a specifically Anglo-Saxon context to Christina's spirituality that is somewhat at odds with the Continentally inspired influence Geoffrey undisputedly exercised over Christina. This Anglo-Saxon context will be central to the next section of this chapter, in which I focus on the composition of Christina's *Life*.

'My Sunday daughter': reading Christina's *Life*

As the *Life* reveals, Christina's existence as a hermit was fraught with danger and anxiety. She had to flee her family, having been coerced into marriage, and to survive in secrecy, hidden by her friends in God, and for some years she had to live in constant fear that she would be discovered and returned to the man to whom she had been betrothed. In a key scene, the *Life* describes a vision that Christina received in which Christ appeared to her carrying a golden cross that he gave to her, promising to take it away again soon. The *Life* records that Christina told her then protector, the hermit Roger, of this revelation, who delighted in the consolation offered. As the *Life* explains, Roger then said to Christina *in English*: ' "Rejoice with me, myn sunendaege dohter" ' [my Sunday Daughter] (*Life*, 107). Although Roger's name suggests that he was French or Anglo-Norman, it is no surprise that he should converse with Christina in her own first language. Nevertheless, this is a remarkable moment. The text foregrounds a term of endearment that must have had great spiritual, emotional and cultural meaning for Christina and her supporters and followers. Christina is here associated with the Lord's day, a day of rest and of devotion, and implicitly, through the revelation of Christ carrying His cross, with the holiest of holy days, Easter Day, the feast celebrating Christ's resurrection. At the same time, her relationship as spiritual child of Roger, a hermit revered by the monks of St Albans, is specified; she is also named as Roger's heir in the *Life*, inheriting his cell after his death (*Life*, 109). But it is particularly striking that the writer of the Latin *Life* chooses to preserve the exact English phrase. In inviting the reader to contemplate its meaning, he fleetingly draws our attention to the importance of the English language as the 'mother' tongue of Christina and many of her circle. In some ways this passage echoes the opening episode of the *Life*, which draws our attention to Christina's origins (spiritual and natal) and in particular, in the narrative of Christina's birth, to the significance of the words of the maternal figure of Beatrix. The transcription of the phrase 'myn sunendaege dohter' is, I will suggest, the moment when the repressed English voice speaks. Furthermore, what is not said here is as significant as what *is* said. What the *Life* does not fully articulate is the linguistic and cultural tension – between English, Anglo-Norman/French and Latin language and culture – that lies at its heart.

The writer of the *Life* describes his undertaking thus: 'my task is to describe quite simply the simple life of the virgin' (*Life*, 157). The writer does not explicitly reveal his own identity, although it is apparent from his partisan attachment to St Albans Abbey, which he repeatedly refers to as 'our monastery', that he must be a monk there. The fact that he is at pains to establish the close bond between Christina and the revered Roger (who enjoyed a posthumous cult at St Albans Abbey, where his tomb is located) indicates his dual loyalties to his own religious house and the subject of his hagiography. The fact that he records Roger's address to Christina in English may indicate that he was of Anglo-Saxon origin or simply that he was told the story by someone who was. Evidently he was a contemporary of Christina and he knew her well. He recounts one incident that he witnessed when sharing a meal with her (*Life*, 191).[38] He makes it clear that in compiling this *Life* he consulted Christina's family, friends and fellow recluses, and also spoke to Christina herself. Thus, when he retells an episode in which the devil failed to distract Roger from his devotions by setting fire to his clothing, he asserts that he heard it from Christina's own mouth (*Life*, 105). It is nonetheless possible that Christina did not want her story written, or at any rate did not actively collaborate in its composition.[39] Certainly, unlike the main secretary of *The Book of Margery Kempe*, for example (see Chapter 5 of this book), the writer does not represent himself as an especial confidant of his subject. Unlike Roger or Geoffrey of St Albans, he is not one of those privileged few who shared Christina's 'secrets'. Rather, the information he received directly from Christina seems, if not to have been overheard exactly, then at least shared amongst his community. Thus on one occasion he refers to Christina's thoughts, and explains that he had knowledge of them because she subsequently spoke of them 'in my hearing' (*Life*, 87). On other occasions it is clear that Christina withheld information from him and from his sources (*Life*, 151). Much of the detailed description of her experiences, visions, and emotional, physical and spiritual states is then evidently indebted to Christina, but possibly only indirectly via her confidants, Geoffrey of St Albans and her sister Margaret, and via other members of her family (including her married sister Matilda) and community.

Within the text itself, and despite the fact that the writer often claims to quote her words directly, Christina's voice remains elusive. Thomas Head's response to the problem of locating Christina's presence within her *Life* is to attempt to discriminate between the 'actions described in the text' and the 'description of those actions'.[40] According to this distinction, although the latter offers 'an entry into the mind of her male hagiographer', the former may be taken as 'an accurate reflection of Christina's lived experience'. Head's analysis places great trust in the authenticity of the record of events at the same time as it attests to the preservation of Christina's agency in her text, but it does not acknowledge fully the implications of the irretrievability of her words, thoughts and perspectives. This irrecoverability is powerfully illustrated in Christina's childhood vow, which is central to Head's reading of the conflicts over the meanings of marriage in Christina's story: 'O Lord God, merciful and all powerful, receive my oblation through the hands of Thy priest. For to Thee as a surrender of myself I offer this penny. Grant me, I beseech Thee, purity and inviolable virginity . . .' This promise, with its 'payment of the symbolic dowry' is effectively a betrothal to Christ.[41] In subsequent arguments with her parents, and in examinations before Fredebert, prior of St Mary's Huntingdon, and Robert Bloet, bishop of Lincoln, Christina's belief in the legally binding nature of her vow strengthened her resolve not to submit to her family's wishes that she should marry. Christina's vow is thus absolutely central to the action of the first part of her story, and indeed to both the entire narrative and her spiritual identity. Yet as Stephanie Hollis and Jocelyn Wogan-Browne observe, the vow is not formulated according to either standard or Anglo-Saxon liturgies for the consecration of virgins.[42]

Christina's actual utterance may well be lost and what Hollis and Wogan-Browne call the 'liturgical flavour' of the vow should perhaps be ascribed to the writer of the *Life*. Christina's (Anglo-Saxon) words are always already mediated in Latin by her male monastic hagiographer. Like legendary saints such as Agnes, whose declaration of her commitment to God, in the Old English version of her life, resonates with the language of the Song of Songs,[43] other parts of Christina's vow (*Life*, 41) echo the Psalms, and it is impossible to know if Christina or her biographer framed it in these terms. Only very occasionally do we really seem to get close to Christina's speech; for example when Christina is reported to have said ' "Tomorrow white stones will be thrown into the pot" ' (*Life*, 147). But even here it is translated into Latin, and furthermore the writer adds an explanation that this is 'A charming proverb which is quoted when success is assured'.

Christina's voice only distantly echoes through this Latin narrative, and although she may have co-operated to some extent in its composition, she was not directly responsible for it. But, if Christina did not decide to have her story written, then who did? The writer cites Christina's sister Margaret as having remarked that Christina's visions were 'worthy to be remembered by those who come after us' (*Life*, 155), but he nevertheless implies that the impetus came from another source. At one point he breaks out of his explanation about why Christina remained near St Albans to appeal with an abrupt directness to an implied and intended reader: 'because, as you have learned by experience, she revered you more than all the pastors under Christ' (*Life*, 127). This reader can only have been Geoffrey of St Albans himself, and this interjection confirms that the *Life*, like the St Albans Psalter, was commissioned by and possibly (in the first instance) for him. Geoffrey certainly dominates the last third of the *Life*, in which we get remarkable insight into the close spiritual relationship between Geoffrey and Christina. The *Life* evidently shares with the 'Discourse on Good and Evil' in the St Albans Psalter the aim of providing a defence of Christina's sanctity and Geoffrey's dependence on and support of her. Yet, somewhat surprisingly, the *Life* also dwells on Geoffrey's own shortcomings and failures. The writer of the *Life* clearly has insight into Geoffrey's inner thoughts, conflicts and anxieties, and also records Geoffrey's own visions (see *Life*, 137, 153–5). In fact it becomes clear that even if the writer was not necessarily privileged with Christina's secrets, he seems to have been privy to those of Geoffrey, in other words that he was Geoffrey's own spiritual confidant, his secretary.

Within the *Life*, Geoffrey of St Albans plays an important role. According to the *Life*, Geoffrey initially refused to believe Christina's visions and

warnings about his own corrupt activities, but learnt through hard experience that he should not ignore them (*Life*, 135–9). Although he found
her foreknowledge disconcerting and on occasion tried to test her (*Life*,
145), the *Life* reports that 'ever after the man often visited the servant of
Christ, heard her admonitions, accepted her advice, consulted her in
doubts, avoided evil, bore her reproaches' (*Life*, 139). The *Life* also records
that, between 1136 and 1139, Geoffrey was summonsed to journey to
Rome, first, for the confirmation of Stephen's election as monarch, then
as a delegate in a Council called by Innocent III, and finally to defend
the rights of the Church after the bishops of Salisbury and Lincoln had
been imprisoned (*Life*, 161–9). On each occasion, we are told, Geoffrey
consulted Christina, whose prayers were answered, and Geoffrey remained
in England. Likewise, around 1140 Geoffrey was summoned to the royal
court, but Christina was able to assure him that all would go well (*Life*,
169–71). These episodes all serve to validate Christina's sanctity, to vindi-
cate the spiritual friendship between Christina and Geoffrey, and thus
Geoffrey's own involvement with Christina, and to authorize the text
itself.

Extra-textually, the relationship between Christina and Geoffrey was
evidently one of interdependency. Elizabeth Alvida Petroff suggests that
'Geoffrey's role as abbot made Christina's life simpler and safer, and Christina's role as prophet and confidante strengthened Geoffrey'.[44] Geoffrey
was head of one of the wealthiest abbeys in England, and as we have noted,
he helped found the priory at Markyate of which Christina was to be superior. Christopher Holdsworth contends that prophets like Christina
achieved their status by existing on 'the frontier, of society'.[45] However,
Christina's marginal status should not be over-emphasized. Christina
is represented in her *Life* as a powerful and influential woman who defied
her family and corrected Church leaders. As French incomer warriors
in post-Conquest England sought alliance with the noblest Anglo-Saxon
women, so Geoffrey (as a controversial and at times unpopular leader
of his religious house) sought out this native holy woman in order to
bolster his position in society at large. As both the 'sunendaege dohter' of
the hermit Roger and the beloved '*puella*' [daughter] of Geoffrey of
St Albans (*Life*, 154, 155), Christina of Markyate forged a crucial spiritual
link between distinct and to some extent disparate elements of twelfth-
century society.

Recent critics reading *The Life of Christina of Markyate* have tended to
adopt an assimilationist model of society in post-Conquest England, arguing
that through intermarriage and other forms of contact the Normans soon

became relatively fully integrated with the English. That the Normans and the Anglo-Saxons interacted with one another is evidenced in the *Life* by the relationship between Christina's aunt Alveva of Ælfgifu and Ranulph Flambard, bishop of Durham from 1099 (*Life*, 41). Henrietta Leyser, in her introduction to the *Life*, asserts that 'Christina's kin had made their peace with their new rulers'.[46] Yet, alongside evidence of co-operation between the foreign incomers and the indigenous population of post-Conquest England are indications of tension between them. I would like to end this chapter by arguing that while the St Albans Psalter (which merges Anglo-Saxon and Norman artistic and cultural traditions) reveals something of the Continental influences exerted on the spiritual lives of Christina and her followers, the *Life* suggests at least an element of Anglo-Saxon resistance. The clearest example of this opposition is found in the contrast between the Old French *Chanson of St Alexis*, one of the later additions to the Psalter, and the story of St Cecilia referred to in the *Life*. The *Chanson* relates the story of a (male) saint who fled marriage to live an ascetic and eremitic life, and who was finally reconciled with his bride in Heaven. Christina may well have identified with or been expected to identify with both the saint Alexis, and his pious and faithful wife; certainly the narrative offers its audience a choice of 'multiple subject-positions'.[47] It is entirely plausible that Geoffrey, with his French background, would have been responsible for proposing St Alexis to Christina as an appropriate model of married celibacy. Geoffrey certainly knew the legend well: there was a chapel dedicated to St Alexis in his monastery at St Albans. In contrast, within *The Life of Christina of Markyate*, it is the example of Cecilia and Valerian (familiar saints to the Anglo-Saxons) that Christina cites when trying to convince her husband Burthred to agree to a vow of chastity (*Life*, 51). Geoffrey's inclusion of the *Chanson* in the Psalter reveals that he tried to frame Christina's piety in terms of Continental exemplars, and is thus indicative of a form of cultural or spiritual colonialism. The *Life* indicates that alternative insular traditions were as, if not more, important to Christina and others of her close associates.

Leyser contends that, within the *Life*, there is 'not even a whisper of sedition against Norman lordship', and thus implicitly takes issue with Talbot's much earlier view that 'there is an undercurrent of national feeling' in the text.[48] The reality may be that the text is more ambivalent than either critic suggests. While Geoffrey of St Albans tried to channel Christina's spirituality along lines more immediately recognizable to him, even going so far as to try to improve her literacy in Latin and French, the writer of the *Life* does little to resist such cultural appropriation. Admittedly the early part of Christina's narrative is concerned with her quest to become a hermit (as has been suggested, a particularly insular form of piety), first at Flamstead with the recluse Alfwen, then at Markyate with Roger. However, this is represented as a necessity rather than a choice, eventually superseded by Christina's integration into the organized Church. As Eddie Jones observes, the teleology of the *Life* is such that it 'seems to be moving inevitably towards the (monastically speaking) happy ending of [Christina's] adoption of regular Benedictinism'.[49] Nonetheless there are, as Dyan Elliott puts it in a different context, 'fissures in [the] divided text'.[50] It is significant, for example, that *if* Christina's mother Beatrix is of French or Norman descent, the *Life* certainly does not suggest that Christina's ethnic identity is hybrid. On the contrary, it stresses that 'she came of a family of ancient and influential English nobles' (*Life*, 83). Furthermore, on one occasion, mentioned in the previous section, the writer notes that Christina turned down an offer by her supporter, the Norman Archbishop Thurstan, to become superior of the convent of St Clement's in York and invitations to join the French communities at Fontevrault and Marcigny (*Life*, 127). This is cited as evidence that Christina 'preferred our monastery' (St Albans), but it may also betray an element of disapproval of the Normans and French and thus reveal something of the conflicting allegiances of the text as a whole. While the *Life* may well be written by a monk of St Albans at the request of Geoffrey, in defence of Christina and Geoffrey, many influences have been brought to bear on it, some of them potentially at war with one another. To some extent then, *The Life of Christina of Markyate*, with its elements of Anglo-Saxon bias represents a counterbalance to those aspects of the St Albans Psalter that betray Geoffrey's particularly French interests. In linguistically foregrounding Roger's term of endearment, 'sunendaege dohter', the *Life* fleetingly allows the suppressed Anglo-Saxon voice to speak, preserving not only Christina's father's language and her mother tongue (if not her mother's tongue), but also speaking back to the Norman and French incomers.

Conclusion

The Life of Christina of Markyate is the product of close collaboration between the anonymous writer and his patron, Geoffrey of St Albans, and reflects the spiritual familiarity between the two. In contrast the Alexis quire of the St Albans Psalter, and especially the 'Discourse on Good and Evil', reveals the intimate interconnections between patron/author/subject (Geoffrey) and recipient/reader/subject (Christina). Nonetheless both the *Life* and the St Albans Psalter make manifest the complexity of the related issues of the material production and readership / reception of medieval texts. The St Albans Psalter was put together over an extended period of time and may have been neither originally nor solely intended for Christina. A number of scribes and artists contributed to it (drawing on French alongside medieval Latin and Anglo-Saxon traditions), and both Christina and her sister Margaret may have made or been responsible for additions in the form of the curtains over the illustrations and family and other obits in the calendar. The writer – or perhaps, more accurately, compiler – of Christina's *Life* evidently turned to a range of sources, including Christina's mother and sisters as well as Geoffrey, thus perhaps explaining the cultural hybridity I have identified within it. Yet despite the fact that the St Albans Psalter and the *Life* both suggest that Christina may have had some reading knowledge of Latin and French as well as English, Christina does not appear to have directly contributed to her *Life*. As a consequence, despite the immediacy and apparent realism of much of the *Life*, Christina's unmediated voice, if not her story, is all but lost to us.

2

Marie de France (*fl.* 1180)

Introduction

Marie de France is one of the most enigmatic women to feature in this study. As we saw in the Introduction, very little is known about her – she hardly seems to have existed beyond her poetic persona. Our sense of Marie de France's authorial identity relies heavily on the 'self' represented in the prologues, dedications and epilogues of the works attributed to her – but these representations may well be unreliable or even entirely fictional. Yet, as we also saw in the Introduction, from the perspective of women's literary history, it is crucial that we do not discount the possibility of Marie de France's existence. Unlike Christina of Markyate, whose engagement with textual culture was more indirect, Marie de France was a writer, and of all the women discussed in this study, she is the only one to have produced what we would now think of as unambiguously literary works. An aristocrat, quite possibly a religious, Marie de France wrote, in French, for the English court of Henry II (reigned 1154–89), husband of the great literary patron Eleanor of Aquitaine.

Whatever her identity, Marie de France's works indicate that she was multilingual; literate in French, English, Latin and apparently also Breton and Welsh. Her works – the *Lais*, the *Fables* and *Saint Patrick's Purgatory* – can all be thought of in some sense as translations. The *Lais* claim to be derived from oral songs from Brittany. They are thought to have been written around 1160 and survive in five manuscripts. The most complete collection, in Anglo-Norman, is found in London, British Library, MS Harley 978, which contains the Prologue and all twelve tales. The same manuscript also contains an authoritative text of Marie de France's *Fables*, which exist in twenty-three manuscripts in all. The *Fables*, which assert that they are based on an English text (which has either been lost, or never existed in the first place), seem to have been written between the 1160s and 1190. Marie de France's third work, a poetic translation into French of H. of Saltrey's Latin prose work, *Tractatus de Purgatorio Sancti Patricii* (*c*.1179–85), is generally thought to have been composed around 1190. It has survived in one manuscript: Paris, Bibliothèque Nationale, MS fr. 24407. As this is the only one of her translations for which we have the source, it provides us with concrete evidence of Marie de France's excellent knowledge of the Latin language as well as further evidence of her remarkable poetic ability.

The name Marie de France, which derives from her authorial self-naming at the end of the *Fables*, associates her not only with her country of origin (whilst implying that she no longer lives there), but also with her mother tongue. Marie de France, not atypically for the period, is poetically self-conscious or articulate about her reasons for writing. Yet although she writes prologues in the learned clerical tradition, she rejects the patriarchal or virile Latin language for what is considered the feminine vernacular. Nevertheless, this linguistic choice does not in itself make Marie de France a feminine writer, and it is striking that, while she reflects on the processes of writing and the problems associated with it in her works, she only implicitly addresses the difficulties of writing *as a woman*. But Marie de France does not simply write in the vernacular: she also writes in the French vernacular in an Anglo-Norman context. Caroline Walker Bynum has argued that, at the end of the twelfth century in Western Europe, a paradigmatic shift took place in response to changing social structures and the development of national identities (and reflecting greater anxieties and fears). People began to conceive of change not, as previously, in terms of the hybrid (the joining together of two incompatibles), but in terms of metamorphosis (a process of transformation from one form into another).[1] I put forward the view in Chapter 1 that the mid-twelfth-century *Life of Christina of Markyate* is a culturally hybrid text. Here I will suggest that Marie de France's somewhat later poems are the product of linguistic and cultural metamorphosis that reflects greater cross-channel interaction. They transform traditions as well as languages, and notably appropriate Celtic (Breton, Cornish, Welsh and Irish) myths and motifs. This is significant in relation to what we can surmise about Marie de France's cultural context. Unlike Christina of Markyate, Marie de France, as a French settler in England, can be thought of (albeit anachronistically, in a pre-national context) as a colonizer rather as than one of those colonized.[2] Anticipating her Norman and Anglo-Norman successors who wholeheartedly embraced Arthurian legend and incorporated it into their own literature and mythology, Marie de France appropriates the culture of the Celts (already long since driven to the geographical and political margins of the British Isles) in order to create a distinctive poetic voice.[3]

In the following sections of this chapter, I examine each of Marie de France's works in turn, paying particular attention to the prologues, prefaces, dedications and epilogues and to what they reveal about her perception of her own role as writer, her reasons for writing and her relationship to her readers. As we will see in the first part, 'The monstrous Marie de France: metamorphosis and reputation', the theme of transformation is central to Marie de France's *Lais*. At the same time, her preoccupation with the problems of readership and reception reflects both her fear of misprision and the resulting transformation of fame into scandal, and at the same time her awareness of the importance of interpretation. In the second part, ' "Who painted the lion?" Ambiguity and interpretation', I argue that Marie de France's poems (with their ellipses and open-ended conclusions and at times ambivalent moral and political messages) not only invite, but actually require the participation of an active reader, who has to bring her or his own meaning to them in order to make sense of them. The final part, 'Powers of horror and of translation', explores further the extent to which Marie de France uses the medium of translation not simply as a means of poetic self-expression but also of religious and political engagement. In all three parts I pay particular attention to the representation of gender.

The monstrous Marie de France: metamorphosis and reputation

The Prologue to the *Lais* that appears in the Harley manuscript begins, self-consciously and with what seems at first sight to be exquisite poetic self-confidence, by asserting that those blessed with 'the gift of knowledge and true eloquence' have a responsibility 'not to remain silent' (*Lais*, 41).[4] Yet the poet does not exist in isolation. It is important, Marie de France suggests, that edifying works should reach a wide audience and receive the recognition that they merit. She cites the example of the authorities from the past, who effectively collaborate with their readers in the creation of meaning (Marie de France's 'surplus').[5] She asserts that the ancients wrote obscurely so that later generations of scholars had to devote time, learning and thought to providing commentaries and explanations. Marie de France thus aligns her narrative voice not only with the wise and talented 'ancients' (in so doing attributing authority to herself) but also with these more recent readers, interpreters and transmitters of knowledge.

Marie de France goes on to assert that, because such learned pursuits bear moral fruits, helping banish sin and anguish, she herself has considered improving her spiritual state by 'translating a Latin text into French' (*Lais*, 41). Nevertheless recognizing that to do so would simply be to follow in the footsteps of many others, she now seeks a different, and she implies more innovative, role.

> So I thought of lays which I had heard and did not doubt, for I knew it full well, that they were composed, by those who first began them and put them into circulation, to perpetuate the memory of adventures they had heard. I myself have heard a number of them and do not wish to overlook or neglect them. I have put them into verse, made poems from them and worked on them late into the night. (*Lais*, 41)

> [Des lais pensai k'oï aveie;
> Ne dutai pas, bien le saveie,
> Ke pur remambrance les firent
> Des aventures k'il oïrent
> Cil ki primes les comencierent
> E ki avant les enveierent.
> Plusurs en ai oï conter,
> Nes voil laisser në oblïer;
> Rimez en ai e fait ditié,
> Soventes fiez en ai veillié. (*Lais*, Prologue, ll. 33–42)]

Here it is the preservation of the *aventures* or courtly events or happenings that is important both for those first responsible for the lais and for Marie de France. Immediately afterwards, however, she offers yet another reason why she has decided 'to assemble lais, to compose and to relate them in rhyme' (*Lais*, 41) – she has done so in order to present them to her king, and by implication, in order to gain patronage and favour. In so doing she steps back from asserting the originality of her enterprise, shielding herself from criticism behind a conventional dedication.

In this Prologue, Marie de France represents herself somewhat ambivalently as both poet, foregrounding her own creative role, and compiler, responsible for bringing together the works of others. But even though she explicitly rejects the role of translator, she also fulfils it, in so far as she implies that her poetry *is* translated from one language (Breton rather than Latin) into another (French), and also from one form (memorized oral recitations) into another (rhymed written texts). Furthermore, Celtic fairytale is transformed into courtly romance. In likening herself to and simultaneously distancing herself from the ancients, the patriarchal authorities so valued by medievals, and praising and simultaneously rejecting Latin – the very language of patriarchy – and *translatio studii* (literally the 'translation of learning' but with much wider implications), she engages with but does not directly articulate the gender politics of medieval authorship.[6] Significantly, Marie de France turns to the oral tradition, often seen as inherently feminine, as well as to her own mother tongue, the feminized vernacular. It is important to keep in mind, however, Susan Crane's observation that, given the elite status of French within England at this time, Marie associates 'her work more fully with high culture and learning than [she] would choosing to write in French on the continent'.[7]

The Harley Prologue is followed by a second prologue, in this case embedded into the beginning of the first of the tales, 'Guigemar'. This second prologue gives the impression of having been retrospectively added, following the circulation of at least some of the poems. Here, after stating the importance of doing one's job well, the poet refers back to the very beginning of the Prologue proper, claiming that she, finally named in the third person as 'Marie', is not one to 'squander her talents' (*Lais*, 43). Nevertheless, even if she has appropriate matter – in the form of the Breton tales that she will go on to relate – and sufficient ability, it would appear that she does not experience the sort of reception that she has observed is so necessary for successful poetic composition. In contrast to the king addressed in the Prologue, who is 'worthy', 'courtly' and full of virtue (*Lais*, 41), this audience is far more hostile:

> Those who gain a good reputation should be commended, but when there exists in a country a man or a woman of great renown, people who are envious of their abilities frequently speak insultingly of them in order to damage this reputation. Thus they start acting like a vicious, cowardly, treacherous dog which will bite others out of malice. But just because spiteful tittle-tatlers attempt to find fault with me I do not intend to give up. They have a right to make slanderous remarks. (*Lais*, 43)

> [Celui deivent la gent loër
> Ki en bien fait de sei parler.
> Mais quant il ad en un païs
> Hummë u femme de grant pris,
> Cil ki de sun bien unt envie
> Sovent en dïent vileinie;
> Sun pris li volent abeisser:
> Pur ceo comencent le mestier
> Del malveis chien coart felun,
> Ki mort la gent par traïsun.
> Nel voil mie pur ceo leissier,
> Si gangleür u losengier

Le me volent a mal turner;
Ceo est lur dreit de mesparler. (*Lais*, 'Guigemar', ll. 5–18)]

Here we find an anxiety about scandal that is reminiscent of the concerns of Christina of Markyate and Geoffrey of St Albans, described so vividly by the writer of the *Life*.[8] However, whereas the cruel gossip surrounding Christina was focused on her piety, and in particular her close relationship with Geoffrey (and his generosity towards Christina and her community), Marie de France is specifically concerned with the negative reception that her *work* will receive. Her talents for storytelling provoke jealousy in others and her works are vulnerable to misinterpretation. Yet it is striking that neither here, nor in the Prologue to the collection as a whole, does she acknowledge that her writing might be perceived as transgressive in terms of sex and gender roles. Marie de France does not address the specific problems of and prohibitions against women's writing, and indeed, on the contrary, she suggests that her own problems are not gender-specific, stressing that people of both sexes can suffer as she does.[9]

Issues of reputation and scandal recur in Marie de France's poems, inevitably in a very aristocratic courtly setting, often tied in the theme of metamorphosis or transformation. They emerge, for example in the story of 'Bisclavret'. This tale is fascinating for a number of reasons, not least because it is possible to read the figure of Bisclavret, a noble knight who has a dark and monstrous secret, as a metaphor for Marie de France's poetic vocation. Bisclavret, who for three days of every week turns into a werewolf, may superficially appear monstrous, but he is in fact the epitome of courtliness. The woman writer, who represents herself as working 'late into the night', and who is vulnerable to slander even as she is celebrated can be viewed in a similar light. Furthermore, Bisclavret's physical metamorphosis from man into beast may be seen to mirror the translation of the lais from oral to literary, from folk and fairy tale to romance, and from Breton to Anglo-Norman. All these transformations might be viewed as producing inferior, corrupted versions of the perceived original. Marie de France draws attention to the connection between translation and monstrosity in the opening lines to this tale, stating: 'In my effort to compose lays I do not wish to omit *Bisclavret* – for such is its name in Breton, while the Normans call it *Garwaf* (*Lais*, 68). The use of both titles in the opening lines draws our attention to the problems of both linguistic plurality and indeterminacy, to the difficulties of finding the 'right' word, and thus to the inadequacies – and also the *potential* – of translation.[10] Within this narrative Bisclavret is both a common noun and a proper noun: as the former,

Marie de France initially interchanges it with the Norman word 'garualf'.[11] Interestingly it is the Norman that indicates the horror of the werewolf, while the Breton designates its more civilized manifestation. Marie de France cannot find within her own language an adequate means of expression but the Breton tongue meets this lack.

Bisclavret as a knight is a good man, devoted to his king, loving to his wife, esteemed by his neighbours and throughout Brittany. His loyalty is emphasized throughout the tale. At the start of the story he is described as the chief confidant to the monarch, before he is cruelly tricked by his wife so that he is unable to transform himself back from wolf into man. Following his capture in a hunt (the courtly inversion of Bisclavret's own secret activity), he pleads for mercy from the king and begins to follow him like a dog. He is welcomed into his castle, where he is fed and nurtured and he sleeps with the knights, at the side of his royal master. This king, like the monarch to whom Marie de France dedicates her *Lais*, is in turn idealized. He is merciful and protective, generous and rewarding, and, perhaps most important of all, receptive to good advice. On two successive occasions, the king listens to and follows the recommendations of one of his courtiers, who speaks out on behalf of Bisclavret. When Bisclavret finally returns to human form, the king ensures his land, which had been lost to him in his werewolf state, is returned. Yet, although justice would seem to be done, this tale demonstrates a curious amorality that is typical not only of many of Marie de France's *Lais*, but also of her writing as a whole, and which can be playful and at the same time rather sinister.

This amorality is demonstrated in the treatment of both Bisclavret, and of his wife and her new husband. In the opening lines of the tale, Marie de France offers an uncompromising definition of the werewolf: 'a ferocious beast which, when possessed by this madness, devours men, causes great damage and dwells in vast forests' (*Lais*, 68). Yet she does not immediately make any connection between this creature and her protagonist, announcing instead: 'I leave such matters for the moment, for I wish to tell you about Bisclavret' (*Lais*, 68). Even though Bisclavret is identified as a werewolf – and by his own admission he roams the woods in pursuit of food, and returns elated from such expeditions – Marie de France does not directly address the devastation he causes. She certainly makes no mention of the fact that his prey is *human*. In other words, Marie de France holds back from condemning Bisclavret, and instead represents him as the victim of the plotting of his wife and her lover. Furthermore, throughout the narrative the transformed Bisclavret is often referred to as a 'beast'. This is mainly because the king and the court do not recognize him for what he is until the climax of the story, but it also has the effect of distancing Bisclavret from his monstrous identity.

The narrator's position is mirrored in the story by the stances adopted by the royal household in general and by the king's new adviser in particular, who react with astonishment when the wolf viciously attacks first Bisclavret's former wife's accomplice, and then the former wife herself. The feeling of the court is that the wolf's aggression towards both the knight and the lady must be in some way justified. Unlike the malicious, gossiping environment that Marie de France describes at the start of 'Guigemar', this court holds back from circulating damaging rumours, and there is only concern for Bisclavret following his disappearance, but no evil talk about him. The court in other words is idealized, much as is the king.

The only real threat to Bisclavret comes then from his former wife and her lover. Bisclavret's wife's sin is disloyalty: she both betrays and abandons the man she once loved. This contrasts with the unswerving fidelity of Bisclavret to his king, and of the court to Bisclavret. The narrator sides with Bisclavret against both the wife and the lover, suggesting that the punishments they both receive from Bisclavret (being bitten and mauled, and in the case of the wife, disfigured) and the treatment the wife gets from the king (being tortured and then exiled) are warranted. While there is a sense of rough justice here, this is hardly conventional morality. Within the world of this lai, Bisclavret's appearance may be bestial, but he is still, it *seems*, considered honourable at all times and his identity remains constant. As I have indicated, there are clear suggestions in the narrative that this is not the whole story. Nevertheless, he is neither shunned nor punished. Rather it is his wife who is not only cast out but also permanently marked by sin. Bisclavret bites off her nose (which connotes castration and sexual punishment), and in the conclusion to the narrative we are told that, Eve-like, she passes on the sign of her transgression to some of her daughters and female descendants. The world that is represented in this tale is profoundly homosocial, even homoerotic (Bisclavret, returned to his human form, is discovered 'sleeping on the king's own bed' (*Lais*, 72) and awoken by the king's kisses),[12] and, at the same time, profoundly misogynist. Strikingly, Marie de France does not seem to question the anti-feminism of her own narrative.

The twinned themes of metamorphosis (or transformation) and reputation come to the forefront in Marie de France's Arthurian tale of 'Lanval'. Here, Lanval, unlike the popular and highly esteemed Bisclavret, but like the unfortunate Marie de France as she represents herself at the beginning of 'Guigemar', is a virtuous and talented individual who falls victim to the envy of the others. The other knights of the Round Table are two-faced towards him, pretending to be his friend, but willing to stab him in the back, metaphorically speaking. As a consequence, Lanval is overlooked by King Arthur, when he gives out rewards to his followers, and finds himself impoverished and disconsolate. Saved by the appearance of a mysterious, beautiful and unfathomably rich maiden, who takes him as her lover and grants him unlimited wealth on condition that he does not reveal the secret of their relationship, he returns to Arthur's court where he is feted by one and all. However, once again, he finds himself the casualty of the jealousy of another. Arthur's own queen sets her sights on him, and when he rejects her advances, becomes incensed. She accuses him of sodomy:

> 'Lanval,' she said, 'I well believe that you do not like this kind of pleasure. I have been told often enough that you have no desire for women. You have well-trained young men and enjoy yourself with them. Base coward, wicked recreant, my lord is extremely unfortunate to have suffered you near him. I think he may have lost his salvation because of it!' (*Lais*, 76)

> ['Lanval', fet ele, 'bien le quit,
> Vuz n'amez gueres cel delit;
> Asez le m'ad hum dit sovent
> Que des femmez n'avez talent.
> Vallez avez bien afeitiez,
> Ensemble od eus vus deduiez.
> Vileins cuarz, mauveis failliz,
> Mut est mi sires maubailliz
> Que pres de lui vus ad suffert;
> Mun escïent que Deus en pert!' (*Lais*, 'Launval', ll. 277–86)]

Lanval finds his hand forced. In defending himself against the charge of sodomy (a crime as well as a sin in the Middle Ages), he blurts out his own secret: 'Lady, I am not skilled in the profession you mention, but I love and am loved by a lady who should be prized above all others I know' (*Lais*, 76). Unfortunately, this admission only increases the queen's fury and she defames Lanval to her husband, claiming that he had sought her love and then, when she rejected his advances, dishonoured her, and thus by implication the king as well. The result is that Lanval finds himself on trial, his only defence being to produce his beloved and thus prove the truth of his rash declaration that she is superior in beauty, wisdom and virtue to the queen.

As with 'Bisclavret', this is a lai about betrayal, alienation, metamorphosis and reversal. Lanval's otherworldly damsel, whose generosity is unlimited and who is ultimately shown to be merciful and forgiving (appearing to rescue Lanval despite his betrayal), is the inverted image of Arthur's cruel, vengeful and disloyal queen. At the same time, the retinue of women over which the damsel presides is an idealized version of the flawed Arthurian court, with its fickle and self-seeking knights and ladies. According to Sharon Kinoshita, 'Lanval' is 'a *male* Cinderella story' or wish-fulfilment fantasy that 'imagines an outside to the feudal order that relegates women to the status of objects of exchange underpinning the patriarchal system'.[13] Unlike Bisclavret, Lanval is represented as an individual who is *always* in the position of outsider and in a perpetual state of alienation. At the start of the *Lais* we are told that he is the son of a king, but from a country far away. His isolation is reiterated later in the narrative, for example to explain why, initially, following his arrest no one agrees to put up bail for him (*Lais*, 78). The mysterious maiden's identity is never fully explained, but she is clearly a supernatural creature, and the resolution of the tale sees Lanval himself translated out of this world into another more ephemeral existence:

> [Lanval] went with her [the damsel] to Avalon, so the Bretons tell us, to a very beautiful island. Thither the young man was borne and no one has heard any more about him, nor can I relate any more. (*Lais*, 81)
>
> > [Od li s'en vait en Avalun,
> > Ceo nus recuntent li Bretun,
> > En un isle que mut est beaus;
> > La fu ravi li dameiseaus.
> > Nul hum n'en oï plus parler,
> > Ne jeo n'en sai avant cunter. (*Lais*, 'Lanval', ll. 641–6)]

The open-ended conclusion to this tale – there is after all something horrific about Lanval's fate – is in keeping with the ambiguity and ambivalence of the collection as a whole; the resistance to offering clear explanations, resolutions and morals that keeps the reader alert and involved in the production of meaning.[14]

One particularly striking aspect of 'Lanval' is of course the explicit expression of homophobia manifested in the queen's initial outraged response to his rejection of her.[15] Indeed fears of various forms of sexual transgression, from sodomy to incest to adultery, repeatedly surface in the *Lais*. Marie de France does not offer any simple or straightforward guidance on courtly love. On the contrary, her perspective is constantly shifting. If 'Lanval' can be read as a proto-feminist critique of the masculine chivalric ethos, 'Bisclavret' takes the side of the knight/werewolf, celebrates the

court and presents Bisclavret's wife in familiar antifeminist terms as a deceptive, treacherous adulteress (or rather bigamist). Bisclavret's wife is represented unsympathetically as a woman who takes a lover in order to rid
herself of a husband who has become too much of an inconvenience to her.
In order to make this portrayal convincing, Bisclavret's monstrosity has to
be underplayed. Yet in other tales such as 'Eliduc', the final lai in the Harley
manuscript, the eponymous hero is caught up in a moral dilemma – married
to one woman, Guildelüec, while in love with another, Guilliadun – and
yet is largely exempted from blame. At the same time the women in this
story, the wife and the lover, are idealized figures; victims of circumstances
over which they have little control, but at the same time, brought together
by relinquishment and atonement. Nevertheless these women are not
entirely passive, and the intervention of Guildelüec results in a close bond
developing between the two women based on mutual (self-)recognition.
Indeed, as Matilda Tomaryn Bruckner points out, Marie de France's preferred title of the story, 'Guildelüec and Guilliadun' (*Lais*, 111) – which
modern editors disregard – draws our attention to 'the way Marie has
allowed two women to take the initiative'.[16] However, unlike that between
the king and Bisclavret in the earlier lai, this bond between the two does
not result in the exclusion of a third party, but is predicated on the women's
common love for Eliduc. It is no coincidence that the names Guildelüec
and Guilliadun are so similar, or that Eliduc's name is 'contained anagram-
matically in that of Guildelüec'.[17] The women are reflections of one another
and Eliduc is unable to leave one for the other.

Eliduc's story begins when he, like Lanval and again like Marie de France
herself, becomes the object of the jealousy of the court and the subject of
malicious gossip: 'The envy of his good fortune, which often possesses
others, caused him to be embroiled with his lord, to be slandered and
accused, so that he was banished from the court without formal accusa-
tion' (*Lais*, 111). Again, like Marie de France herself, Eliduc crosses the
channel to a new life. Eliduc's exile takes him away from his wife and into
the service of a king across the sea, from Brittany to the mythic Celtic
realm of Logres. In Logres, the king's daughter Guilliadun falls in love with
him, and despite his guilt over betraying his wife (to whom he has promised to remain faithful), he accepts her love-tokens and returns her feelings,
but is subsequently summonsed back to Brittany. Guilliadun does not,
however, discover that Eliduc is married until he has come back for her
and they have fled together by boat back to his homeland. She then falls
into a death-like swoon, and Eliduc places her body, in secrecy, in a hermitage near his own home. Just as in 'Lanval' the mysterious damsel is

all-forgiving so in 'Eliduc' Guildelüec demonstrates incomprehensible generosity and self-sacrifice, first in bringing Guilliadun back to life with the aid of a miraculous flower, and then in resolving to become a nun in order to enable her husband to marry Guilliadun. In 'Eliduc' then there occurs transformation from a death-like state back to life and translation from the secular and courtly to the spiritual. Eliduc provides Guildelüec with land to found an abbey, where she presides over thirty nuns. Then, many years after his remarriage, he himself turns to religion and founds his own monastic order, while Guilliadun joins Guildelüec, who 'received her as her sister and showed her great honour, urging her to serve God and teaching her the order' (*Lais*, 126). Ultimately, then, it is Guilliadun who is reunited with Guildelüec, although there are no overt articulations of female same-sex sexuality.[18] As Bruckner explains, 'the final configuration shows the women as a couple vis-à-vis Eliduc: all three are united with reference to God, as the women pray for their beloved's salvation and he for theirs'.[19] Reconciliation and renunciation offer a recovery of reputation for posterity for all three: 'Each one strove to love God in good faith and they came to a good end thanks to God, the true divine' (*Lais*, 126).

The conclusion of 'Eliduc', with its transformation or translation of secular love into divine service might be seen to parallel the development of the collection as a whole. Indeed critics have been of the view that Marie de France's oeuvre moves from the secular (the *Lais*) to the didactic (the *Fables*) to the explicitly religious (*Saint Patrick's Purgatory*); a reading in keeping with Marie de France's putative identity as an aristocrat and a religious. However, Roberta L. Krueger offers a powerful counter-argument:

> Such a biography, however, arises less from Marie's words than from the will of readers who would seek to impose an authorial identity upon writing that remains, in many ways, fragmentary, enigmatic, and 'obscure'. If there is coherence and continuity in the narrative voices of the *Lais*, the *Fables*, and the *Espurgatoire*, it is because these texts lead the reader, at every turn, to reflect upon their interpretative questions.[20]

It is these very 'interpretative questions' that I will now consider in relation to the *Fables*.

'Who painted the lion?' Ambiguity and interpretation

In the Prologue to the *Fables*, Marie de France reflects further on her role as a writer, and, more specifically, as a translator.[21] Here, as we might expect, her stance to some extent mirrors that taken in the Prologue to the *Lais*. Yet at the same time it seems, at least initially, more cautious and conventional. Marie de France begins with an indirect address to 'Those persons, all, who are well-read' (*Fables*, Prologue, l. 1), reflecting on the importance of studying the works of philosophers of old as a means to moral self-improvement. Inserting her own literary undertaking within a tradition that she presents as patriarchal, that of the 'ancient fathers' (*Fables*, Prologue, l. 11), Marie de France goes on to cite the examples of earlier writers: Romulus, who was credited with translating a collection of fables for the edification of his son; and of course Aesop working for his master. As in the Prologue to the *Lais*, Marie de France emphasizes the importance of the role of the ideal reader as the interpreter of the text, finding, if not the *true* meaning of the text, then its relevance and usefulness:

> To many it was curious
> That he'd [Aesop would] apply his wisdom thus;
> Yet there's no fable so inane
> That folks cannot some knowledge gain
> From lessons that come subsequent
> To make each tale significant.
>
> [Merveille en eurent li plusur
> Qu'il mist sun sen en tel labur;
> Mes n'i ad fable de folie
> U il n'en ait philosophie
> Es essamples ki sunt aprés,
> U des cuntes est tut li fes.] (*Fables*, Prologue, ll. 21–6)

Marie de France then proceeds to align herself with Romulus and Aesop as a compiler and translator of fables for the benefit of another – the male patron whom she claims asked her to produce the work. In so doing, she implicitly takes upon herself the mantle of philosopher and also that of teacher (fables were key school texts for boys in the Middle Ages). Yet, she also undermines her own status by distancing herself from both her authors and her ideal reader, by suggesting that, like those who cannot understand Aesop, she does not fully understand the task she has undertaken:

> To me, who must these verses write,
> It seemed improper to repeat
> Some of the words that you'll find here.

[A mei, ki dei la rime faire,
N'avenist nïent a retraire
Plusurs paroles que i sunt.] (*Fables*, Prologue, ll. 27–9)

Furthermore, Marie de France once more reveals her enduring preoccupation with reputation and reception, lamenting that, like Aesop's, her audience will not understand her work and dismiss it as 'crude' (*Fables*, Prologue, l. 36).

The identity of Marie de France's patron is unknown, although in the Epilogue to the *Fables* she names him as 'Count William' (*Fables*, Epilogue, l. 9). He may, of course, be a fictional creation. The claim to be writing in response to a commission is a widespread convention in medieval literature. We have no way of verifying the accuracy of what Marie de France says about herself or her dedicatees (and this also holds true of the king to whom the *Lais* are dedicated). Predictably enough the patron of the *Fables* is idealized in the same way as the king addressed at the beginning of the *Lais*: 'the flower of chivalry, / Gentility and courtesy' (*Fables*, Prologue, ll. 31–2), and later, 'the doughtiest in any realm' (*Fables*, Epilogue, l. 10). In this way, Marie de France locates her *Fables* within the same courtly milieu as her *Lais*. In the Epilogue, she also takes the time to spell out the exact nature of her literary undertaking. In composing the *Lais* she rejected the well-trodden path of translating from one language into another. Here she follows it (or so she claims), choosing however not to translate her *Fables* into French directly from Latin originals but from a previous English translation, which she attributes to King Alfred, apparently Alfred the Great, famous for his piety and educational projects, and especially his translations into Old English. That Alfred had a reputation for wisdom in this period is attested to by the fact that a collection of proverbs were (wrongly) attributed to him. Marie de France distances herself from her classical sources, finding in the Anglo-Saxon King Alfred a precedent from her adopted country for vernacular translation.

Yet, just as the commissioning of the *Fables* may be fictitious, so may the source. Certainly, although works associated with Alfred the Great continued to be copied in the twelfth century, he is not accredited anywhere else with a translation of the fables, and no Old English collection of fables has survived. Rather, Marie de France seems determined not simply to insert herself into a literary patrilineage extending from the sixth century BC through the tenth century AD to the present day, and encompassing both philosophers and kings, but, if necessary, to fabricate such a genealogy. At the same time in the Epilogue, as in the opening to 'Guigemar', Marie de France names herself in her text, claiming recognition as the translator of this work, while at the same time associating herself with her mother country and mother tongue: 'I am from France, my name's Marie' (*Fables*, Epilogue, l. 4). Again, she asserts the importance of receiving recognition for one's merits and achievements. Indeed, it is for this very reason that she decides to reveal her identity. While 'many a clerk' (*Fables*, Epilogue, l. 5), in other words many a *male* scholar, may well attempt to claim, and even succeed in claiming, her work as his own, she, Marie de France, will do what she can to ensure that her memory is preserved and 'not forgot'. Here then Marie de France addresses (more than in the prologues to the *Lais*, if still only implicitly) the gender war she is fighting over learning, literature, reputation and fame.

Given the extent to which Marie de France constructs and reflects upon her own roles as poet-scholar, compiler and translator in the prologues and epilogues to the *Lais* and the *Fables*, it is unsurprising that within the *Fables* themselves we also find moments of literary self-consciousness. Marie de France's fable of 'The Lion and the Peasant' tells the story behind the Wife of Bath's immortal invocation 'Who painted the lion, tell me who?'[22] In her Prologue, the Wife of Bath quotes the question asked by the lion on being shown a picture, by a man, of a man killing a lion, as part of a diatribe on the misogyny of representations of women. She continues:

> By God, if women had written stories,
> As clerks have within their oratories,
> They would have written of men more wickedness
> Than all the mark of Adam may redress.
>
> [By God, if wommen hadde writen stories,
> As clerkes han withinne hire oratories,
> They wolde han writen of men moore wikkednesse
> Than al the mark of Adam may redresse.][23]

Anticipating Chaucer's use of the fable, Marie de France evokes the story of an 'unnatural' friendship between man and beast to comment on the unreliability of the text, whether written or painted:

> From this example we should know
> Not to accept that something's so
> From fables which are but false seeming
> Or paintings similar to dreaming.
> Believe only in what you see:
> The truth revealed openly.

> [Par essample nus veut aprendre
> Que nul ne deit nïent entendre
> A fable, ke est de mençuinge,
> Ne a peinture, que semble sunge.
> Ceo est a creire dunt hum veit l'ovre,
> Que la verité tut descovre.] (*Fables*, no. 37, ll. 59–64)

Here the moral of the fable contradicts the claims made in the Prologue about the usefulness of the genre. Marie de France, in playfully undercutting the educational, instructive function of her own literary undertaking (a 'fable' is of course also a 'lie'), draws our attention to its limitations. Yet at the same time, she reinforces her claims that the reader and audience play a part in interpreting the text. After all, not *all* fables and paintings are deceptive, and the answer seems to lie in reconciling authority with experience.

However, whereas some two centuries later, Chaucer's fictional champion of the reputation of womankind made this allusion as part of an explicit, and highly satirical, response to the antifeminist writings of the great medieval authors, Marie de France's fable is much more circumspect and makes no reference to women at all. In Marie de France's fable, the lion asks the same question:

> 'This painting here – How was it done?
> By man or lion – Say which one!'
>
> ['Ki fist ceste semblance ici?
> Humme u lïuns – Itant me di!'] (*Fables*, no. 37, ll. 13–14)

Yet the context is quite different. Here the lion and the man are comrades not antagonists, engaged in friendly debate rather than outright hostility. Their topic is status, and the man (a peasant) shows the lion the wall painting in response to the lion's claim that he is of royal birth, and thus the man's superior. In turn, the lion tries to prove his point by taking the man to watch the execution of a traitor: the criminal is thrown to a lion and is unable to save himself. The moral ultimately drawn by the lion is that one should believe what one sees with one's own eyes above all else. The lion, it would seem, not the man, is in the position of true supremacy. But the fable is more complex than this analysis would suggest, because the lion's superiority over the peasant is not based on brute strength alone. The lion also demonstrates the chivalric virtues of loyalty and grace. After witnessing the prisoner's death, the peasant and the lion encounter another lion, and another perspective: the second lion warns the first that men know how to trap them, and therefore they should join together to kill the peasant. The first lion's refusal to turn on his human companion serves to reinforce the mutual bond between them in a way that no demonstration of greater might can. The truth that the man has seen demonstrated and to which the lion testifies is concerned with the symbiosis of sovereignty and courtesy.

Karen Jambeck has argued that the *Fables* fall within the category of the 'mirror of princes', a politically inflected genre concerned with good governance and self-conduct, and have to be understood in terms of the bureaucratic and legal changes introduced by Henry II.[24] Certainly many of the *Fables*, for example 'The Wolf and the Lamb' (*Fables*, no. 2), address issues of kingship, lordship and service, and either praise them or speak out against corrupt practices and vice. Once again the courtly milieu of Marie de France's work is manifest. Fables such as 'The Sick Lion and the Fox' (*Fables*, no. 36) provide timely warnings against the dangers of life in the entourage of the monarch. The wise, we are reminded, are wily like the fox and hold back and pay heed to what they see and hear. 'A Man, his Stomach, and his Members' (*Fables*, no. 27) – also found in John of Salisbury's *Policraticus* (1159) – describes the need for harmony in the body politic.[25] At the same time it establishes the connection between macrocosm and microcosm, or between the political and the personal. The hands and feet that deprive the greedy stomach of sustenance until it is too late for recovery to be possible serve as a reminder both to the lord and his servants of their mutual dependency. Both should honour one another to preserve their own honour. Typically, these *Fables* appear very conservative: although corruption and the exploitation of power are criticized, the social hierarchies are fixed and inflexible, and those in the lower ranks are expected to keep to their places.

Yet, in keeping with other mirrors of princes, there is a playful quality to these *Fables*, many of which are characterized by an amorality that would seem to undermine their didactic purpose. 'The Peasant and the Beetle' is a case in point. Here the scatological humour is directed towards a peasant who falls asleep naked in the open air, and suffers great discomfort after a beetle crawls into his anus. Unaware of what is causing him such pain, he consults a physician, who tells him he is pregnant. The moral of the narrative is directed against the 'foolish folk' (*Fables*, no. 43, l. 24) who believe the physician's story and wait with trepidation for the birth.

> This example serves to say
> The ignorant are oft this way:

Believing that which cannot be,
They're swayed and changed by vanity.

[Par ceste essample le vus di:
Del nunsavant est autresi,
Ki creient ceo que estre ne peot,
U vanitez le oste e muet.] (*Fables*, no. 43, ll. 25–8)

This moral is implicitly homophobic, depending upon opposition of the perceived sterility of sodomitic practices to the fecundity of heterosexual reproduction. In a collection so overtly concerned with the responsibilities of knowledge and with conveying and discerning good advice, it is remarkable that the deceptive and irresponsible behaviour of the physician is not commented upon. Yet again and again, shrewdness and ingenuity are praised alongside honesty and integrity. Indeed on occasion, two very similar fables appear side by side, but are differently inflected. Thus the fabliau-esque 'The Peasant who Saw Another with his Wife' (*Fables*, no. 44) celebrates the cruel cunning of the adulterous woman. In contrast 'The Peasant who Saw his Wife with her Lover' (*Fables*, no. 45) comes to the predictable conclusion that women are as deceptive as the devil. Such a conclusion is typical of the antifeminist tradition against which Chaucer's Wife of Bath rails, but which her Prologue paradoxically reinforces and reproduces.

As in the *Lais*, Marie de France provides positive and negative representations of both sexes in her *Fables*.[26] At times the overt misogyny of her tales and morals is extremely disturbing. 'The Peasant and the Snake' revolves around another 'unnatural' friendship between man and beast, where the former was granted wisdom and great wealth by the latter in exchange for a regular supply of milk, but lost everything after he attempted to kill the snake on the advice of his wife. Here, however, the moral of the fable does not turn on questions of loyalty or mercy between companions, but centres on the risks of listening to 'woman's guiding word' which often proves treacherous (*Fables*, no. 73, l. 109). Yet while many of the *Fables* draw on such hostile female stereotypes (for example 'The Thief and the Witch' (*Fables*, no. 48)), others (such as the fable of the female bear raped by a fox (*Fables*, no. 70)) are far more sympathetic to the female predicament.[27] Furthermore, unlike 'The Peasant and the Snake', most of the *Fables* which depict women as cruel, deceptive or sexually immoral claim a more general applicability. 'The Widow who Hanged her Husband' (*Fables*, no. 25) is a warning against the unreliability of the world in general. Nevertheless, the twinned tales of 'The Peasant and his Contrary Wife'

(*Fables*, no. 95) and 'The Peasant and his Cantankerous Wife' (*Fables*, no. 96) may caution, respectively, against persisting in giving foolish advice or with arguing with one's master, but it is the cruelty of the husbands that is most memorable. It is impossible to forget the haunting images of the woman whose tongue is cut out, Philomela-like, by her husband, or the body of the drowned wife floating upstream in the river. The ambiguities, ambivalences, inconsistencies and contradictions within the *Fables* are part of their point. Marie de France invites her audience to make sense of her collection as a whole. Like the parent in 'The Crow Instructing his Child' (*Fables*, no. 93), Marie de France sees her task as being to communicate knowledge and to convey learning, but she acknowledges that it has its limits. Just as the crow sends its child off to fend for itself, so Marie de France leaves the final acts of interpretation and application to her readers.

Powers of horror and of translation

Marie de France provides a new prologue, dedication and epilogue to her version of *Saint Patrick's Purgatory* in which she, once again, reflects on her writing processes.[28] In this case, Marie de France foregrounds the moral purpose of her work, written as 'a recollection and record' of the vision of Purgatory that is the focus of her text (*Saint Patrick's Purgatory*, l. 6). She minimizes her own creativity, stressing that she has simply 'put into writing in French, / The Pains of Purgatory / Just as the book tells us about them' (*Saint Patrick's Purgatory*, ll. 3–5), although the author of her 'book', H. of Saltrey, remains unacknowledged. Nevertheless, as in the *Fables*, Marie de France quite deliberately inserts herself within and, in so doing, disrupts a venerable tradition of masculine authorities. It is God who is the ultimate author behind this work, and St Patrick the human intermediary. As we have come to expect, and as convention requires, Marie de France's patron or 'dear father' (*Saint Patrick's Purgatory*, l. 16), who, she emphasizes, asked her to produce this poem (*Saint Patrick's Purgatory*, ll. 9, 23), is represented as her ideal reader, and is characterized by his virtue. Yet Marie de France also has a further, secondary audience in mind: people who might be improved by reading her work, and who might repent and turn to God. Furthermore, whereas in the Prologue to the *Lais* Marie de France explicitly rejected the task of translating Latin into French, even as she acknowledged the moral benefits of such studious activity, now she freely submits to such an undertaking. Here her primary concern is avowedly no longer personal recognition. She celebrates the fact that her scholarship has engendered within her a 'greater love for God, / And desire to serve him, my Creator' (*Saint Patrick's Purgatory*, ll. 27–8). Marie de France, in emphasizing her own personal spiritual gain from her translation, aligns herself with her own readership.

In Marie de France's epilogue to *Saint Patrick's Purgatory* she once again names herself within her work. Yet on this occasion she does not express any concern with preserving her own reputation or fame:

> I, Marie, have put
> The Book of Purgatory into French,
> As a record, so that it might be intelligible
> And suited to lay folk.
> Now we pray God through his grace
> To cleanse us of our sins.
>
> [Jo, Marie, ai mis, en memoire,
> le livre de l'Espurgatoire
> en Romanz, qu'il seit entendables
> a laie gent e covenables.
> Or preium Deu que par sa grace
> de noz pechiez mundes nus face!
> Amen.] (*Saint Patrick's Purgatory*, ll. 2297–302)

Here author and readers, equally edified by the preceding text, are bound together as joint recipients of God's mercy with Owen, the Irish knight who is the protagonist of the narrative. Sharing the gift of salvation is the ultimate purpose of this work. Although this sort of closing prayer is again traditional, it does also add to our knowledge of Marie de France's inscribed and presumably intended readership. Marie de France, a woman and a member of the court, is not and can never be a cleric and she here makes explicit what is implicit in the *Lais* and *Fables*: that she writes for an audience that is, like herself, lay. Whereas in the *Fables* Marie de France was concerned that a clerk might effectively steal her work, here, in laying claim to a text from the clerical tradition, her act of translation is also an act of appropriation.

Conversion, it might be argued, is itself a form of translation. As Howard R. Bloch convincingly shows, the notion of translation – which is itself akin to metamorphosis – is central to the *Purgatory*: whether this be the translation between languages (from Latin into French), the translation of souls (in and out of Purgatory), the translation of a vision into a poem, or, as we will see, the translation of the cultural and religious concept of Purgatory (from a religious to a secular context and, geographically, from France to England).[29] Despite her modesty, Marie de France once again demonstrates considerable self-confidence in her writing in so far as she seems determined to place her own stamp on her material. Rather than denigrate the role of translator, she elevates it. The extent to which Marie de France is in control of the text she translates is manifest not only in the additions and revisions she makes to her sources, but also in the way she is able to choose what to include and what to leave out. H. of Saltrey's *Tractus* was to prove a popular text in the Middle Ages, and a large number of other vernacular translations followed Marie de France's, including English and Welsh versions. Marie de France's narrative centres on the journeys of the Irish knight Owen into and out of Purgatory – the entrance of which is located in Lough Derg in Ireland – and includes detailed and gory accounts of his revelations of ten torments and a description of his vision of paradise. However, she also preserves a number of other elements found in her source, including, of course, a discussion of St Patrick's original revelation of Purgatory, with its significant account of a wise old Irish man who had committed many murders and was brought to penance. For Bloch, *Saint Patrick's Purgatory*, with its emphasis on converting and civilizing the 'fickle and savage' Irish (*Saint Patrick's Purgatory*, l. 204) has to be understood in terms of Henry II's contemporary colonialist ambitions in Ireland.[30] If we accept this reading, then Marie de France's final work has a greater political urgency than her previous poems.

Marie de France's dedication is followed by a preface, largely derived from her sources, discussing the theological background to visions concerning one's fate after death. Crucially this preface also explains the concept of Purgatory – which was only beginning to gain wide currency at the end of the twelfth century – to an audience of 'simple folk' (*Saint Patrick's Purgatory*, l. 48). Marie de France as translator is mirrored in the figure of Owen, who first meets with Gilbert of Lough in Ireland when he is appointed by the king to act as his interpreter (*Saint Patrick's Purgatory*, ll. 1955–60, 1980), although it is Gilbert who transmits Owen's story to the wider world. Michael J. Curley points out that Marie de France adapts her text to make it less clerical and more courtly and that Owen's journey is thus translated into a chivalric *aventure*, reminiscent in many ways of the *Lais*.[31] Some subtle changes to the source reinforce the secular thrust to Marie de France's tale. In her version, for example, Owen's king specifically instructs him not to take holy orders following his spiritual journeying but to remain as knight, engaged in the active life: 'He counselled him to retain this station / So that he might serve God well' (*Saint Patrick's Purgatory*, ll.

1929–30; compare ll. 1971–88). This is Marie de France's addition to the text, and is in line with a general tendency to deviate from the monastic emphasis of the original. As Curley observes, it signifies 'a clear assertion of the equal value of the secular and religious vocations as pathways to salvation'.[32] At the same time, however, it chimes with the message of many of the *Fables* which stress the importance of accepting one's status and proper place in society.

Clearly, then, the central purpose of Marie de France's text is the *translation* of the doctrine of purgatory – a hot topic at the end of the twelfth century – to a secular Anglo-Norman audience.[33] In the preface, Marie de France offers the story of Owen's adventures as evidence to confirm the teachings of the Church Fathers:

> Indeed, who would not believe this
> If he did not have proof
> That what we have described here
> Were the truth?
>
> [Ki crerreit ço veraiement,
> se nen eüst demustrement
> ceste chose estre verité,
> que nus avuns ici mustré?]   (*Saint Patrick's Purgatory*, ll. 181–4)

Superficially, the didacticism of *Saint Patrick's Purgatory* would seem to set it apart from the *Lais*, while the theological focus distances it from the *Fables*. However, one point much remarked on by critics is that taken together Marie de France's works demonstrate a clear knowledge of the geography of the Celtic regions – from Brittany to South Wales and from Cornwall to Ireland. Furthermore there are strong thematic continuities between the *Purgatory* and the *Lais* in particular, many of which are linked to the shared Celtic background of both texts. The journey to the otherworld has its origins in ancient pagan mythology and such voyages in the Celtic tradition often incorporate imagery and motifs that anticipate the Christian depiction of Purgatory. Indeed the very idea of Purgatory as a place, not only of punishment, but also of transition (between Heaven and Hell) and metamorphosis (from sinner to redeemed) is reminiscent of Celtic fairy traditions. The experiences of the knight Owen, who meets with the walking – and speaking – dead, thus to some extent mirror those of Bisclavret, who, neither fully human nor fully beast, finds himself temporarily trapped within his own bestiality. Yet while Owen, like Bisclavret, is able to return from his supernatural adventure and rejoin the human race, there are others, such as Lanval, who ultimately depart for ever into another realm. This brings us to a further link between the *Lais* and *Saint Patrick's Purgatory*, and one that does not depend on the Celticism of the texts: both are centrally concerned with identity. Central to *Saint Patrick's Purgatory* are the extended accounts of the torture of those wretched souls tormented by the devils, with their focus on the horror of grotesque physical suffering. According to Julia Kristeva, 'abjection [is] what disturbs identity, system, order'.[34] Although both protagonists emerge with their sense of their own identity intact, Owen's *aventure*, like that of Bisclavret, is predicated on anxieties about notions of selfhood.

Saint Patrick's Purgatory, with its emphasis on visions about the fate of the dead, seems to anticipate later medieval women's writing in England, such as *The Book of Margery Kempe*, or – even more strikingly – an epistolary revelation of purgatory written by an anonymous fifteenth-century woman to her confessor.[35] Unlike this latter text, which describes the torments of a former nun, there is no focus in Marie de France's work on female suffering. Her account of Owen's fifth torment tells of those 'hung cruelly / From flaming hooks' (*Saint Patrick's Purgatory*, ll. 1083–4), some by their eyes, nose, ears and so forth, and some by their genitals, but does not comment specifically on their sex.[36] Marie de France does not exclude women from the torments of purgatory, but nor does she victimize them. In the subsequent retelling of the Archbishop's exposition on the Fall, following Owen's vision of paradise, the sin of Adam is stressed but no mention is made of the role of Eve or the serpent (*Saint Patrick's Purgatory*, ll. 1689–720; this nevertheless accords with the Latin source). The image of woman as temptress *is* preserved in the final anecdote appended to Owen's tale: a story about an anonymous priest who is overcome with desire for his 15-year-old foster daughter. Despite its clerical focus, this narrative about a foundling, and the desire of the father figure for his motherless daughter, is reminiscent of Marie de France's *Fables*. It resonates with both 'Le Fresne' (which centres on a maiden, abandoned as a baby in a churchyard, who ran away with her lover) and 'Les Deus Amanz' (in which the widowed father, unwilling to let his daughter marry, sets her suitors a seemingly impossible task). Even the ending, with the priest entrusting the young woman to a convent, echoes the conclusion of 'Eliduc'. In the story in *Saint Patrick's Purgatory* the young woman is no more exempt from blame than many of the female protagonists of the *Lais* (Bisclavret's wife being a case in point). The woman agrees to the priest's propositions and both are saved only by the resolution of the man himself: rather than succumb to sin he castrates himself with a knife. Yet, in this case, the corrupting power of the woman is not dwelled upon. It is a devil, determined to do mischief, who is held ultimately responsible by both the narrator (the devil sets out to trap the man) and the other demons (who punish him for the failure of his plan). *Saint Patrick's Purgatory* veers away from apportioning blame to the human participants, stressing instead the redeeming power of divine grace (*Saint Patrick's Purgatory*, l. 2269; compare l. 2301).

Conclusion

Common themes run through the three works generally accepted to be written by Marie de France. Whether or not Marie de France herself was a religious, all three texts appear to be directed towards a secular courtly audience of women as well as men. Although her poems engage only implicitly with the problems of writing as a woman, and although they are still (like Bisclavret's wife) marked with misogyny, they demonstrate a sophisticated awareness of issues of gender. Metamorphosis, transformation and translation are also recurring preoccupations, closely tied to questions of identity and language. As a French writer associated with the English court, Marie de France appropriates (or so she claims) traditions from Brittany, Ireland, Wales, Cornwall and pre-Conquest England. But she is also highly innovative, and in her last poem she takes responsibility for introducing her readers to the newly promulgated concept of purgatory. Significantly, the *Lais*, *Fables* and *Saint Patrick's Purgatory* are all self-conscious texts. They are preoccupied with questions about the role of the poet, compiler and translator, about her relationships with patrons and readers and with patriarchal tradition, about the reasons for writing and the purposes writing serves, and about problems of reception and reputation. However, although Marie de France is now most famous for her *Lais* and *Fables*, it is *St Patrick's Purgatory* that reveals most clearly the power or potentiality of translation as a form of literary production on a par with original poetic composition.

3

Legends and Lives of Women Saints (Late Tenth to Mid-Fifteenth Centuries)

Introduction

Vernacular saints' lives, in Old and Middle English and French, which were often composed with oral delivery in mind, must have appealed to a lay as well as religious audience, to women as well as men. In the lives of women saints (in particular, but not exclusively, those of virgin martyrs), the trials of the saints centre on the preservation of their chastity, which to varying extents results in a focus on female sexuality and the female body. This chapter looks at lives of women saints written between the late tenth and the mid-fifteenth centuries. It thus cuts across and disrupts the chronological structure of this study as a whole. In so doing, the chapter emphasizes the need to consider the context and circumstances of the production of the texts in understanding works which, because of their formulaic aspects, may superficially appear very similar. The texts chosen include male-authored and anonymous lives in Old English with an implied male audience; a life written by a woman in French for other women but which also inscribes a male audience; and lives written by a man in Middle English but commissioned by both women and men. The key question addressed in this chapter is how saints' lives written about, by or for women offer evidence of the readership or reception of the lives themselves and of other works by women. I look in particular at examples of intertextuality that link these lives of women saints to the other writings considered in this study, such as *The Life of Christina of Markyate*, the works of Marie de France and *The Book of Margery Kempe*.

Reading the lives of saints: Christina of Markyate and the Anglo-Saxon tradition

In Chapter 1, I examined similarities between *The Life of Christina of Markyate* and Bede's account of Abbess Hild, who was one of three Anglo-Saxon women saints whose names appeared in the St Albans Psalter, the others being Æthelthryth of Ely and Frideswide of Oxford. Lives of saints composed in Anglo-Saxon continued to be circulated in England after the Norman Conquest.[1] Here I examine further the possible influence of the virgin martyrs in the Old English tradition on Christina's book, focusing on the lives of women saints attributed to Ælfric of Eynsham (c.950–c.1010).[2] These are part of a larger collection of saints' lives by Ælfric, found in an eleventh-century manuscript (London, British Library, MS Cotton Julius E.vii), and include two women's lives (Mary of Egypt and Euphrosyne) not composed by Ælfric. Only one of the saints included, Æthelthryth, is Anglo-Saxon. The *Lives* are explicitly aimed at a pious lay audience. In his Preface, Ælfric dedicated his *Lives* to two noble patrons, the father and son Æthelweard and Æthelmær, 'because of this history that you have never before had in your language' (*Women Saints' Lives*, 18). As Catherine Cubitt has pointed out, the women martyrs are intended by Ælfric as 'vehicles for ideas of virginity, not as exemplars of femininity'.[3] For such male readers, the universal significance of sanctity, regardless of the sex of the saint, was crucial. At the same time, Ælfric also makes it clear that he had a wider audience of fellow Christians (religious and secular) in mind when he decided to translate these hagiographies into the vernacular. He states that he wishes 'to profit others by edifying them in the faith whenever they read this relation, as many, namely, as are pleased to study this work, either by reading or hearing it read' (*Women Saints' Lives*, 19). Clare A. Lees has suggested that 'the *Lives* offer internal evidence for the monitoring of audience and reception' in so far as we are told that a number of the saints, including Agnes, Agatha, Lucy, Eugenia, Claudia and Cecilia inspire female as well as male emulators.[4] Furthermore, regardless of whether or not Ælfric's implied audience was male, the actual audience of the *Lives* must have included women.[5] While it is impossible to tell how women responded to these *Lives* at the time of composition in Old English, the twelfth-century *Life of Christina of Markyate* offers us some evidence of the later reception of those such as Mary of Egypt, Cecilia, Æthelthryth, Agatha, Eugenia and Euphrosyne. In particular, these Old English lives seem to underlie the representations of Christina of Markyate's spiritual friendships (especially that with the hermit, Roger) and of the struggle to preserve her virginity.

At the heart of the Old English Life of Mary of Egypt occurs the haunting sequence in which the aged monk Zosimus chases after a fleeing naked figure across the desert. The chase ends at a dried-out creek, where Zosimus, weeping, calls out to Mary and she replies, addressing him by name and asking for his cloak to cover her body. Astonished that she knows who he is, but aware 'that she was enlightened by divine foresight' (*Women Saints' Lives*, 105) he hastens to grant her request, and in so doing turns his gaze away from her. Having covered herself, Mary speaks again:

> 'Lo, abbot Zosimus, why did you have so great a need to see me, a sinful woman? Or what do you want to have from me or to know that would not allow you to slow in accomplishing such a great effort on my account?'
>
> Immediately, he prostrated himself on the earth, and asked her blessing.
>
> Asking his blessing, she then prostrated herself to him. (*Women Saints' Lives*, 105)

> [Hwi wæs þe la abbod Zosimus swa micel neod me synful wif to geseonne. Oððe hwæs wilnast þu fram me to hæbbenne oþþe to witenne þæt þu ne slawedest swa micel geswinc to gefremmanne for minum þingum. He þa sona on þa eorðan hine astrehte and hire bletsunga bæd. Heo ongean hine astrehte and his bletsunga bæd.][6]

This scene, and the narrative as a whole, is sexually charged (the reader's point of view is closest to that of Zosimus in that, like Zosimus, we pursue Mary and struggle to see her). Nevertheless, as Clare A. Lees and Gillian R. Overing have argued, the Old English Mary of Egypt is not just about gender or sexuality, but concerned with conversion, interpretation and knowledge. In this text 'Mary, the object of Zosimus's desiring sight, stands in place of, or for, another object – God'.[7] Lees and Overing suggest that Mary herself, a former prostitute, 'turns away from sexual knowledge . . . toward spiritual knowledge', while the reader (male or female) is required to identify with Zosimus, and 'like Zosimus, the reader's belief is to be confirmed, or changed, in the process of spiritual reading'.[8]

This same scene resonates, perhaps coincidentally, with the account in *The Life of Christina of Markyate* of the hermit Roger's first encounter with Christina, after she has left the recluse Alfwen to live near Roger's cell; although in many ways the episodes seem like inverted images of one another. Although Roger invites Christina to join him, rather than seeking to see her or speak with her directly, he decides to avoid contact. 'Nevertheless' we are told, 'they saw each other the same day':

> The virgin of God lay prostate in the old man's chapel, with her face turned to the ground. The man of God stepped over her with his face averted in order not to see her. But as he passed by he looked over his shoulder to

see how modestly the handmaid of Christ had composed herself for prayer, as this was one of the things which he thought those who pray ought to observe. Yet, she, at the same instant, glanced upwards to appraise the bearing and deportment of the old man, for in these she considered that some trace of his holiness was apparent. And so they saw each other, not by design and yet not by chance, but, as afterwards became clear, by the divine will.

[Virgo Dei prostrata iacebat in oratorio senis, demersa facie ad terram. Super quam vir Dei transibat averso vultu ne videret eam. At ubi pertransierat respexit ut videret quam apte Christi ancilla sese composuisset ad orandum, quoniam hoc quoque censebat orantibus esse observandum, et illa nichilominus eodem puncto suspexit ad videndum incessum et habitum senis, in quibus credebat non nullum vestigium apparere tante religionis. Et ita sese mutuo viderunt non sponte, sed nec fortuitu: ceterum sicut postea claruit divino nutu.] (*Life*, 100–1)

Just as Mary appears vision-like to Zosimus as he wanders in prayers and fasting in the desert, Christina is unexpectedly present in the hermit's chapel when he enters to perform his devotions or to meditate. Yet the aged Mary is a reformed whore and her exposed body, which causes her shame, must be covered and hidden, while the youthful Christina is a virgin, and it is her chaste demeanour that is displayed to the watching man. Whereas Zosimus averts his eyes, and, when Mary turns to him, prostrates himself, Roger, going against his previous resolution, looks over his shoulder as the supine Christina looks up.

This episode in *The Life of Christina of Markyate* is revealing when placed alongside that in the Old English *Mary of Egypt* for a number of reasons. If *Mary of Egypt* is, as Lees and Overing suggest, concerned in part with interpretation, and if the episode in *The Life of Christina of Markyate* is indebted to that text in some way, however tenuously, then Christina's *Life* offers evidence of how *Mary of Egypt* was actually read. To what extent does Christina's *Life* respond to the invitation in the Old English text to understand the female saint in figurative terms? Do Roger, or Christina, or the author of her *Life* discover or rediscover God in the aged naked fleeing woman? Roger is converted in a sense, in that he realizes his mistake in trying to avoid Christina, but Christina, who takes the place of Mary of Egypt in this episode, does not carry the same weight of figurative meaning. Christina may represent God's will rather than God, but she also has agency in her own right. She is not merely looked at; she also looks.

This is indicative of the larger differences between the two texts. In Mary of Egypt the saint is both elusive in a literal sense (she runs away) and in a metaphorical sense (in terms of her figurative meaning). *The Life of Christina of Markyate*, in contrast, is concerned with a real, living and *familiar* woman (familiar to the author, and to the initial audience). To put it another way, Christina cannot be read as God because she is known to be Christina. Further, even if we are unconvinced of any direct connection between the two narratives, both are nevertheless concerned with the representation of spiritual friendship between men and women. The Old English narrative may direct the reader towards a figurative reading of such friendships (interpreted as the relationship between the soul and God) but it allows the sexual element in this relationship to remain. Indeed, with its focus on pursuit, nakedness and former sinfulness, it foregrounds this sexual element. Similarly, the Old English narrative is concerned with ineffability as well as interpretation. This is manifest in the treatment of Mary of Egypt's name: we, as readers, know her name from the beginning but Zosimus does not until after she is dead. The narrative, from Zosimus's perspective (if not, in this case, from the reader's), is enigmatic, haunted by ambiguity and uncertainty. Christina's *Life* presents the spiritual friendship between Roger and Christina in literal rather than figurative terms. The 'mutual glance' inspires 'heavenly desire' (*Life*, 103) and a fire of burning love but the episode is immediately explained in terms of Roger and Christina choosing to live together 'in chastity and charity' and in terms of their fear of scandal. As a consequence, the *Life* betrays a much greater anxiety about the sexual element to their relationship and tries (perhaps not entirely successfully) to overwrite it. Christina's book therefore resists – or tries to resist – multiple interpretations. Any identification between Christina of Markyate and Mary of Egypt can only be fleeting and partial as the virgin must not be conflated with the reformed harlot. As for Roger, it is our belief in Christina rather than our faith in God that has to be confirmed, although the former is clearly predicated upon the latter.

If the similarities between the Old English Mary of Egypt and *The Life of Christina of Markyate* may be accidental, the connection with another female saint's life popular in the Anglo-Saxon period cannot be denied. In Christina's *Life*, as we saw in Chapter 1, explicit mention is made to the life of Saint Cecilia, one of the legends amongst those retold by Ælfric. As Leslie A. Donovan has observed, this narrative 'offered medieval woman a more practical possibility for achieving sanctity than the violence and refusal to marry presented in many other virgin martyrs' lives'.[9] Again one key highly charged scene in the Old English life – in this case one *explicitly* concerned with sex – connects it to Christina's book. Christina takes upon herself the role of Cecilia with her betrothed Burthred playing the saint's husband Valerian as they are brought together to consummate their relationship. Christina relates the story of Cecilia and Burthred: 'And sitting on her bed with him, she strongly encouraged him to live a chaste life, putting forward the saints as examples' (*Life*, 51; compare *Women Saints' Lives*, 58). The rereading of the story of Cecilia and Valerian that is here attributed to Christina is both literal and figurative. Christina and Burthred will live in a chaste marriage like Cecilia and Valerian, but for them the 'crown' of martyrdom (*Life*, 51) is reinterpreted as a religious vocation as Christina proposes that both will in due course enter a monastery or convent. The reworking of the life of Saint Cecilia in Christina's biography is written in such a way that it also anticipates the account of her spiritual friendship with Roger. Christina's initial attempt to emulate Cecilia does not succeed. This is, at least in part, because Burthred's 'conversion' is short-lived. He is immediately persuaded by her family to renew his attempts on Christina's virginity and also retracts a subsequent offer to release her from her betrothal and to support her financially to join a religious community (*Life*, 69–71). Nevertheless, Christina ultimately achieves her imitation of Cecilia in her chaste cohabitation in the hermit's cell. Indeed Christina's desire that she and Burthred make a vow of chastity so that 'neither will look upon the other except with a pure and angelic gaze' (*Life*, 51) finds its fulfilment in the modest exchange of glances between Christina and Roger discussed earlier.

Karen A. Winstead argues that Christina of Markyate's biographer deviates from tradition when he 'fixes his attention on his heroine's *failure* to imitate a famous saint'.[10] However, as Dyan Elliott points out, the motif of the saint who 'fails to convert her husband to chastity but refuses to consummate her marriage, much to his chagrin' was a feature of insular Anglo-Saxon female sanctity.[11] The twice-married Æthelthryth of Ælfric's collection (*Women Saints' Lives*, 32–5) provides just one example. As Jocelyn Wogan-Browne neatly puts it, 'In the lives of forcibly betrothed and married native virgin saints, the pagan tyrant role [of the virgin passion narrative] is filled by unwanted British husbands.'[12] Yet, in one significant respect, Christina's *Life* diverges from the model of virgin martyrdom found in Ælfric in particular: in dwelling on Christina's conflict with her parents, and in keeping with post-Conquest vernacular traditions, it places far greater emphasis on what Wogan-Browne calls 'female desire and dissent'.[13] Other, less obvious, Old English saints' lives that echo through Christina's include those of Agnes and Agatha. Agnes is forced by the judge Simpronius to proceed naked, but miraculously covered by her hair, to a brothel (*Women Saints' Lives*, 49), and Agatha is handed over by the persecutor Quintianus to prostitutes 'to learn their practices so that her mind would be perverted' (*Women Saints' Lives*, 38). Similarly, Christina's father stripped her (although she remained 'clothed with the gems of virtue') and wanted to drive her from his house (*Life*, 73). Meanwhile her mother 'wasted a great deal of money on old crones who tried with their love potions and charms to drive her out of her mind with impure desires' (*Life*, 75). In the latter case, physical sexual initiation is replaced by magical concoctions, but the intention is comparable and the role of women in the corruption of innocence crucial. In Ælfric, the prostitute Aphrodisia laments that ' "Stones may soften and stiff iron become like molten lead, before the faith in Agatha's breast can ever be extinguished" ' (*Women Saints' Lives*, 38). In Christina's *Life*, the 'Jewess' complains, ' "Our trouble has been all for nothing: I can see two phantoms, two persons, as it were, dressed in white, who accompany her at all times and protect her from assaults at all points" ' (*Life*, 75). In both of these examples from Christina's *Life*, it is the parents rather than pagan oppressors who act tyrannically to overcome their daughter's defiance, but, as in the Old English narratives, divine will prevails.

Equally strikingly, echoes of Ælfric's life of Eugenia (*Women Saints' Lives*, 68–77) and the Old English Euphrosyne (*Women Saints' Lives*, 80–90), narratives of pious women who live their lives as men, can be found in Christina's *Life*.[14] The life of Eugenia centres on a young pagan noblewoman who, accompanied by two eunuchs, sets off on a journey to find someone to teach her about Christianity. Cutting off her hair, she disguises herself as a youth and is soon converted. With her two male companions, she joins a monastery, and three years later is made abbot. The life of Euphrosyne tells of a virtuous and well-educated young woman whose Christian father has promised her in marriage to a wealthy suitor, but who desires to dedicate herself to God by joining a monastery for which her father has a particular attachment. Seeking the advice of one of the brothers, she is urged to flee from her father and her betrothed, dressed as a monk. The most obvious parallels are between the legend of Euphrosyne and *The Life of Christina of Markyate*. Christina also expresses a desire at a young age 'to share in [the] fellowship' of a monastery (St Albans) to which her parents introduce her (*Life*, 39). She too, with the help of male companions – the solitary Eadwin and his servant Loric – uses a male disguise to escape from her family (*Life*, 81–97). Both narratives stress the grief and anger of parents and bridegrooms, and in particular the extensive but fruitless searches that they carry out. But for Euphrosyne, as for Eugenia, the adoption of male clothing signals a more long-lasting change in gendered identity (Euphrosyne also succeeds in entering the monastery, claiming to be a eunuch, and in fact lives out her days as a man). In contrast, in *The Life of Christina of Markyate*, although the flight itself is described at some length, Christina's disguise is short-lived as she escapes to the anchoress Alfwen and a community of women, and immediately resumes female attire. Furthermore, Christina's temporary gender transgression is given a metaphorical interpretation, which deflects the reader from understanding it too literally:

> Why delay fugitive? Why do you respect your feminine sex? Put on manly courage and mount the horse like a man. At this she put aside her fears and, jumping on the horse as if she were a youth and setting spurs to his flanks, she said to the servant . . .
>
> [Quid fugitiva moraris? Quid sexum feminei vereris? Virilem animum indue, et more viri in equum ascende. Dehinc abiecta pusillanimitate: viriliter super equum saliens atque calcaribus eius latera pungens famulo dixit . . .] (*Life*, 92–3)

Christina exchanges female modesty for masculine bravery, defending her virginity with virility and heroism.

Like the Old English narratives of Mary of Egypt, Cecilia, Agnes and Agatha, those of Eugenia and Euphrosyne emphasize the sexuality and desirability of the saintly protagonist. Eugenia, as a monk, is subjected to the attempted seduction of the widow Melantia. Euphrosyne is not only sought after by her bridegroom, but also, when passing as a eunuch, lusted after by the brothers in the monastery. In *The Life of Christina of Markyate*, the sexual threat, Burthred's continued pursuit of Christina, manifestly drives her escape, but it is also represented symbolically. As she flees her father's house, Christina is 'swathed in a long cloak that reached to her heels' to cover her male disguise, but on being followed by her sister Matilda, she drops 'one of the sleeves of the man's garment which she was hiding beneath her cloak' (*Life*, 91). Thinking quickly she manages to distract Matilda by passing her an item of female clothing (a veil) as well as her father's keys to return to the house. As Elizabeth Alvilda Petroff has pointed out, this incident replays and inverts a vision earlier in the *Life*.[15] In this Christina sees Burthred 'prostrate on the ground swathed in a black cape with his face turned downwards' reaching out and trying to seize Christina, who 'gathering her garments about her and clasping them close to her side, for they were white and flowing, passed him untouched' (*Life*,

77). Here, the colour of the clothing is clearly symbolic, Burthred's black cloak signifying his sexual desire and sinister intentions, Christina's white dress her chastity. Christina's virginal robes protect her from Burthred's desperate lustful clutches. Later, when Christina actually puts on a cape like that of Burthred, a mantle of masculinity, it too serves to protect rather than threaten her.

Fascinatingly, Christina's vision is also inverted in the episode discussed at the beginning of this section, when Christina is prostrated before Roger and Burthred's unseeing grasping is replaced by the pious exchange of looks of the pure in spirit. Indeed when these two episodes are read side by side the full meaning of the 'mutual glance' of Roger and Christina becomes clear. Whereas in the vision, Burthred's sinful sexual desire for his betrothed is equated with spiritual blindness, Christina's chaste friendship with Roger is sparked by their shared spiritual insight. Throughout the Old English lives of the women saints, with their foci on chaste encounters and celibate marriages, seduction, humiliation and prostitution, and flights in male disguise, sexuality is always an issue. Christina's *Life* draws on narratives such as these to describe her defence of her virginity and to explore spiritual friendship – two subjects that are of necessity closely interrelated. In so doing, Christina's *Life* overtly explores issues such as threatened rape and physical torment, although her suffering never approximates the tortures and martyrdoms of her role models. Nevertheless, perhaps because it deals with living people rather than legendary saints, compared with that in the legend of Mary of Egypt, its treatment of spiritual friendship is extremely cautious and tries to overwrite the erotic. What should be clear, however, is that in *The Life of Christina of Markyate*, we can find evidence of how the Old English lives of the women saints might have been read. Here, after all, is one woman who, in her pursuit of a life devoted to God, either imitated these virgins herself, or was seen by her own biographer to be part of their tradition, or both. Clemence of Barking's *Life of St Catherine*, in contrast, provides an example of a woman writer rewriting in translation the life of a woman saint for her own religious community and beyond.

The saint's life and the woman writer: Clemence of Barking's St Catherine

A substantial number of Anglo-Norman saints' lives have survived of which three are known to have been authored by women. These include a life of Edward the Confessor, by an anonymous nun of Barking Abbey in Essex; a life of Æthelthryth of Ely (St Audrey) written by one Marie, possibly of Chatteris Abbey in Cambridgeshire; and the *Life of St Catherine* by Clemence of Barking (*fl.* 1163–c.1200).[16] The identities of these authors are far from secure: the life of St Audrey has been attributed to Marie de France;[17] while the life of Edward is sometimes seen as an early work by Clemence of Barking.[18] Other lives were written for female patrons, such as the life of St Margaret of Scotland (1046–93), written for her daughter Matilda, wife of Henry I, or the anonymous female patron of the late-twelfth-century French *Life of St Lawrence*. What becomes clear even from these few examples is that French hagiography is an important aspect of female textual production and dissemination in post-Conquest England. Clemence of Barking's *Life of St Catherine* illustrates just how distinctive a woman's version of a well-known narrative can be, even one written in such a highly formulaic genre as this.

As with Marie de France, little is known of Clemence of Barking beyond what she herself tells us in her conclusion:

> I who have translated her life am called Clemence by name. I am nun of Barking, for love of which I took this work in hand. (*Life of St Catherine*, 43)

> [Jo ki sa vie ai translatee,
> Par nun sui Clemence numee.
> De Berkinge sui nunain.
> Pur s'amur pris cest oevre en mein. (*Life of St Catherine*, ll. 2689–92)][19]

In contrast to Marie de France at the end of the *Fables*, in her act of authorial self-naming, Clemence of Barking identifies herself in relation not to her country but to her vocation and her convent, revealing herself to be an English Benedictine. In contrast with Marie de France in the conclusion to the *Fables* (and more like the Marie de France of the epilogue to *Saint Patrick's Purgatory*), Clemence of Barking is less concerned with preserving her own fame as writer than with salvation. Immediately before these lines she invites her community of readers to join with her in prayer to her subject, St Catherine. She then follows them with the formulaic request to 'all who will hear this book and who listen to it with a receptive heart to pray to God on my behalf' (43).

Yet, strikingly, Clemence of Barking's introduction to her *Life of St Catherine*, which appears to be her own innovation, closely resembles the Prologues to Marie de France's *Lais* and *Fables*. Like Marie de France in these texts, Clemence emphasizes the moral responsibility of those who have knowledge to share it with others:[20]

> All those who know and understand what is good have a duty to demonstrate it wisely, so that by the fruit of its goodness others may be encouraged to do good deeds and to want what is good, as far as they are able. (*Life of St Catherine*, 3)
>
>> [Cil ki le bien seit e entent
>> Demustrer le deit sagement,
>> Que par le fruit de sa bunté
>> Seient li altre amonesté
>> De bien faire e de bien voleir
>> Sulunc ço qu'en unt le poeir. (*Life of St Catherine*, ll. 1–6)]

With its botanical metaphor, this claim resonates with Marie de France's assertion in her *Lais* that 'When a truly beneficial thing is heard by many people, it then enjoys its first blossom, but if it is widely praised its flowers are in full bloom' (*Lais*, 41).[21] Both writers draw on images of fecundity and generation to describe textual composition. Clemence of Barking's authority is Christ himself, who 'gave us both precept and example', anticipating her later description of Christ as the 'fruit' of the cross, rather than the venerable writers and thinkers that Marie de France cites in her Prologues. In contrast to Marie de France, she does not place particular significance on eloquence, but both women writers dwell on the moral benefits achieved by taking upon themselves the 'task' – Clemence of Barking's word is 'labur' (*Life of St Catherine*, l. 24) – of teaching others. For Clemence of Barking, as for Marie de France at the end of *Saint Patrick's Purgatory*, translation is an act of devotion. Furthermore, whereas in the *Lais*, Marie de France emphasizes the originality of her enterprise of preserving the lais, for Clemence of Barking it is the urgency of her task of translating a saint's life 'from Latin into the vernacular' that has to be stressed.

In an important passage, Clemence of Barking explains that she does not simply undertake her translation to make her text 'more pleasing' but because of necessity:

> It was translated before and well set out according to the standards of the time. But people then were not so hard to please or so critical as they are in our day, and will be even more so after we are gone. Because times and men's quality have changed, the poem is held in low esteem, for it is somewhat defective in places. So it is necessary to correct it and make the

times conform to the people. I am not correcting it out of arrogance, for
I seek no acclaim. He alone should be praised from whom I derive my
small amount of knowledge. (*Life of St Catherine*, 3)

> [Ele fud jadis translaté
> Sulunc le tens bien ordené;
> Mais ne furent dunc si veisdus
> Les humes, ne si envius
> Cum il sunt al tens ki est ore
> E aprés nus serrunt uncore.
> Pur ço que li tens est mué
> E des humes la qualité
> Est la rime vil tenue
> Car ele est asquans corrumpue.
> Pur ço si l'estuet amender
> E le tens selunc la gent user.
> Ne l'aiment pas pur mun orgoil,
> Kar preisie estre n'en voil;
> Il sul en deit loenge aveir
> De qui sai mun povre saveir. (*Life of St Catherine*, ll. 35–50)]

As Catherine Batt points out, for Clemence of Barking, 'reading is presented as a pleasure both aesthetic and doctrinal'.[22] Clemence of Barking
is fully aware of the evolving literary tradition within which she is writing.
Like Marie de France, she understands its limitations (for Marie de France,
there are too many translations; for Clemence of Barking, those that
already exist are inadequate) and thus its opportunities. At the same time
(and like Marie de France in the prologue to 'Guigemar'), Clemence of
Barking is aware of the dangers of hostile reception and misprision. Her
source text (also in the vernacular – she is *not* translating from Latin), outdated and flawed as it is, is now badly received at least in part because *men*
have become corrupted. Given how difficult it is to satisfy contemporary
audiences, her own translation may suffer a similar fate in the future.
Despite the (highly conventional) assertion of humility in the final sentence, Clemence of Barking does not directly address the difficulties of
writing as a woman any more than does Marie de France in her *Lais*.
Nevertheless, implicitly, through her account of St Catherine's verbal
conflict with the philosophers, she does assume a defiant stance against
clerical privilege.

The legend of this female saint was hugely popular in the later Middle
Ages. Nevertheless, like Marie de France, in the process of translating her
source, Clemence of Barking makes the text her own. Most strikingly, she

identifies with her saintly protagonist, whose wisdom she shares.[23] In retelling her tale of St Catherine, Clemence of Barking mirrors her subject's narration of 'la fable' (*Life of St Catherine*, l. 745) or the tale of Christ. Clemence of Barking shares with St Catherine an understanding of the necessity of instructing others. Indeed the French term 'plaideresse' (*Life of St Catherine*, l. 335), which Jocelyn Wogan-Browne and Glyn S. Burgess gloss as 'speaker'[24] but which also has legal connotations of 'advocate', applied to the saint by her antagonist, the pagan emperor Maxentius, could equally describe the Clemence of Barking of the Prologue. Clemence of Barking's authorial voice blurs with the authoritative speech of her subject.

St Catherine is described at the outset as uniquely learned: '[Her father] had her taught letters and how to argue a case and defend her position. There was no dialectician on earth who could defeat her in argument' (*Life of St Catherine*, 5). In other words, Catherine has received the sort of advanced education usually limited to clerics. In her first confrontation with Maxentius, who rejoices in persecuting the Christians and in forcing them to sacrifice to false gods, we are reminded, before she speaks, that 'she was well trained in fair speech' (*Life of St Catherine*, 6). Again and again in this narrative, the potency of her words is emphasized. These rhetorical skills are perceived by the Emperor directly as a challenge to masculine power, as his letter summonsing his philosophers reveals:

> 'Let it be known by everyone far and near – especially rhetoricians, who are experts in fine and effective speech – that the emperor has a great need for everyone to come to him and maintain his honour and his law, for he finds himself confronted by a powerful woman advocating that he should abandon his law. If he can confound her so that she can make no further reply and has to surrender publicly, when she prides herself so much on her skills in debate, he will make them his personal advisers and they will be honoured above all others.' (*Life of St Catherine*, 8)

['Ço sachent tuit e pres e loin
Que l'emperur ad grant besoin
– E meimement rethorien
Ki parler seivent e bel e bien –
Quit tuit a l'emperur viengent,
S'onur e sa lei maintiengent,
Kar une plaideresse ad forte
Ki de sa lei guerpir l'enorte.
Si il ceste poent cunfundre,
Que ne lur sache mais respundre,
Que devant tuz seit recreante

> Del desputer dunt tant se vante,
> De ses cunseilz les frad privez
> E sur tuz serrunt honurez.' (*Life of St Catherine*, ll. 329–42)]

The conflict between Maxentius and Catherine revolves around the question of whose 'masters' are better. Maxentius tells Catherine that her wisdom would have been greater if she had learned from his pagan clerics (*Life of St Catherine*, 7). Catherine in turn insists that her own teachers were greatly skilled, but that once she had encountered the Christian Gospel, she realized the inadequacy of anything but spiritual knowledge (*Life of St Catherine*, 9).

In response to Maxentius's summons, fifty philosophers arrive at the Emperor's palace. On discovering the nature of their opponent they are dismayed. In an addition to her source, Clemence of Barking describes how their spokesperson is overcome by envy. Here we find a concern with the negative consequences of jealousy similar to that found in the prologue to Marie de France's 'Guigemar':

> To this day many people feel great chagrin at virtues possessed by others. When the good receive more praise than they do, they feel that they are being reproached. An arrogant man cannot admit that someone is his equal in goodness unless it be someone who enjoys his favour, shares his habits and follows his example. If he knows what is good, he refuses to declare it; if another proclaims it, he refuses to listen. When he hears another praised, he often takes on something he later regrets. (*Life of St Catherine*, 10)

> > [Uncore unt cel us li plusur,
> > Que d'altrui bien unt grant dolur.
> > Avis lur est qu'il sunt blasmez
> > Quant li bon sunt plus d'els loez.
> > Orguillus huem ne put granter
> > Que nul par bunté li seit per,
> > Si n'est alcun ki ait sa grace
> > E sun us tienge e siut sa trace
> > S'il seit le bien, nel velt geir;
> > Si altre le dit, nel velt oir.
> > Pur altrui los enprent suvent
> > Tele chose dunt puis repent. (*Life of St Catherine*, ll. 457–68)]

Here Clemence of Barking uses the same sort of proverbial language as Marie de France although here, of course, she is applying it not to her own detractors, but to the opponent of her protagonist. Whereas Marie de France claims her enemies are within their rights to behave as they do and implies that there is little she can do about it, Clemence of Barking stresses that the philosopher 'was later forced to repent and to confess the real truth' (*Life of St Catherine*, 10).

Perhaps the most marked contrast between Clemence of Barking's *Life of St Catherine* and Marie de France's *Lais* and *Fables* in particular (and also the *Purgatory*, if to a lesser extent) is that Clemence of Barking represents women in far more *consistently* positive terms. Thus in her account of the Fall she presents women and men as equals:

> He made men and women to be rational beings and then placed them in paradise. The enemy deceived the woman through the apple that she ate. She gave some to her husband. He ate it and thereby went astray. (*Life of St Catherine*, 13)

> > [Humes e femmes raisnables fist
> > E pois en pareis les mist.
> > L'enimi la femme enginna
> > Par la pume qu'ele manga.
> > Ele en mangad e sun segnur,
> > Il en manga si fist folur. (*Life of St Catherine*, ll. 701–6)][25]

Clemence of Barking does not depict Eve as disobedient or deceptive, but as the victim of treachery that in turn brings down Adam. Neither is inherently evil; both have free will.[26] Later in her discussion of Christ as fruit of the cross, Clemence of Barking again avoids condemning Eve. She states: 'When the father . . . had created man and woman and given them power over good and evil, that man sinned through the fruit of the tree which God forbade him' (*Life of St Catherine*, 17–18). The former retelling of the Fall is juxtaposed with a celebration of the Virgin Mary (like Eve, created by God): 'When [Christ] came down to earth, he clothed himself in flesh and blood, which he took from a chaste maiden; she was his creation and his handmaiden. Without defilement he placed himself in her, and without pain he was born of her' (*Life of St Catherine*, 14). Here Clemence of Barking honours the patron saint of her own religious community.

The ascription of rationality to Eve as well as Adam is entirely consistent with Clemence of Barking's portrayal of the female as intelligent and sagacious, demonstrated so clearly in the tremendously detailed rendering of Catherine's defeat of the philosophers. Scholarship and logic – male clerical preserves – are appropriated by Clemence of Barking through

Catherine. As Simon Gaunt has observed, in this narrative male learning may be pitted against female faith, but female learning is key to Catherine's victory.[27] Mention is also made of St Helena (mother of the emperor Constantine), who found the true cross (*Life of St Catherine*, 4), and St Catherine herself cites the example of the Sibyl, who was believed to have foretold Christ's mission (*Life of St Catherine*, 16–17). Critics have often noted that other representations of female virgin martyrs dwell voyeuristically on the tortured, suffering female body. A notable example of this is the Middle English *Life of Saint Katherine* where the torments of the virgin martyr at the hands of her (sexually?) frustrated antagonist are graphically described:

> The king had no power over his senses, but began to tremble and did not know what to say. He madly commanded that she be stripped stark naked and her bare flesh and her beautiful body beaten with knotted scourges, which was immediately done, so that her lovely body was all lathered with blood.

> [Þe king ne cuðe nawit ah bigon to cwakien & nuste hwat seggen. Het o wode wise strupen hire steort naket. & beaten hire bare flesch & hire freliche bodi wið cnotte schurgen. And swa men dide sone þet hire lefliche lich liðerede al o blode.][28]

Clemence of Barking, in contrast, is relatively restrained in her portrayal of such violence:

> Then the evil tyrant ordered the soldiers to take her, beat her with iron rods and put her in the dungeon. They did his bidding and beat her very savagely, wounding her tender body so brutally that the blood flowed out from every part. (*Life of St Catherine*, 25)

> > [Dunc cumande li fel tyrant,
> > Que la preissent li sergant,
> > De verges de fer la batissent,
> > E pois en chartre la meissent.
> > Cil firent sun cumandement;
> > Mult la batirent asprement.
> > Tuit pleinstrent sun tendre cors,
> > Que par tut raeit li sans ors. (*Life of St Catherine*, ll. 1457–64)]

Furthermore, in Clemence of Barking's narrative, but not in the Middle English version, the description immediately shifts from the scourging back to St Catherine's verbal exchanges with the Emperor. As

Wogan-Browne and Burgess point out, Clemence of Barking's Catherine is never just 'a stripped, naked, female body'; rather her intellectual and rhetorical skills are always foregrounded.[29] Clemence of Barking not only identifies with St Catherine but also offers her as a figure that her readers (both men *and* women) might emulate.

Clemence of Barking's text 'inscribes' audiences for Catherine's saintly history within the text, in the sense that it imagines the 'situations of telling and listening'.[30] The philosophers provide one such audience – confounded by Catherine's arguments they declare their faith in the Christian God (*Life of St Catherine*, 19–20). However, not everyone who hears her speak is so convinced: 'If one said that she was right, another said that she was deceiving them' (*Life of St Catherine*, 18). Again, Clemence of Barking describes Catherine's detractors in sententious terms, likening them to those false flatterers who cultivate the wealthy, but who quickly turn against them if their luck changes. Thus Clemence of Barking once more seems to anticipate a hostile readership who will refuse to learn from this exemplary life.

Yet, significantly, Clemence of Barking's *Life* also has inscribed within it an idealized female reception. A central focus of the second half of the narrative is Maxentius's wife, who, along with the royal adviser Porphiry, is also converted by Catherine, and who endures cruel torture (her breasts pierced by nails and torn off) and martyrdom for her faith. At the moment of her greatest trial, the queen turns to Catherine in supplication, requesting her to intercede on her behalf: ' "Oh, royal maid, offer prayers for this handmaiden of the lord to your great God, who is so good and who provides complete reassurance for his own" ' (*Life of St Catherine*, 37). Critics have noted the courtly, lyrical register of Clemence of Barking's text, and this is particularly evident in this section of the narrative. Remarkably, the Emperor's words to his wife echo Tristram's message in Marie de France's 'Chevrefoil', ' "Sweet love, so it is with us: without me you cannot survive, nor I without you" ' (*Lais*, 110). Nevertheless, when the Emperor asks rhetorically, ' "How will you live without me and how shall I live without you?" ' he speaks not as a languishing lover but as a judge announcing a sentence of execution (*Life of St Catherine*, 35).[31] St Catherine's response to the queen's invocation translates the courtly into the spiritual, with the promise to the queen that she will find in Christ a more beautiful lover, a more stable kingdom, greater joy and overwhelming sweetness (*Life of St Catherine*, 37). Subsequently, before her own eventual death, Catherine also addresses a crowd of female spectators, encouraging them to rejoice in her fate and to weep for their own sins (*Life of St Catherine*,

41), in words which echo Christ's speech to the women of Jerusalem (Luke 23. 27–8).[32]

The closing sections of the *Life of St Catherine*, while formulaic, are reminiscent of the epilogue to Marie de France's *Saint Patrick's Purgatory*. As noted above, Clemence of Barking names herself as the translator of her work. At the same time as she aligns herself with Catherine, with the queen, and with her readers, as recipients of God's grace. Having described Catherine's demise, and the miracles that immediately followed it, she invites her readers (in words that resonate with Catherine's to the queen) 'to desire his love and eschew all worldly love' for the one 'who alone is king and lord' (*Life of St Catherine*, 42). Like the queen, Clemence of Barking prays to Catherine for 'the will to love God and to serve him and come to a happy end' (*Life of St Catherine*, 43). Finally, she directly addresses her implied, ideal audience – 'all who will hear this book and listen to it with a receptive heart' – asking that they too should pray for her own salvation (*Life of St Catherine*, 43).

What of the intended audience of the *Life of St Catherine*? Clemence of Barking must certainly have produced this work for her own community of enclosed nuns. For Gaunt, this makes the *Life* 'an unusual, though not unique example, of a woman writing for other women'.[33] At times, the text certainly implies a female readership, or at least one sympathetic to female suffering. When describing the grief of the queen's people at her death, Clemence focuses on the women and comments: 'Certainly, anyone who has ever loved a woman would feel compassion' (*Life of St Catherine*, 38). Nevertheless (and somewhat surprisingly, given the focus on women within the narrative), Clemence of Barking directly addresses an audience that is male and aristocratic. She reminds them: 'Lords, you have heard very clearly how these martyrs met their end' (*Life of St Catherine*, 20). Within the narrative Catherine addresses a male audience *and* a female audience (*Life of St Catherine*, 22, 33, 41). Furthermore, in describing herself as a nun of Barking, Clemence both sanctions her own community, and, as William MacBain observes, implicitly directs her text beyond her own convent.[34] In choosing to write in the French vernacular, and in choosing to stress that her saint is noble as well as spiritual, Clemence of Barking, like Marie de France, assumes a non-Latinate but elite, privileged and very probably aristocratic or courtly reception. Certainly, the nuns of Barking would have been members of the nobility or upper gentry and the convent would have maintained close links to the Anglo-Norman court. Clemence of Barking assumes, in other words, a textual community that would have included the upper ranks of the laity (of both sexes) and clerics as well as religious women.

According to Wogan-Browne, who emphasizes the theological sophistication of the *Life*, and its debts to Anselm of Canterbury (*d*.1109), 'Clemence transforms both vernacular and Latin source materials, and challenges
or repositions the discourses of other audiences – clerical and seigneurial
– *beyond* the Barking community'.[35] In terms of actual audience, we know
that the *Life* survives in three manuscripts in France and England. The
earliest of these – in a collection that includes the *Life of St Alexis* – is dedicated to the wife of Henry I (Paris, Bibliothèque Nationale, MS nouv. acq.
fr. 4503). Another (London, British Library, MS Additional 70513) appears
in an important compilation of hagiographic texts (which also includes the
two other French lives known to have been written by women), that may
have been commissioned by Isabella, countess of Arundel.[36] It was presented to the nuns at Campsey Priory for refectory readings. Wogan-
Browne also notes Clemence of Barking's influence on later texts, including
the ascription of some lines to Mary Magdalene in a West Midlands preaching text. She concludes, 'on the indications of responses to her work as we
so far have them, Clemence's voice was received as authoritative'.[37] Despite
the fears expressed by Marie de France, and more indirectly by Clemence
of Barking herself, it seems that writings by women could be both highly
regarded and influential. Yet, as the example of Osbern Bokenham illustrates, women's engagement with textual culture was not limited to
reading and writing and could manifest itself in a myriad different ways.

Women patrons and female saints: Osbern Bokenham's *Legends of Holy Women*

Osbern Bokenham (1393–*c*.1464) was a friar of the Augustinian priory of
Stoke Clare in East Anglia. His hagiographic collection, *Legends of Holy
Women*, was compiled between 1443 and 1447.[38] This survives in its entirety
in one manuscript: London, British Library MS Arundel 327. Bokenham's
source texts for his English translation include the thirteenth-century
Golden Legend by Jacobus de Voragine (1230–98). Critics have made the
case that the lives gathered in the Arundel manuscript were originally
composed and circulated piecemeal as a series of separate devotional booklets.[39] Yet the recent discovery of another, much more extensive, hagiographic collection by Bokenham lends support to Sheila Delaney's argument
that he was also responsible for organizing the individual lives into a composite whole.[40] In producing what may be the first free-standing collection
of female saints' lives, Bokenham may indeed (as Delaney contends)
have set out to write a spiritual response to *The Legend of Good Women*

by Geoffrey Chaucer (*c*.1342–1400), and also, as I will argue here, *Confessio Amantis* by John Gower (1330–1408). Other influences include John Lydgate (1370–1450), *The Life of our Lady* and John Capgrave (1393–1464), *The Life of St Katherine*. Bokenham translated some of his saints' lives for patrons within East Anglia – including women. The paratextual evidence (in the form of his dedications, and the inscription of presentation at the end of the manuscript) indicates that he was part of a thriving literary, and spiritual, network within Cambridge and East Anglia that included lay as well as religious men and women. Indeed his text carefully negotiates a range of inscribed, implied and intended audiences. Bokenham's *Legends* thus provides an important context for the East Anglian women's writing that is the focus of the last three chapters of this study.

In contrast to women writers such as Marie de France and Clemence of Barking, right at the start of the *Legends* Bokenham is able to, and indeed does, claim clerical authority. Bokenham opens the Prologue with a reference to 'euery clerk' [every cleric],[41] and proceeds to articulate what and why he is writing. He frames this discussion of author, matter, order and intention in terms of the scholastic literary theory of the Aristotelian 'four causes'.[42] In an extended humility topos, Bokenham refuses at this stage to name himself, because he fears that 'because of personal dislike and malice, few would have the pleasure of reading it and the work would be thrown into oblivion's corner' (*Legends of Holy Women*, 3) or, in the Middle English, 'the angle of oblyuyoun' (*Legendys of Hooly Wummen*, l. 40). While this concern about the jealousy of others and their slanderous reaction to his work may be reminiscent of that of Marie de France, the tone is much more overtly humorous, and it becomes apparent that Bokenham is writing in an intellectual rather than courtly environment. Shortly afterwards, Bokenham dismisses (under the cover of praising) 'the school of the clever writer Geoffrey of England [Geoffrey of Vinsauf]' by juxtaposing the elaborate rhetorical colouring of Geoffrey's work, the *Poetria Nova* or *New Poetry*, to his own simple, plain style, with its fidelity to its original (*Legends of Holy Women*, 4). At the end of the Prologue, Bokenham gives an account of the commissioning of his life of St Margaret – the first in the collection (as it appears in the sole complete manuscript witness) – by a fellow Augustinian friar, Thomas Burgh, who is named shortly afterwards. Here he picks up again the themes of envy, detraction and scandal. He insists that Burgh preserve his anonymity and protect his writing:

> . . . that you not display it where villainy might have it, and primarily at Cambridge in your establishment, where many capacious and subtle wits would soon discern my ignorance. (*Legends of Holy Women*, 6)

[. . . that ye detecte
It in no wyse wher that vylany
It myht haue, and pryncypally
At hoom at Caunbrygge in your hows,
Where wyttys be manye ryht capcyows
And subtyl, wych sone my lewydnesse
Shuld aspye . . . . (*Legendys of Hooly Wummen*, ll. 204–10)]

And if Burgh feels compelled to circulate the text, Bokenham asks him to pretend that he received it from a man who sells horses.

Bokenham's playful attack on the Cambridge clerics superficially seems to exclude them as readers of his text. Nevertheless, when seen in the context of his earlier allusions to the philosophers and his appropriation of the scholastic academic prologues it reveals that to some extent he sees his ideal audience as made in his own image. Yet at the same time, Bokenham also appeals to a greater authority and a more universal audience. 'To stimulate people's emotions to take pleasure in loving and serving' the virgin martyr St Margaret is the principal motive behind Bokenham's translation (*Legends of Holy Women*, 5). Consequently, his implied audience is not limited to Burgh and his companions. Two of the lives in the collection claim to have been commissioned by noble female patrons, and another four also name women dedicatees.[43] The life of Mary Magdalen was composed at the request of Isabel Bourchier, countess of Eu, sister of Richard, duke of York (*Legends of Holy Women*, 101–5); the life of Elizabeth of Hungary at that of Elizabeth de Vere, countess of Oxford (*Legends of Holy Women*, 102, 176, 195). The life of Katherine of Alexandria was written 'for the spiritual consolation of Katherine Howard and also to the comfort of Katherine Denston'(*Legends of Holy Women*, 126). The former is likely to have been the first wife of John Howard, future duke of Norfolk. John Howard was a cousin of Elizabeth de Vere.[44] Katherine Denston is also mentioned along with her husband and daughter in the life of St Anne (*Legends of Holy Women*, 30, 41); her husband was a local coroner and Justice of the Peace. The life of St Dorothy ends with a prayer for its commissioners, John Hunt and his wife Isabel (*Legends of Holy Women*, 99). The life of St Agatha intercedes on behalf of Agnes Flegge, the wife of a businessman and administrator for Richard of York (*Legends of Holy Women*, 158). These paratextual references indicate that Bokenham was writing, at least in part, for a tight network of aristocratic and gentry women, most either from, or with close connections to, East Anglia. Further, they suggest a direct intellectual and spiritual connection between Cambridge and its environs. The note appended to the end of the manuscript, in which Thomas Burgh states that he transcribed the collection himself in 1447, reveals that Burgh did not take seriously Bokenham's request that he preserve the anonymity of the text. Burgh not only names Bokenham, but he also confirms his order and community. However, at the same time, Burgh respects the spirit of Bokenham's *Legends of Holy Women* in so far as he directs it to a female audience and shows a concern with not only his own spiritual welfare but also that of a particular woman. Burgh reveals that he presented the manuscript to a convent 'so that they should remember him and his sister Dame Beatrice Burgh' (*Legends of Holy Women*, 195).

Bokenham shares with Clemence of Barking, and the Marie de France of *Saint Patrick's Purgatory*, the motivation of personal devotion combined with the desire to teach others. In his Prologue he depicts himself as a pilgrim; one who has travelled in Italy on more than one occasion and visited the shrine of St Margaret of Antioch at Montefiascone, and also her relics in England. He even includes the detail that he had touched the foot of St Margaret with his ring and that this saved him from danger during his travels (*Legends of Holy Women*, 5). This representation of the author as a pilgrim-narrator is picked up on elsewhere in the *Legends*. In the preface to the life of St Mary Magdalene, Bokenham refers to a pilgrimage he undertook to the shrine of Santiago de Compostela in 1445 (*Legends of Holy Women*, 103). In the life of St Margaret, Bokenham draws upon this self-representation in order to establish a connection between the actual translation of the remains of St Margaret and his own literary translation of the narrative from Latin into the vernacular.[45] Like the Augustine responsible for carrying the holy relics, Bokenham is a weak and weary pilgrim struggling to bring his task to completion (*Legends of Holy Women*, 18–19). If the *Legends of Holy Women* is a devout response to Chaucer's *Legend of Good Women*, as Delaney contends, Bokenham's pilgrim-narrator is also reminiscent of that of Chaucer in *The Canterbury Tales*. Of course the former is a religious rather than a secular figure, and the stories he tells are entirely spiritual. Bokenham deliberately invokes Chaucer throughout his text, repeatedly naming him as one of the great writers whom he cannot expect to emulate. These are, however, just some examples of the dense intertexuality of Bokenham's work. Bokenham also directs his audience to devotional works in the vernacular by other contemporary writers. When he retells the story of St Anne (*Legends of Holy Women*, 40) he refers to the *Life of our Lady* by Lydgate, who was a Benedictine monk of nearby Bury St Edmunds. He also alludes to the *Life of St Katherine* by his fellow Augustinian friar from Norfolk, Capgrave (*Legends of Holy Women*, 126).

The frequency with which Bokenham praises Gower alongside Chaucer and Lydgate suggests that this eulogy may be simply formulaic. However, Delaney makes the case that Bokenham, with his Yorkist political sympathies, may also be in the business of producing a 'negative critique' of the 'Lancastrian' poets, Chaucer, Lydgate and Gower.[46] I remain unconvinced that Bokenham is rejecting rather than emulating his predecessors, as the following brief analysis of Gower's influence on Bokenham will illustrate. The prolocutory to the life of St Mary Magdalene, which Bokenham opens with an elaborate astronomical passage establishing the date of the poem's commission, is reminiscent, for example, of the opening of the first chapter of Book i of Gower's Latin work *Vox Clamantis*.[47] Here, Bokenham establishes both his familiarity with classical literature and tropes (alluding, for example, to Ovid's *Metamorphoses*). Yet, at the same time, Bokenham separates himself from the smooth-tongued courtiers who 'like to make ballades and little booklets for their ladies' sakes, in which they feign sorrow and weeping as if death constrained their heart' (*Legends of Holy Women*, 105). He declares that 'to aspire to learn such craft of language in my old age and my condition would be foolish' and insists that his service to the female sex will be to offer 'spiritual comfort' alone. Bokenham's pilgrim-narrator thus bears similarities not only to Chaucer the pilgrim of *The Canterbury Tales*, but also to the *senex amans* or the aged lover of Gower's *Confessio Amantis*. Bokenham's poetic persona is particularly reminiscent of that at the end of the *Confessio*, when Amans is finally identified with the 'feeble and impotent' poet Gower and revealed to be too old for love.[48] Like Gower also, Bokenham repeatedly distances himself from the elaborate colours of rhetoric, insisting that his own plain style is suitable for his subject matter (for example, *Legends of Holy Women*, 4, 105).[49] Bokenham even apologizes for writing in a plain Suffolk dialect (*Legends of Holy Women*, 82).

But, equally interesting as the similarities between Bokenham's *Legends of Holy Women* and Gower's *Confessio Amantis* are the differences between them, and especially those found in their respective employments of the commissioning topos. Gower, famously, dedicated the first version of his *Confessio Amantis* to Richard II. Gower relates how, rowing along the Thames one day, he by chance met with King Richard. Having been invited on board the royal barge, Gower claims that the monarch issued him a command to write 'some new thing':[50] the poem that he is now producing. In revising the poem, Gower removed these and other lines and re-directed the poem to the future Henry IV and in his later poetry he depicted Richard not as a generous benefactor but as an abusive oppressor.

Bokenham provides us with two detailed accounts of the commissioning of his legends. In the first, the opening Prologue, as part of his descriptions of his Italian pilgrimages he tells us in a description that intriguingly resonates with the opening of Gower's poem how only five years previously he was saved by the saint's intercession. This occurred 'when a cruel tyrant drove me out of a barge into a swamp just outside Venice' (*Legends of Holy Women*, 5). Here Bokenham deliberately juxtaposes spiritual and secular power (while, it seems, avoiding making any specific political references), stressing that it is to honour 'that holy virgin who is willing to turn her ear to sinful prayers' that he finds himself 'impelled to translate her life' (*Legends of Holy Women*, 5–6). Bokenham's second extended description of the commissioning of one of his lives occurs in the prolocutory to the legend of St Mary Magdalen. Here he gives a lively account of his attendance at the Twelfth Night festivities held by the countess of Eu, where he fell into conversation with Lady Bourchier, and she requested that he make the Magdalen's life 'in English' for her (*Legends of Holy Women*, 102). This commissioning account testifies to the social immediacy of the relationship between patron and poet. As part of this prefatory material, Bokenham outlines the lineage of the countess and the possible inheritance of the throne of Castile (*Legends of Holy Women*, 101–2). Delaney makes the case that in so doing Bokenham is also expressing his support for the countess's brother, Richard, duke of York, as the legitimate heir to the English throne.[51] Bokenham's Yorkist sympathies are corroborated by Simon Horobin's argument that the surviving manuscript of Bokenham's larger collection of saints' lives was a presentation copy produced for Richard of York, and intended for the mealtime readings of his wife, Cecily Neville (known for her piety and vernacular book ownership).[52] But whether or not one reads into these lines a deliberate political intervention in support of the Yorkist claim, it is clear that Bokenham, in contrast to Gower, places great emphasis on and defers to female authority, whether saintly (St Margaret) or secular (the countess of Eu).

Bokenham's emphasis on female authority is manifest in his treatment of these female saints' lives. His version of the life of St Katherine, for example, bears comparison with that of Clement of Barking: Bokenham's life also avoids expanding upon the violent torture and suffering bodies of the saint and her follower, the empress. Similarly the former sinful life of Mary Magdalene, who 'spent her youth so shamelessly in promiscuity' is not dwelt upon unnecessarily (*Legends of Holy Women*, 108). The three sword strokes to the neck of St Cecilia are given a figurative slant, being explicitly linked to the 'three days' respite' granted her by God in which she was able to instruct and convert the people (*Legends of Holy Women*, 154). Interestingly, this is reminiscent of Julian of Norwich's desire to suffer, figuratively, the three wounds of St Cecilia and the subsequent three days and nights of illness that preceded her revelations.[53] At the time she first made this prayer, Julian was not an anchoress, although she may have been a nun. Felicity Riddy points out, however, that Bokenham's St Cecilia is presented as a model of *lay* piety, 'a pattern of the mixed life of action and contemplation . . . put into practice by devout women, including the appropriately named Cecily, duchess of York'.[54] Perhaps most interesting is Bokenham's treatment of the life of the married saint Elizabeth of Hungary (otherwise Elizabeth of Thuringia (1207–31)). Margery Kempe mentions the treatise of a St Elizabeth in her *Book* (154), but although that reference is probably to the *Revelations* of Elizabeth's great-niece, Elizabeth of Toess (*c*.1294–1336), clear parallels emerge between Kempe's *Book* and Bokenham's version of Elizabeth of Thuringia's life.[55] The most obvious comparison – beyond the fact that both were wives and had children but wished they could have retained their virginity – is that both devout women find themselves overcome with 'copious weeping' (*Legends of Holy Women*, 180). Both Elizabeth and Margery Kempe also embrace extreme aestheticism and voluntary poverty, tend the sick whom other people shun, fast and abstain from fine food, and eventually make vows of chastity. One episode in particular in Elizabeth's life resonates with *The Book of Margery Kempe*; Elizabeth earns the violent disapproval of her confessor, Conrad of Marburg, after she visits a convent without his permission (*Legends of Holy Women*, 190). Although this incident is also found in the *Golden Legend*, Bokenham's Conrad appears less unreasonable, and his Elizabeth more wilful.[56] Margery Kempe goes even further and sets off on pilgrimage to Northern Europe without consultation, but although her confessor rebukes her, he soon forgives her (*Book*, 247). Similarly, Elizabeth confronts a fashionable young man about his sinfulness, and as a consequence he joints a religious order (*Legends of Holy Women*, 192–3). Margery Kempe likewise converts her own dissolute son; and subsequently encourages a youth who has resolved to enter a monastery (*Book*, 221–3, 246).

Given its later date of composition, Bokenham's life of Elizabeth of Hungary could be read as a defence of aspects of Margery Kempe's controversial life and piety. A recurring theme in *The Book of Margery Kempe* is the disruption and hostility caused by her loud weeping and crying. One renowned visiting preacher refuses to allow her into the Church and turns many of her supporters against her (*Book*, 148–54). One of those who tolerates her regardless is a member of Bokenham's own order, an Augustinian

Friar from Capgrave's house at Lynn (*Book*, 167). Yet it is striking that Bokenham has Elizabeth herself condemn those ' "who inordinately contort their faces in weeping" ' and thus take the practice too far (*Legends of Holy Women*, 191).[57] Similarly, critics have noticed that Bokenham's life of St Katherine – a saint to whom Margery Kempe is unfavourably compared by one of her persecutors (*Book*, 111–12) – changes the most controversial aspects of her sanctity; aspects which Kempe herself emulated. Bokenham's revisions include omitting her mystical marriage to the Godhead and replacing her skills in disputation with more straightforward piety.[58] Paul Price argues that Bokenham deliberately revises the *Legends* for a specifically female audience to avoid encouraging 'transgressive female religious conduct' and to offer 'a stern rejoinder to those ambitious lay persons who do not know their place'.[59] Margery Kempe, who probably died just a few years before Bokenham was writing, would have been just such a lay person. Bokenham may have disapproved of any fledgling un-official local cult surrounding the holy woman of Lynn.

As a young man, Osbern Bokenham may well have known both Julian of Norwich and Margery Kempe. It is inconceivable that his friend, Cap-grave, who spent most of his life in Kempe's hometown of Lynn in Norfolk (where he became prior and then prior provincial) would not have been acquainted with them. Although Bokenham's *Legends* post-dates Julian of Norwich's *Revelations* and *The Book of Margery Kempe*, it clearly provides a context for understanding their religious lives and visionary writings. At the same time, it is crucial to note that the secular branch of the reading community that Bokenham anticipates overlaps with the actual commu-nity in which the Paston family lived and with which they interacted in the second half of the fifteenth century. For example, three letters survive from Elizabeth de Vere to John Paston,[60] and she recurs in the correspon-dence, as do the husbands of Lady Bourchier and Katherine Howard. Katherine Denston's half-brother, John Clopton, who was sheriff of Norfolk and Suffolk between 1451 and 1452, also figures (usually negatively) in the letters. Most notably there exists amongst Agnes Paston's papers a draft indenture, dated around 1454, of the settlement for the proposed marriage of John Clopton to Agnes's daughter Elizabeth.[61] This illustrates the will-ingness of the family to use marriage to forge alliances, even with enemies, although in this case the union did not actually go ahead. Given these con-nections, and our knowledge that books were lent, presented and willed to others, often within and between religious houses and the wider com-munity, and across social classes, it is entirely possible that Bokenham's *Legends* might have reached the Paston women or others like them. Agnes's son John was a keen book collector. The Paston women themselves may not have been great readers, but John's daughter Anne is reported to have lent a copy of *The Siege of Thebes* to the Earl of Arran.[62] It is therefore important to recognize that both they and Bokenham were connected by the same religious and patronage networks, spiritual and literary communities that, in earlier generations, also extended back to include Margery Kempe and Julian of Norwich.[63]

Conclusion

The Life of Christina of Markyate provides evidence of the reception of the Old English lives of women saints in the post-Conquest period; evidence which suggests that women actively modelled themselves on the virgin martyrs so popular in the late Anglo-Saxon period. The *Life* also indicates that women were able to offer their own interpretations of their exemplars to suit their own circumstances. The *Life* provides further evidence that these women's supporters (in this case, Christina's biographer) understood them in terms of their saintly predecessors, and expected their audience or readership to do likewise. Reading *The Life of Christina of Markyate* alongside the Old English lives of women saints enables us to see just how densely textured the former is with hagiographic allusions, themes and topoi. As my analysis has indicated, this is particularly marked in the representation of Christina's preservation of her virginity and of her spiritual friendship with Roger. At the same time, such a comparison enables us to see the ways in which *The Life of Christina of Markyate* differs from these earlier legends, especially in its representation of Christina of Markyate's active resistance to marriage and ensuing conflict with her own family. Clemence of Barking's *Life of St Catherine,* in contrast, suggests a connection with the writings of another woman, Marie de France. While it may be impossible to prove the direction of the influence, or even, conclusively, that the influence exists, it is clear that both Anglo-Norman writers were working within overlapping textual communities. Even though we know for certain that Clemence of Barking was a nun, and we are uncertain whether Marie de France was or not, both writers address a privileged aristocratic audience. Although Clemence of Barking may address her own nuns in the first instance, she evidently envisaged a wider courtly audience for her work. Like Marie de France, Clemence of Barking is aware of the difficulties of writing as a woman, and one of the strategies she develops to overcome these is to identify with her own saintly protagonist. These strategies seem to have worked: the manuscript evidence would suggest that Clemence of Barking's *Life of St Catherine* was regarded as authoritative. Osbern Bokenham's *Legends of Holy Women* illustrates the extent to which, directly and indirectly, texts authored by men might be influenced by women, as patrons as well as readers, and as positive and negative exempla. Although Bokenham as translator and compiler of the legends of female saints was able to claim the sort of clerical authority denied to Marie de France and Clemence of Barking, like them he expresses anxieties about how his work will be received. Bokenham locates himself in relation to a literary tradition that includes writers such as Chaucer, Lydgate, Capgrave and Gower. Nevertheless, he also defers to female authority, whether that be heavenly (that of the saints of whom he writes) or secular (the aristocratic and gentry patronesses of his work). *Legends of Holy Women* is the product of a thriving literary community, which required the production of works of vernacular devotion. Bokenham was writing for a coterie audience of religious and lay women and men, largely but not exclusively in East Anglia, an area associated with intense piety, orthodox and heterodox. His work is nuanced by an awareness of the religious tensions within Bokenham's own community, tensions that will be further examined in the next two chapters of this study.

4

Julian of Norwich (1342/3–after 1416)

Introduction

Very little is known about Julian of Norwich, beyond what she reveals about herself in her accounts of her visions or showings, and a handful of references in other documents. Even her birth name is unrecorded. Her writings focus on the divine revelations she received when she was 30½ years old and lying on her sick bed, with her friends, mother and priest gathered around her. The showings began on the eighth or thirteenth of May 1373 at 4 o'clock in the morning and lasted until after noon. She describes fifteen in all, starting with a vision of the Passion, and subsequently one of the Virgin Mary, and encompassing explanations of and reflections on the Trinity, Creation and sin. The following night, Julian received a sixteenth showing. In the intervening period she experienced doubt, despair and diabolic temptation as well as a return of her physical illness, and the devil also came back to torment her after the final showing. Two versions of her account of her showings have survived: the earlier, shorter *Vision Showed to a Devout Woman*, which was probably written in the 1380s or 1390s; and the longer *Revelation of Love*, composed possibly in the late fourteenth or early fifteenth century.[1] Julian records in the *Revelation* a supplementary showing that she received in 1388, and includes additional material that arose from greater understanding that she gained in 1393, some twenty years after her first experiences. Julian may not have been a recluse at the time of her original showings, and we do not know when she became one, but by this year she was certainly living as an anchoress in Norwich (a will of 1393/4 testifies to this). Julian is also mentioned in wills dating to 1404/5, 1415 and 1416. In 1413, Margery Kempe visited Julian in Norwich to seek spiritual advice. In the same year the original manuscript was produced from which the surviving version of the *Vision* was copied: Julian is described therein as being still alive. She must certainly have been dead by the time Margery Kempe wrote her *Book* in the late 1420s or 1430s.

This chapter offers a reading of the *Vision* and the *Revelation* that tries to balance attention to Julian's theology with attention to Julian as a woman writer. The first section, ' "I am really nothing" ', begins by looking at Julian's representation of herself as 'nothing' and explores the ways in which this links to the discussions of Creation, sin and Christ. Through her suppression or denial of her individuality and through her humility, Julian stresses her identification with her spiritual community of fellow Christians. The little she chooses to reveal about herself in the *Vision* connects with the theology of the *Vision*. While it is possible only to guess Julian's background at the time of her showings, we can make some assumptions about her level of education (which may, in any case, have been similar whether she were a nun or a privileged lay woman). Furthermore, the imagery of motherhood, childbirth and childlessness that resonates through the *Vision* does suggest a particularly feminine mysticism. The exploration here of Julian's accounts of sin (including her own fall) and of the secrets of God illustrates some of the ways in which the *Vision* anticipates the *Revelation*. The second section, ' "The Service and Labour of Motherhood" ', examines the connection between Julian's universalism and two overlapping innovations in the *Revelation*: the Parable of the Lord and the Servant and the metaphor of Jesus as mother. Another less commented upon addition to the *Revelation* – a brief account of St John of Beverley, brings together Julian as sinner, the servant from the parable, and also Christ as mother. Here, however, we also see that Julian's feminine theology does not always transcend medieval antifeminism. The additions in the *Revelation* further illustrate the accretive process of composition and point towards a more collaborative model of composition, where Julian not only reflects on the original visions but also shares them with others and brings new learning into play. At the same time she betrays anxiety that they might be misunderstood and reveals her desire to control interpretation.

The third section, ' "This Revelation is High Divinity and High Wisdom" ', looks at the evidence concerning the reception and transmission of Julian's writings. All the extant medieval and Early Modern texts of Julian's work appear to be descended from the *Vision* or the *Revelation*.[2] There is a single manuscript of the *Vision* that dates to the mid-fifteenth century: London, British Library, MS Additional 37790. There are three complete manuscripts of the *Revelation* that date to the seventeenth century. The two earliest of these are Paris, Bibliothèque Nationale, MS Fonds Anglais 40, and London, British Library, MS Sloane 2499. There is also a manuscript made up of selections from the *Revelation*, datable to *c*.1500

(London, Westminster Cathedral Treasury, MS 4); a seventeenth-century printed text, based on the Paris manuscript, by the English Benedictine monk, Serenus Cressy; and a seventeenth-century series of excerpts in a devotional anthology, known as the Upholland manuscript. For the most part, these texts are revealing about the secondary audience of Julian's writing, although the Sloane manuscript also provides more concrete evidence of collaborative composition. A better sense of the relationship between her implied audiences and her immediate reception, and of her literary as well as spiritual network, can be gained from the references to Julian in *The Book of Margery Kempe* and the evidence of contemporary bequests. Far from being isolated as a recluse, Julian seems to have been part of a thriving East Anglian community made up of aristocratic and middle-class, lay and religious men and women.

'I am really nothing': *A Vision Showed to a Devout Woman* (the short text)

Julian of Norwich's earlier *Vision* is a quarter of the length of the later version. It appears to have been intended as a completed piece with the decision to rework it (largely through adding new material and commentary, rather than revising what is already written, although some deletions are also made) only being made later. There are, of course, substantial differences between the *Vision* and the *Revelation*. With the *Revelation* came greater theological understanding and new insights and interpretation. The more succinct *Vision* can, perhaps, be characterized by its immediacy and urgency: particularly striking are the autobiographical details revealed as if incidentally in the retelling of the mystical experience, a number of which seem to be deliberately sacrificed as part of the process of revision.

In the fourth section of the *Vision*, Julian of Norwich tells the reader that she saw 'three noughts' (*Vision*, 69–71). The first of these 'noughts' or 'zeros' is what Creation, described as the size of a hazelnut, lying in the palm of her hand, would be but for the love of God (*Vision*, 69). Later, in the eighth section, Julian explains that she realized that sin is also nothing (*Vision*, 77), and she goes on to talk about how God nullifies the devil. In the thirteenth section, it is Christ, who, in His life and dying, is negated, as well as His creatures, who have to be negated in order to be redeemed (*Vision*, 91). Yet, between the descriptions of both Creation and sin as nothing appears a crucial discussion of Julian's own role as visionary and intermediary. In the sixth section, Julian directs her audience and readership as individuals, 'you who hears and sees this vision and this teaching' (*Vision*, 73), away from herself and towards their own spiritual health and consolation:

> And therefore I pray you all for God's sake, and advise you for your own profit, that you stop beholding the wretched, sinful creature to whom this vision was shown, and that you mightily, wisely, lovingly and meekly behold God . . .
>
> [And therfore I praye yowe alle for Goddes sake, and counsayles yowe for youre awne profit, that ye leve the behaldinge of the wrechid, sinfulle creature that it was shewed unto, and that ye mightlye, wiselye, lovandlye, and mekelye behalde God . . .] (*Vision*, 73)

This evocative passage indicates that, at the time of composition, Julian's showings and her reputation as a visionary have already begun to circulate. She goes on to insist that in making her showings public in this way she is following God's will, but she also intends to ensure that they are correctly understood. Julian thus emphasizes that her showings are not personal but, in a sense, anonymous. They have a universal applicability: when she talks about her own experiences she is also talking about all others who will be saved. She explains that, like Creation and sin, she too is 'nought' except in so far as she is Everywoman and Everyman: 'For if I look at myself individually I am really nought. But in relation to everyone else, I am in unity of charity with all my fellow Christians' (*Vision*, 73). Julian of Norwich's elucidation of her status is tied into her assurances concerning the orthodoxy of her text: here and elsewhere she reiterates that her showings entirely conform to Church doctrine and teaching. Julian stresses that she has not been chosen as the conduit for God's message because she is any the more deserving than anyone else. Indeed she asserts that many of those who are not blessed by visions love God more than she does. To reinforce this point, she appears to undercut her own authority in matters of doctrinal instruction:

> But God forbid that you should say or understand it that I am a teacher. Because that is not what I mean, nor did I ever mean thus. For I am a woman, uneducated, feeble and frail. But I know well that what I say I have from the showing of Him who is supreme teacher. But truly charity stirs me to tell it to you . . . But because I am a woman must I therefore believe that I must not tell you of the goodness of God, when I saw at the same time that it is His will that it should be known?

[Botte God forbede that ye shulde saye or take it so that I am a techere. For I meene nought so, no I mente nevere so. For I am a woman, lewed, febille, and freylle. Botte I wate wele, this that I saye I hafe it of the shew-inge of him that es soverayne techare. Botte sothelye charite stirres me to telle yowe it . . . Botte for I am a woman shulde I therfore leve that I shulde nought telle yowe the goodenes of God, sine that I sawe in that same time that it is his wille that it be knawen?] *(Vision, 75)*

Here Julian indirectly responds to Church anxieties concerning women as teachers (See 1 Timothy 2. 12: 'But I suffer not a woman to teach, nor to usurp authority over the man, but to be in silence'). Yet in describing herself as a vessel for divine inspiration, she makes it clear that she has no choice but to communicate to others the messages that she has received. While Julian insists that we look away from her, a mere 'wretch' *(Vision, 75)*, she also insists that we follow her gaze and see and comprehend her showings, the teachings of Christ, through her eyes and mind and soul.

Julian of Norwich's understanding of both Creation and sin as nothing follows from what she sees and what she does not see: from her perception of Creation as a hazelnut in the palm of her hand and from the absence of a vision of sin at that time. Similarly, in the *Vision*, Julian of Norwich offers us some compelling, but elusive, glimpses of herself, even as she reiterates that her individuality and identity are insignificant. She is both seen and not seen. Thus, for example, from the *Vision*, it seems unlikely that at the time of the showings in 1373, Julian of Norwich was living in an anchoress's cell; rather, from what we are told about her sick room, she could either have been in a convent or her own home. In the second section, she describes how her companions, believing her to be near the point of death, summon her parish priest, who attends her accompanied by a boy *(Vision, 65)*; the boy is not mentioned in the *Revelation*. In the tenth section, Julian's own mother steps forward to her bedside:

My mother, who stood amongst the others and watched me, lifted her hand up to my face to shut my eyes. For she believed I had been dead for a while or else I had just died . . .

[My modere, that stode emanges othere and behelde me, lifted uppe hir hande before my face to lokke min eyen. For she wened I had bene dede or els I hadde diede . . .] *(Vision, 83)*

The tender action of the mother, who gently cares for her daughter even at the point of death, mirrors 'the compassion of our lady, Saint Mary' which Julian sees shortly afterwards (*Vision*, 85). Certainly, there is a strong sense of imitation of Christ in Julian's death-bed experience. Not only is she afflicted when she was 'thirty and a half years old', the age of Christ when He began his active ministry, but her illness, described as lasting for two three-day periods, is suggestive of the duration of the Passion (*Vision*, 65). When Christ dies, Julian is thought to die. Even at the points when the *Vision* is the most rooted in a specific moment in Julian's personal history, it is still concerned with the eternal.

In the *Vision*, then, Julian's mother is allocated a key role in the mystic's own Passion drama, but in the *Revelation* she is absent. One explanation for this is that the intervention of Julian's biological mother may be seen to detract unnecessarily from the emphasis in the *Revelation* on Christ as the one true mother, and from the comparisons between the Virgin Mary and Christ that run through that text. What is lost in the omission of Julian's mother from the *Revelation*, however, is a glimpse of death-bed ritual,[3] and also a positive representation of a mother–daughter relationship and of maternal care and compassion that is remarkably rare in medieval English writing. In Chapter 1, we saw that the relationship between the recluse and her mother was deeply ambivalent, with Christina of Markyate's mother both sharing and violently opposing her daughter's spiritual vocation. Chapter 6 will similarly demonstrate the often fraught intergenerational interactions of women within the family unit. Intriguingly, and in contrast to Julian of Norwich, Margery Kempe's father figures in the narrative of her life, alongside her husband, one of her sons and her daughter-in-law, but no mention is made of any other female family members.

If Julian of Norwich is unlikely to have been a recluse at the point when she first received her showings, she nevertheless appears to have been deeply devout. In the eighth section, following her showing of Christ defeating the devil, Julian laughs out loud and those by her bedside join in. The Lord then speaks to her, saying ' "I thank you for your service and your labour and especially in your youth" ' (*Vision*, 79). While the nature of Julian's service and labour is not further defined, it is clear that prior to her showings, she must have devoted herself to contemplation for many years. Indeed, the *Vision* begins with Julian's account of how she prayed to God for three gifts, the first of which – a physical experience of the Passion – arose out of her spiritual contemplation (*Vision*, 63). Her request for this gift, and the second (physical sickness), was then forgotten (*Vision*, 65), which indicates that it was made some considerable time previously. Nicholas Watson and Jacqueline Jenkins argue that the reference to Julian's service in her youth provides evidence that she was a nun, consecrated at an early age.[4] They make the convincing case that she was a member of the Benedictine convent of Carrow in Norwich. Nevertheless, there are other possibilities. For example, Julian could have been married and (given that no husband is mentioned) widowed. As either pious housewife or vowess, she could have spent considerable time on prayer, reflection and affective devotion, re-enacting in her mind's eye scenes from Christ's life and cultivating appropriate emotional responses. Given the emphasis on motherhood in the *Revelation* in particular, it is certainly tempting to speculate, as some critics have, that she was a widow and had had children.[5] In Middle English the quotation above reads: ' "I thanke the of thy service and thy travaile and namly in thy youth." ' In context, Julian's 'travaile' echoes that of Christ, whose hard work is in turn opposed to the unsuccessful toil of the devil, but the word 'travaile' can also refer to 'the pains of childbirth'.[6] Of course Julian could also have had no children and still been married or widowed. Certainly Julian does not identify herself as or liken herself to a mother in either the *Vision* or the *Revelation*, but, as will be seen, she does also draw upon metaphors of infertility and childlessness. One under-explored possibility is that she remained single, either in her parents' home or in service elsewhere. As will be seen in the final chapter, in the mid-fifteenth century, Elizabeth Paston did not marry until she was almost 30. Whatever was the case, Julian's bonds with spiritual advisers (the priest who comes to her death-bed, the man of religion to whom she first mentions her showings) and other women (her mother, a devout woman and close friend about whom she seeks reassurance from God) were equally important to her.

Just as we can only surmise about Julian of Norwich's lifestyle before she became an anchoress, so we can only make broad assumptions about her education. We do not even know for certain if she wrote her works herself or if she relied on a secretary to write them down for her. It is, nevertheless, important to remember that the education of nuns or lay gentlewomen in the late fourteenth century would have been very similar. While the courtliness of Julian's language suggests a privileged background, according to her own account, Julian was not a scholar. At the start of the *Revelation*, she describes herself as 'a simple, unlearned creature' (*Vision*, 125). This may simply be another example of the sort of passive humility conventional in women's visionary writing, or even internalized anti-feminism. Nevertheless, as Felicity Riddy argues, Julian puts it to very positive use in creating 'a textuality of the spoken as well as the written word'.[7] Furthermore, it is clear from the evidence of her writing that, despite her protestations to the contrary, she was an intellectual. Certainly, in rewriting her account of her showings, she reveals that she has deliberated on them for a long time and offers new and refined interpretations. The subtlety and originality of her theology and the sophistication of her language must derive from years of absorbed study, for which she must have had access to a library and an educational community, whether male, female or mixed. Yet, while she envisages her own work being listened to *and* read, she does not actually discuss what she herself read or directly cite other medieval authors and authorities, preferring to refer to teaching available to everyone, no matter how uneducated. Thus, at the beginning of the *Vision*, she mentions images of the Passion, as well as Church teaching on the subject (*Vision*, 63) and shortly afterwards talks about hearing a man of God relating the life of St Cecilia (*Vision*, 65). In the *Revelation*, she describes the knowledge that God reveals as elementary and accessible as 'an A.B.C.' (*Revelation*, 371; see also 285). Her disingenuous self-fashioning as one who has only basic learning is linked to her deliberate anonymity, enabling her oneness with her fellow Christians, lay and religious, women as well as men.

While the nature of Julian of Norwich's service to God, prior to her showings, is not explained, she does have a great deal to say about the relationship between God and His servants. Julian is careful to distinguish between the teaching concerning salvation which is available to all, through the instruction of the Holy Spirit and Holy Church, and the knowledge that 'is locked away from us and hidden' (*Vision*, 95). Using the imagery of contemporary secular kingship, Julian stresses that God's servants, Christians such as herself, should not seek access to 'our Lord's privy counsels' which are confidential and secret. In insisting that God withholds as well as reveals his secrets, Julian of Norwich is distinguished from Margery Kempe, who (as we will see in the next chapter) represents herself as a divine counsellor by likening herself to 'our Lord's own secretaries whom He has endued with love' (*The Book of Margery Kempe*, 71).[8] What is more, Margery Kempe is one who does have access to His 'privy counsels' (*Book*, 144). Julian's examination of the relationship between God and His servants in the *Vision* anticipates the Parable of the Lord and the Servant which is introduced into the *Revelation* and which, as we shall see, is absolutely central to its meaning. In the twenty-third section, in which Julian describes her delivery from the devil's second assault upon her, she reiterates that sin is nothing, and offers a sympathetic understanding of transgression, which holds on to the promise of redemption:

> And during that time that man or woman loves sin, if any are like this, he suffers pain that surpasses all pain. And when he does not love sin, but

hates it and loves God, all is well. And he who truly does this, though he may sometimes sin by frailty or ignorance in his will, he does not fall, for he will mightily rise again and behold God whom he loves with all his will.

[And for that time that man or woman loves sinne, if any be swilke, he is in paine that passes alle paines. And when he loves nought sinne, botte hates it and luffes God, alle is wele. And he that trewlye does thus, though he sin sumtime by frelty or unkunninge in his wille, he falles nought, for he wille mightely rise againe and behalde God wham he loves in alle his wille.] (*Vision*, 115)

Julian's incredulity that there are any who actually love sin – expressed in the clause 'if any are like this' – anticipates her intimations in the *Revelation* concerning universal salvation (a heresy) – which will be discussed in the next section. Here, however, it should be noted, first, that Julian explicitly addresses both sexes. Second, in describing sin as due to 'frailty or ignorance', rather than deliberate and blameworthy iniquity, Julian not only looks forward to the servant of the Parable in the *Revelation*, but also back to the twenty-first section in which she discusses her own, temporary, falling from grace. There she describes how, having awoken in pain and anguish from her mystical trance on the first day, she dismissed her own visions as delirium before a man in holy orders, and, racked by self-doubt, felt unable to share them with a priest. 'But like a fool,' she says, 'I let it pass from my mind' (*Vision*, 109). Suffering, remorse, ingratitude and foolishness all distract Julian from the comfort of God, until He, having mercy on her, brings her respite. This is the same Julian, who, in explaining the feelings of desolation that sometimes follow prayer, establishes a connection between herself and her readership with the assurance, 'I have felt thus in myself' (*Vision*, 103). One word used in both passages to describe this sense of emptiness – 'barren' – has obvious connotations of infertility or childlessness, and is implicitly opposed to the fecundity of motherhood, both human and divine (*Vision*, 103, 109).[9] Julian of Norwich, in representing herself as an Everywoman and Everyman, explores in her *Vision* her own sense of failure, described in terms of infertility, and insignificance (her nothingness), as well as her blessings.

'The service and labour of motherhood': *A Revelation of Love* (the long text)

Central to the theology of the *Revelation* is the Parable of the Lord and the Servant, not included in the *Vision*, which is closely linked to another innovation in the *Revelation*, the extended metaphor of Jesus as mother. We have already seen that the ground is laid for the Parable of the Lord and the Servant in the *Vision* in the exploration of the interaction between God and His servants. In chapter 7 of the *Revelation* – following on from the vivid new similes of the blood dripping from Christ's head under the crown of thorns as pellets, rain dropping from the eaves, and herring scales (*Revelation*, 147) – is an explanation of God's homeliness or intimacy and courtesy. Here God is likened to a king or lord, who is not aloof but whose esteem for his servant is expressed through friendliness, intimacy 'both in private and in public' (*Revelation*, 147). Later in the *Revelation* Julian warns that divine intimacy, or courtesy, is so freely given that it can be wrongly taken for granted (*Revelation*, 365). Julian's assertion concerning the closeness of God to His servants is the counterbalance of her warning in the *Vision*, reiterated in the *Revelation* (chapter 30), that God's privy counsel is closed to us, and consequently that some divine knowledge and understanding is rightly withheld from us. Subsequently (in chapter 34; see also chapter 46), she expands on the distinction between those secrets that are hidden only because of our ignorance and inability to see, and which God chooses to reveal to draw us closer to Him, and those that will remain hidden until the end of time.

Julian's concern with God's secrets in the *Revelation* is closely tied to her apocalyptic prophecy that the Trinity will perform a deed 'unknown to all creatures that are under Christ' by which 'He shall make all things well that are not well' (*Revelation*, 223–5). Julian here seems to hold on to an unspoken promise of universal salvation, as she struggles with the teaching of Holy Church that some – the devil and his fallen angels, heathens, Jews and unrepentant sinners – will be damned eternally in hell.[10] Without knowledge of the nature of this deed, she has to rely on her faith that God can perform the seemingly impossible. Indeed she stresses that we should not strive to find out about it, because 'the more we busy ourselves to know His secrets about that or any other thing, the further we shall be from knowing them' (*Revelation*, 227). Julian also discusses another deed, distinct from the first, that shall be performed for her sake for all who are saved on reaching heaven, 'which may be partly known here' (*Revelation*, 233). Despite straying dangerously close to heterodoxy (and her insistence that her beliefs are doctrinally orthodox demonstrates her awareness of the risks she is taking), Julian continues to insist that she was not granted a vision of hell or purgatory (*Revelation*, 225; compare 245; contrast *The Book of Margery Kempe*, 141–4, 204). The absence of a revelation of a general hell seems implicitly to admit the theologically radical possibility that, in Julian's understanding, it does not exist. Furthermore, Julian's decision to write in the vernacular, a far less exclusive language than Latin, mirrors the way her showings reach out to those the Church rejects as damned. Less controversially, however, Julian also relates that she was denied a specific revelation concerning the spiritual pathway of a close friend. When she asked God for knowledge about the state of grace of another woman whom she loved and who had committed herself to God, she was denied it on the grounds that it was a 'singular desire' or a desire to know about an individual (*Revelation*, 229; compare *Vision*, 97). Later, Julian distinguishes between two judgements: the first, which is that of God, is a 'fair sweet judgement'; and the second, that of Holy Church, teaches 'that sinners sometimes deserve blame and wrath' (*Revelation*, 261). It is as a response to Julian's struggle to reconcile these two judgements that she is offered the answer of the Parable of the Lord and the Servant (*Revelation*, 261).

In chapter 38 of the *Revelation*, Julian introduces a discussion of St John of Beverley (*d*.721), who is described as 'a close neighbour' and Julian assumes that, like her, her audience will know him well (*Revelation*, 239). The Anglo-Saxon saint was, in his youth, a monk of Whitby, before becoming bishop of Hexham and then of York, and finally retiring to the monastery of Beverley which he had founded, and which became the location of his shrine. He has no close associations with Norwich, and East Yorkshire is some distance north of East Anglia by both land and water routes. Yet he may have had personal associations for Julian, who some scholars have argued, on the basis of manuscript dialect evidence, may have moved from Yorkshire or Lincolnshire down to Norwich.[11] Certainly, according to the Sloane manuscript (but not Paris), her showings began on the day after his feast on 7 May.[12] Julian explains that St John of Beverley came to her mind to illustrate the intimacy and courtesy with which the Lord treats His servants: 'And God called him St John of Beverley, simply as we do, and with a very glad and sweet demeanour' (*Revelation*, 239). St John of Beverley also illustrates the pattern of falling and redemption that is key to the *Revelation*:

> [God] mentioned that in his youth and at a tender age he was a precious servant to God, very greatly loving and fearing God. And nevertheless God allowed him to fall, mercifully protecting him, so that he did not perish or lose any time. And afterwards God raised him into many times more grace. And for the contrition and meekness with which he lived, God has given him in heaven many joys, surpassing those he would have had if he had not sinned or fallen.

[And with this he made mention that in his youth and in his tender age he was a dereworthy sarvant to God, full mekille God loving and dreding. And neverthelesse God suffered him to falle, him mercifully keping, that he perished not ne lost no time. And afterward God raised him to manifolde more grace. And by the contrition and the mekenesse that he had in his living, God hath geven him in heven manifolde joyes, overpassing that he shuld have had if he had not sinned or fallen.]   (*Revelation*, 239)

Bede's Ecclesiastical History of the English People provides the basis for subsequent lives of John of Beverley, and records a number of occasions when he healed the dying and the afflicted (women as well as men and boys) but makes no mention of a youthful iniquity.[13] Edmund Colledge and James Walsh note that 'many Irish and Anglo-Saxons were sent to the Continent to live in solitude as penance for their sins' and suggest, on the evidence of a passing reference in a late fifteenth-century manuscript that John of Beverley followed this pattern.[14] However, according to an apocryphal life that has survived in an early sixteenth-century Dutch chapbook, John of Beverley, as a young man, was deceived by the devil, and when drunk, raped and murdered his own sister.[15] Whether or not we accept that this startlingly shocking series of sins is indeed the fall to which Julian refers, she is evidently alluding to a legend or tradition that has not survived in English. Significantly, in so doing, she seems to draw a parallel with her own younger adulthood, described in the *Vision* and reiterated in the *Revelation*, in which she both served and suffered for God. As we saw in the previous section, Julian represents her own doubts and despair following her first fifteen showings as a personal fall, from which God, in His mercy, raises her. The pattern of suffering followed by joy which pervades the *Vision* is repeated in the *Revelation*, 'because our courteous Lord does not want his servants to despair because they fall often or fall grievously' (*Revelation*, 241–3).

In chapters 50 and 51, Julian explains that she was shown the Parable of the Lord and the Servant in response to her attempt to reconcile her understanding of divine grace and mercy with the teaching of Holy Church that all are sinners, from Adam onwards. This Parable does not appear in the *Vision*, but Julian, in outlining the processes through which she came to a point of more complete comprehension, provides a justification for this. She explains that, although, at the time of the showing, she realized that the Parable must provide her with an answer to her questioning concerning sin, she was granted only a partial understanding, which she describes as 'the beginning of teaching which I understood therein at the time' (*Revelation*, 277). This, however, left her feeling more confused than ever. It would seem, then, that Julian – presumably following the counsel of her spiritual advisers – was not willing to include any aspects of her showings in the *Vision*, no matter how wonderful and mysterious, that she felt unable to explain. This may have been because Julian herself was uncertain about the orthodoxy of her showings, or it may have been that she was concerned about how her audience and readers might respond to them. She felt that she needed to be able to control their reception through her own, divinely inspired, commentaries. Subsequently, however, Julian received a fuller understanding of the Parable in the form of further 'inner teaching' and from contemplating the 'whole revelation' (*Revelation*, 277). Her later teaching, which came to her 'twenty years after the time of the showing, save three months', directed her to take note of all the details in the showing, no matter how minor. These different processes of understanding merge into one, so that Julian has to admit that she cannot fully distinguish between them. What is so significant about this is that it makes it very clear that Julian's texts, both the *Vision* and the *Revelation*, are not simply records of a single mystical experience, but also of continual processes of contemplation and elucidation taking place over many years after the initial event. These processes may result in sudden crystallizations of understanding. In the intervening years between the showings and the acts of writing and rewriting, Julian must have developed intellectually. Before entering the anchorhold she may even have travelled abroad: certainly the *Revelation* adds allusions to the relic of the vernicle (the cloth with which St Veronica wiped Christ's face before the Crucifixion) in Rome and to pilgrimage (*Revelation*, 159, 373). After the showings she must surely have extensively studied other theological and visionary texts. She will have been part of a learned and spiritual community and have been instructed by men of religion (in the *Revelation* (227) she praises the 'preaching and teaching of Holy Church'), and indeed instructed others. She will also have shared her ideas with her own peers, including nuns, anchoresses and other devout women. The final chapter of the *Revelation* announces: 'This book has been begun by God's gift and His grace, but it has still not been performed, in my view' (*Revelation*, 379). The *Revelation* is imperfect in the sense of being incomplete, but also in the senses of not being put into daily practice or even perhaps discussed by its readers.[16]

What causes Julian particular difficulty in understanding the Parable of the Lord and the Servant is comprehending the meaning of the servant, who, in rushing to fulfil his lord's request, falls into a ditch and is injured, trapped and isolated. Julian initially understands the servant to represent

Adam, and identifies the Parable as a retelling of the fall of humankind, but only later recognizes that the servant is also Christ, and that the Parable is also concerned with the Incarnation, the Crucifixion, the Harrowing of Hell and Redemption. The Parable follows on from Julian's earlier discussions of the Father rewarding Jesus Christ (*Revelation*, 195), and of Adam's sin as the *felix culpa* or fortunate fall (*Revelation*, 213–15). The downfall of the servant is in keeping with Julian's understanding of sin, which is expressed in Boethian terms: 'In our blindness and lack of foresight, we say that these things [which befall us] are by chance or accident' and are unable to recognize the workings of providence and God's 'foreseeing wisdom' (*Revelation*, 163). What is most remarkable, however, is the absence of any sense of sin or blame. The servant's fall is caused by his obedience and enthusiasm, rather than by his disobedience. The suffering of the servant is exacerbated because 'he could not turn his face to look upon his loving lord, who was very close to him' and he is characterized by his weakness and foolishness (*Revelation*, 275). The anguish of the servant is also in keeping with Julian's portrayal of herself in chapter 66 as a mystic who, on waking from her visions, is racked by physical pain and desolation, and so, like a fool, doubts the nature of the revelations she has received. Here in chapter 67, and again in chapter 69, she is tempted to despair by the torments of the devil. Elsewhere, it is revealed to Julian that she will fall in the future, but not the nature of the sin, nor its gravity (*Revelation*, 235, 367–9). The servant of the Parable, then, is not only Adam and Christ, but also Julian and every Christian, who, blinded by the cares of the world, cannot see God, even though He is near at hand (see *Revelation*, 369–70). In the Parable, the service and the labour of the servant are acknowledged fully, just like that of Julian. Likewise, the description of the lord, who looks at his servant with love and kindness as well as pity, recalls both God's affection for St John of Beverley, whose reward also greatly outweighed his fall, and the intimacy with which God interacts with Julian herself.

Within the Parable of the Lord and the Servant neither Eve nor the serpent is evoked; indeed neither is mentioned in either the *Vision* or the *Revelation*. The female and femininity have positive associations. Julian has three showings of the Virgin Mary, and, as Sarah McNamer has pointed out, the blue clothing of the lord in the Parable resonates with the colour traditionally associated with the mother of God, and carries with it connotations of intercession and mercy.[17] Shortly before relating the Parable, Julian links mercy to motherhood, 'protecting, tolerating, reviving and healing', and grace to lordship, 'raising, rewarding . . . spreading abroad and revealing the high, plentiful largess of God's royal lordship in His marvellous courtesy' (*Revelation*, 268–9). This anticipates Julian's declaration that the three persons of the Trinity, the Father, Son and Holy Ghost, are father, mother and lord (*Revelation*, 297). Julian further explains:

> In our almighty Father we have our preservation and blessing, as regards our natural substance, which is ours through our creation in eternity. And in the second person, who is intellect and wisdom, we have our preservation as regards our sensory aspects, our restoration and our salvation. For He is our mother, brother and saviour. And in our good lord the Holy Ghost we have our reward and payment for our living and our labour, and endlessly surpassing all we desire in His marvellous courtesy and high plentiful grace.

> [In oure fader almighty we have oure keping and oure blesse, as anemptes oure kindely substance, which is to us by oure making fro without beginning. And in the seconde person, in wit and wisdom, we have oure keping, as anemptes oure sensualite, oure restoring, and oure saving. For he is oure moder, broder, and savioure. And in oure good lorde the holy gost we have oure rewarding and oure yelding for oure living and oure traveyle, and endlessly overpassing alle that we desyer in his mervelous curtesy of his hye, plentuous grace.] (*Revelation*, 307)

Julian's representation of the Holy Ghost as patron and protector of course refers back to the depiction of the lord in the earlier Parable. Julian goes on to describe substance as 'the higher part' which comes from the Father and the 'sensory being' as that which comes from our 'mother in nature', Christ, who in becoming a man shared in our material existence (*Revelation*, 307–9). Julian follows Aristotelian thinking then in associating the Father with the superior male role in reproduction, which is formative, while the Son is linked to the lesser female role of providing the matter.[18] In attributing the qualities of intellect and wisdom to the Son as mother, she also draws on the traditional personification of wisdom as female, while at the same time fusing the Son with His mother, who is also characterized by her wisdom (*Revelation*, 145).

The notion of Jesus as mother is by no means original to Julian, although she develops the metaphor more fully than previous theologians and in new directions.[19] Indeed Julian's exaltation of motherhood *is* unusual amongst religious authors and authorities for whom virginity remains the preferred state until the Reformation. In chapters 60 and 61, she expands on the qualities of mother Jesus, whose love was so great that he took on human form and 'arrayed himself and prepared himself in our poor flesh, to do the service and office of motherhood himself in every way' (*Revelation*, 313). Julian attributes to motherhood faithfulness, suffering and self-sacrifice: a willingness to endure the pains of labour, even though it will result in the mother's own death; surely a particularly poignant image in an era of such high child-bed mortality. Just as the mother feeds her child, so Christ feeds His children of Himself, in the form of the sacrament, and as the mother holds her child to her breast, Christ takes His children into the wound in His side. The mother tends to, nurtures and allows her child to be disciplined, as does Christ, and she allows her child to fall, as long as it is not in danger, and offers it comfort, help and reassurance. Throughout her *Revelation*, Julian repeatedly draws parallels between the Virgin and her son, Jesus Christ, stressing that both are mother to the Christian who shall be saved (*Revelation*, 305). Christ is the true mother. Julian states, 'this fair, lovely word "mother", it is so sweet and so natural in itself that it cannot truly be said of any, nor to any, but of Him and to Him who is the true mother of life and of everyone' (*Revelation*, 313). Indeed even though a human mother may sometimes allow her child to perish, Christ will never do this (*Revelation*, 317). Yet, once again, Julian reassures her audience and readers of the orthodoxy of her showings, stressing that the Church is also the mother with whom all Christians should be united (*Revelation*, 317, 319).

The 'service and office' of motherhood that Christ performs creates a further link between not only divine motherhood and divine lordship but between also the Son and the servant of the Parable. Indeed, as we have just seen, Christ as mother 'was in labour for the full term until he suffered the sharpest pangs and the most grievous pains that ever were or shall be, and died at last' (*Revelation*, 313). Likewise, in the Parable, the servant, who is both Adam expelled from Eden and forced to work the land, as well as Christ, is a gardener who is glad to undertake 'the greatest labour and the hardest labour of all' (*Revelation*, 281–2). Motherhood and gardening have complex associations of work, obligation, fecundity and love. At the same time, Christ's children, whom He allows to fall and to feel pain and fear, and to dirty themselves (*Revelation*, 317), also recall the servant, in his ditch, broken and frightened, in a torn and filthy tunic. The 'service' of Christ's motherhood also creates a connection between Christ's mission and Julian herself, whose 'service' and 'labour' are twice mentioned in the Paris manuscript of the *Revelation* (*Revelation*, 173, 377).[20] The mystic, in her imitation of Christ (and also in her imitation of the Virgin Mary, who in chapter 7 is offered as a model contemplative), also, in a sense, fulfils the service and duties of motherhood. In this context, it is then all the more shocking to encounter Julian's representation of 'the great wretchedness of our deadly flesh' and 'the cleanness and the purity of our soul':

> And at this time I saw a body lying on the earth, which body looked gross and fearful and without shape or form, as if it were a bog of stinking mire. And suddenly out of this body sprang a very beautiful creature, a little child, fully shaped and formed, swift and alive and whiter than the lily, which glided quickly up into heaven.
>
> [And in this time I sawe a body lyeng on the erth, which body shewde hevy and feerfulle and withoute shape and forme, as it were a swilge stinking mire. And sodeynly oute of this body sprong a fulle fair creature, a litille child, full shapen and formed, swift and lifly and whiter then the lilye, which sharpely glided uppe into heven.] (*Revelation*, 325)

This depiction of the soul, portrayed as a child, leaving the body, is traditional and the description of physical corruption is a conventional enough expression of *contemptus mundi* or contempt for the world. The supine body also resonates with the earlier depiction of the servant trapped in the ditch. But, appearing as it does following an extended discussion of motherhood, it may also seem to the reader to be a counter-image of child-bed mortality, exposing its physical horrors. Certainly it resonates with images found in other works of vernacular piety, such as the mid-fourteenth-century *Prick of Conscience*:

> There dwelled a man in a dark dungeon,
> And in a foul place of corruption,
> Where he had no other food
> Except hateful mucus, and coagulated blood,
> And stink and filth, as I said before,
> With which he was first nourished there.
>
> [þar duellid man in a myrk dungeon,
> And in a foul sted of corupcion,
> Whar he had na other fode
> Bot wlatsom glet, and loper blode,
> And stynk and filthe, als I sayde ar,
> With þer he was first norisshed þar.][21]

Whereas *The Prick of Conscience* depicts the soul trapped in the putrescent flesh in terms of the foetus enclosed in the womb, Julian in her *Revelation* describes its escape. Nevertheless her vivid image of physical decay and pollution suggests some internalization of misogynist attitudes to the reproductive female body.

The *Revelation* ends with an additional showing that serves as the summation of all of the previous showings. As with the Parable of the Lord and the Servant, Julian's constant search for comprehension is rewarded in this case, 'fifteen years and more after' (*Revelation*, 379), when she is told that the meaning of all that has gone before is 'Love'. Julian offers some explanation as to why she has written and rewritten her account of her visionary experiences: the decision to make her showings known has been made because God wants this message of love to be 'better known than it is' – simultaneously better understood and more widely circulated.

'This revelation is high divinity and high wisdom': reception and transmission

How was Julian's work received in her own lifetime and how was it circulated? Since only one medieval manuscript (that containing the *Vision*) has survived, these are particularly difficult questions to answer. The early reception and transmission remains unclear. Nevertheless, fascinatingly, Julian of Norwich is mentioned in the writing of her younger contemporary, also from East Anglia, Margery Kempe. In Chapter 3 of this study, the *Revelations* of Elizabeth of Toess was noted as one text mentioned in her *Book* as having influenced Margery Kempe (*Book*, 154). As will be seen in Chapter 5, this is only one of a number of religious texts and figures cited by Margery Kempe and her secretary to justify her controversial life as a celibate married woman, her visions and her devotions, especially her crying and weeping. Other female mystics referred to include Mary of Oignies (*Book*, 153) and St Bridget of Sweden (*Book*, 39, 47, 143). Closer to home are the Yorkshire recluse Richard Rolle and the Nottinghamshire mystic Walter Hilton (*Book*, 39, 143, 154) who both addressed female readers in their writings. Yet, Julian appears not as the author of either the *Showings* or the *Revelation*, but as an anchoress who was an 'expert' in contemplation and revelations, versed in spiritual discernment and able to give 'good counsel' (*Book*, 42). She figures alongside the Norwich priest Richard Caister and the Carmelite William Southfield, amongst others: all individuals whom Kempe consulted before setting off on her pilgrimage to Jerusalem. Nicholas Watson points out that there was growing concern about the proliferation of visionary experiences from the late fourteenth century.[22] Recluses, anchoresses and visionaries were often consulted within their communities as spiritual guides, and according to Margery Kempe's *Book*, she herself performed the same role for others. Margery Kempe recalls how she described to Julian her feelings, contemplations, 'dalliances' and revelations, in an exchange that lasted 'many days' (*Book*, 42–3). Julian's reported response, with its emphasis on holy living and Holy Writ, seems to cohere with the sort of instruction found in one late four-teenth-century treatise, *The Chastising of God's Children*.[23] Nevertheless it is notable that she implicitly approves of Margery Kempe's chastity and tears, and makes no reference to the importance of following the instruction of male spiritual advisers, or (significantly, given the stress on this in her own writings), that of Holy Church. Furthermore, she encourages Margery Kempe, whom she addresses as 'sister', in the face of persecution to 'fear not the language of the world, for the more contempt, shame, and reproof that you have in this world, the more is your merit in the sight of God' (*Book*, 43). Julian's warning to Margery Kempe against the man who is 'forever doubting', whom she likens to 'the flood of the sea, which is moved and born about with the wind' (*Book*, 42), resonates with the end of the *Vision*. There Julian of Norwich distinguishes between 'reverent dread' and other kinds of 'false dread', including 'doubtful dread . . . [which] is sort of despair' and which 'torments and agitates and troubles' or, in the Middle English, 'travailes and tempestes and trubles' (*Vision*, 118–19).

The obvious inference to draw from the absence of direct reference to Julian of Norwich's own writings is that Margery Kempe either did not know of or had not had Julian's treatises read to her. This would suggest that neither the *Vision* nor the *Revelation* were in general circulation, even in Julian's own town of Norwich, during her lifetime. It is possible that such 'suppression' could have been in line with Julian's own wishes. We might be reminded here of other mystics, such as the thirteenth-century German nun, Mechtild of Hackeborn, who, out of a sense of their own worthlessness, but perhaps also out of caution, were wary of sharing any part of their revelatory experiences with others, unless compelled to do so by their spiritual advisers.[24] Margery Kempe also claims to have resisted having her *Book* written for more than twenty years (*Book*, 3, 6, 34). Furthermore, she makes it explicit that she does not want it circulated while she is still alive (*Book*, 4). Yet, neither the *Vision* nor the *Revelation* indicates that this was the case for Julian of Norwich. Although, in the *Vision*, Julian is careful to deny that she is herself a teacher, suggesting instead that she merely assembles her God-given showings, rather like Marie de France claims that she assembles her lais, by the time of the writing of the *Revelation*, her position appears to have shifted. Indeed, according to Watson, the very opening of the *Revelation* 'announces that the book is written by one who means to shape what she says: an *auctor* [author], not the mere *compilator* [compiler] she is in *A Vision*'.[25] In making this transformation, Julian of Norwich no longer alludes to her gender, either as a paradoxical claim to authorial status (the 'least . . . shall be great': Luke 9. 48) or as a shield to deflect criticism.

Just as Julian's self-representation changes between the *Vision* and the *Revelation*, so too does her representation of her audience and readership. In Julian's account in the *Vision* of her revelation that Creation is nothing, she reveals something of her implied audience at this time, when she explains that this is something 'of which each man and woman who wishes to lead the contemplative life needs to have knowledge' (*Vision*, 71). Such individuals are opposed to 'those who are wilfully occupied with earthly business, and always seek worldly success' (*Vision*, 71) and who thus cannot know God. These lines are dropped from the *Revelation*. In the *Revelation*, as in the *Vision*, Julian of Norwich urges her audience and readers to look away from her and towards God. In both versions, she insists that all she sees and learns applies only to herself in so far as she stands for her fellow Christians. In chapter 8 of the *Revelation*, however, she refers to herself simply as a 'wretch' (*Revelation*, 153), rather than as the 'wretched, sinful creature' of the *Vision* (*Vision*, 73). The change is of a kind with the *Revelation*'s omission of Julian's protestations that she is not a teacher but only a woman and a vessel for divine instruction. In the *Revelation*, Julian is more anonymous and less abject and this comes with a reconfiguration of her intended audience beyond fellow contemplatives to all her 'evencristen' or fellow Christians. Nevertheless, whereas the *Vision* addresses one 'who sees and hears this vision and this teaching' (*Vision*, 73), the *Revelation* is directed explicitly 'not to those who are wise, for they know it well' but 'to you who are simple, for support and comfort' (*Revelation*, 153). As noted earlier, Julian figures her showings – the secret matter revealed to her – as elementary rather than advanced learning: the spiritual equivalent of knowing the alphabet. Certainly in writing in the vernacular, she deliberately addresses her audience not in the *lingua franca* of the clergy and the educated, but in the mother tongue of her neighbours and the laity.

Fascinatingly, however, there exists a tension between this claim in the body of the text of Julian's *Revelation*, and the final scribal remarks in the Sloane manuscript, which include the following injunction:

> I pray to almighty God that this book will come only into the hands of those who are his faithful lovers, and of those who are willing to submit

themselves to the faith of holy church, and to obey the wholesome understanding and teaching of men who are of virtuous life, mature years, and profound learning. For this revelation is high divinity and high wisdom, so it must not dwell with him who is thrall to sin and to the devil. And beware that you do not take one thing according to your desire and liking and leave another, for that is the condition of a heretic.

[I pray almyty God that this booke com not but to the hands of them that will be his faithfull lovers, and to those that will submitt them to the feith of holy church, and obey the holesom understondyng and teching of the men that be of vertuous life, sadde age, and profound lernyng. For this revelation is hey divinitye and hey wisdam, wherfore it may not dwelle with him that is thrall to synne and to the devill. And beware thou take not on thing after thy affection and liking and leve another, for that is the condition of an heretique.][26]

One of Julian's own spiritual community, presumably a cleric, may have added these directions, which reveal that he regarded the text as having the greatest authority. He seems to have produced the instructions with the idea in mind that it would be more widely circulated; thus clear guidelines need to be given about exactly how to approach the work. Felicity Riddy has discussed the probability that Julian's writing was the product of collaboration, and the Sloane manuscript provides evidence that the *Revelation* was edited by or in conjunction with a secretary with whom she worked closely.[27] Evidence of editorial presence in Julian's writings includes, for example, the list of contents which prefaces the *Revelation* or the cross-referencing within it. More significant, however, are the chapter headings, which in this manuscript refer to Julian as narrator in the third person, and thus mark Julian's gender, whereas in the body of the text the first person is almost always used. In one chapter heading, for example, Julian is spoken of as 'this blessed woman'.[28] The tone is 'masculine and clerical' in the way it interprets and evaluates.[29] Chapter 66, we are told in the Sloane heading, describes 'her frailty and mourning in discomfort, and speaking lightly of the great comfort of Jesus, saying she had raved. Which, in her great sickness, I suppose was only venial sin.'[30] Riddy also notes, however, that Julian might herself have been responsible for these headings, which in any case signify 'only a further stage in the gradual process of textualization which began with Julian's sense that the visions were not hers alone'.[31] If this were the case, then Julian herself in her role as glossator ventriloquizes the clerical male voice.

The editorial apparatus takes the *Revelation* seriously (just as did the man of holy orders to whom she first confessed), sanctioning and authorizing both the showings themselves and Julian's own understanding. This is comparable, although not identical, to the way the voice of Margery Kempe's clerical secretary seeks to confirm the veracity of her revelations and the orthodoxy of her piety, as we will see in the next chapter. Yet, at the same time, the instructions at the end of the Sloane manuscript, which distinguish between good and bad ways of reading, indicate some anxiety that the *Revelation* is susceptible to misprision if it falls into the hands of the wrong sort of reader. According to this a heretical reader would read selectively and without spiritual insight, would not be governed by the Church, or guided by the Bible, by God and by the instruction of the holy men. Margery Kempe's clerical secretary in contrast plays out on a personal level his own experiences, providing in his account of the resolution of his own doubt a model for how to respond correctly, and with charity, to the text. Another, in this case extreme, example of intra-textual concern is found in the condemned work, *The Mirror of Simple Souls*, written by the French béguine Marguerite Porete and disseminated in Carthusian circles in England in the late fourteenth or early fifteenth century. Its English translator, apparently unaware either that it was written by a woman or that it had been condemned as heretical, but responding to the need on the part of his readers for interpretative guidance, included glosses in order to explain passages that he feared might be misunderstood.[32] Yet, the Sloane injunction merely picks up on the apprehensions about the possible heterodoxy of the showings implied within the *Vision* and particularly within the *Revelation*. It is clear that at the points in the text when Julian's theology is the most controversial – when it discusses sin and damnation and moves towards universalism – she is then most insistent that it conforms fully to the teaching and correction of the Church. Likewise, the Sloane chapter headings at times foreground this conformity over and above the content of the chapter itself (for example chapter 33).[33]

The desire expressed in the Sloane manuscript to limit the readership of Julian's showings to those who will read appropriately may have been fulfilled by those who controlled the dissemination of her work. The *Vision*, for example, which survives in only one mid-fifteenth-century manuscript derived from an early fifteenth-century one, may never have been widely or systematically circulated. Meanwhile the *Revelation* may have been distributed amongst Julian's primary audience – which itself may have constituted a fairly narrow circle of readers – in only an ad hoc fashion. Although the main manuscript witnesses to the *Revelation* are postmedieval, one compilation, the Westminster manuscript, which includes extracts of the *Revelation* first produced in the first half of the fifteenth century, would seem to have been put together for either a religious or lay audience close to Julian herself.[34] Even though Margery Kempe does not mention Julian's writing in her accounts of the books she had read to her, or in her retelling of her visit to Julian, she would clearly have qualified as a member of the audience for whom Julian's vernacular theology was aimed. Furthermore, there are obvious overlaps between the two women's affective meditations on and visions of the Passion and the Virgin Mary, and their concerns about the limits of salvation. There are also linguistic echoes in their shared references to themselves as 'creatures' and to their communities of 'evencristen' or fellow Christians. It makes sense to figure Margery Kempe as in some senses typical of Julian's primary audience, which we can also infer from the evidence of surviving bequests to Julian and her companions and former companions (one Sarah; an anonymous maid; and a former maid, Alice). It included local priests, a Norwich merchant, John Plumpton, and an aristocratic nun of Campsey in Suffolk, Isabel Ufford. Through the names mentioned in Ufford's will Julian is indirectly connected to the Paston family via their circle of correspondents and connections.[35] As Riddy observes, the chance of manuscripts from lay households surviving is much less than for those kept in religious houses, so lack of evidence of lay ownership of either the *Vision* or the *Revelation* does not provide conclusive proof of circulation.[36] Far from being isolated in her anchorhold, Julian was living in the heart of a busy mercantile centre and she was evidently part of a thriving spiritual and indeed literary community.

The transmission and dissemination of the manuscripts and texts of Julian's showings also reveal something of the secondary audience of both versions. The one surviving copy of the *Vision* appears in a late medieval anthology of devotional and mystical texts that includes extracts by male and female writers from England and the Continent such as Richard Rolle, John Ruysbroek, Henry Suso, Marguerite Porete (but not attributed) and St Bridget of Sweden. It clearly reached its intended audience of contemplatives, since it was copied by and belonged to Carthusian monks, an order devoted to meditation. One possibility is that the English Bridgettine nuns of Syon Abbey also read this manuscript.[37] The scribes of Sloane 2499 and the Paris manuscript were English Benedictine nuns from Paris and Cambrai in the first half of the seventeenth century, and the text seems to have been copied for the sisters and preserved in their French convents. Even if one were of the view that Julian's own devout lay female contemporary, Margery Kempe, had no access to, or even knowledge of, her writing, it nevertheless seems to have had an unusually female dominated line of descent and reception after the Reformation through female religious houses abroad.[38] London, British Library, MS Sloane 3705, has at the end the following scribal addition, partly written in the shape of an inverted triangle:

> Here end the sublime and wonderful revelations of the unutterable love of God in Jesus Christ vouchsafed to a dear lover of His and in her to all His dear friends and lovers whose hearts like hers do flame in the love of our dearest Jesu.[39]

These lines unite visionary and audience, as does the text itself, evoking a network of readers (whether female or male, lay or clerical) who share Julian's spiritual desire. But, as seventeenth-century scribal additions, they also reach across time and space into a future unimaginable to Julian.

Conclusion

The writing down of Julian's showings seems to have been her life's work and comparisons are often drawn with William Langland's continual reworking of *Piers Plowman*. The comparison between Julian of Norwich and William Langland bears further scrutiny. Although Langland wrote about fictional dream visions in a conventional first-person voice, while Julian of Norwich related self-experienced mystical revelations, both have a deep-seated respect for the word of God and struggle to express urgent theological and personal issues not in Latin but in the vernacular. Both are concerned with expressing religious truths and as a result find themselves in conflict with established tradition and belief and with what they see as their own limited powers of expression. As a result they share a developed awareness of their own responsibilities as authors – an awareness reflected in the processes of revision and their willingness to start all over again from the very beginning and to rethink all that has gone before. Nevertheless, it is equally, or even more, useful to read Julian's writings alongside Osbern Bokenham's *Legends of Holy Women*, Margery Kempe's *Book* and the Paston letters. This is because it was from within a milieu such as this that the quotidian sublimity of Julian's mysticism emerged and in this milieu that her writings would have been first heard, read and discussed. We have plenty of evidence that Julian was not an isolated contemplative. Whether or not she was professed as a nun in her youth, she had her mother and friends, as well as male spiritual advisers, around her when she thought she was dying, and she had a close female friend for whom she prayed to

God for reassurance. We know from contemporary wills that she had female companions in her anchorhold, and that priests, laymen and nuns valued her, and we know from Margery Kempe's *Book* that she was consulted as a figure of authority. As Riddy observes: 'To see Julian as a solitary is to ignore a central feature of her self-representation, which is relational.'[40]

5

Margery Kempe (*c.*1373–after 1439)

Introduction

In chapter 75 of the first part of *The Book of Margery Kempe* appears a vivid testimony to Margery Kempe's miraculous ability to heal others (*Book*, 177–9).[1] We are told of Margery's encounter in her parish church, St Margaret's Church in Lynn, with a local man, whose wife had been driven insane after childbirth. The man described how his wife was unable to recognize either him or their neighbours, and how she roared and cried so much that she terrified everyone, and hit out at and bit those around her, so much so that she had to be restrained by manacles. Margery offered to visit the woman, and was welcomed by her because, the woman said, ' "You are . . . a very good woman, and I saw many beautiful angels around you" ' (*Book*, 178). The woman may well have been comforted by the empathy of one who had suffered in a similar fashion.

The first chapter of *The Book of Margery Kempe* begins with an account of the inner torment experienced by Margery following a difficult first pregnancy and labour (*Book*, 6–8). This deep sense of despondency, combined with guilt over an unspecified sin that she felt unable to confess to her unsympathetic priest, had terrible consequences. Margery went out of her mind, believing herself to be tormented by devils who urged her to abandon her faith. She said terrible things of her family and friends, bit herself and tore at her skin with her nails, and had to be forcibly restrained. Margery recovered only when Jesus Christ appeared to her and offered her consolation. The parallels between the story of the new mother in chapter 75 and that of Margery's first visionary experience in chapter 1 are striking. Both women are driven to despair by their experience of parturition, no doubt in part because the risk of dying while giving birth was high (Margery Kempe vividly describes her fears of damnation and sense of horror), and because childbirth rendered a woman's body impure in the eyes of the Church. Both women are also treated in a similar fashion: Margery was tied up and overseen by keepers; the new mother was eventually moved to a room on the edge of the town and fastened with iron chains.

The analogies between these two chapters draw the reader's attention to the significance of the episode involving the new mother, which encapsulates a number of themes central to this chapter. It illustrates the extent to which *The Book of Margery Kempe* is a woman-oriented text. Clearly *The Book* addresses issues such as the perceived sinfulness of women's bodies and the impact it had on women's lives which must surely have had a particular appeal to a female readership, especially a lay one. At the same time, it is a useful starting point for addressing the issues of the extent to which we can think about *The Book* as woman-authored and of the functions *The Book* is actually intended to serve. It was as a result of Margery's frequent visits and daily prayers that the new mother recovered completely and was able to attend the church for purification. The chapter ends with a celebration of Margery's role as healer:

> It was, as it seemed to those who knew of it, a very great miracle, because he who wrote this book had never before that time seen a man or a woman, so it seemed to him, so far out of herself as this woman was, nor so difficult to control or govern, and after he saw her serious and sober enough, may Our Lord be eternally honoured and praised for His great mercy and great goodness who always helps when there is need.

> [It was, as hem thowt þat knewyn it, a ryth gret myrakyl, for he þat wrot þis boke had neuyr be-for þat tyme sey man ne woman, as him thowt, so fer owt of hir-self as þis woman was ne so euyl to rewlyn ne to gouernyn, & sithyn he sey hir sad & sobyr a-now, worschip & preysyng be to owr Lord wyth-owtyn ende for hys hy mercy & hys goodnes þat euyr helpith at nede.] (*Book*, 178–9)

This passage poses the reader with a problem: what are we to make of the intervention into the narrative of the voice of the individual who describes himself as 'he who wrote this book'? This voice invites identification with Margery Kempe's principal secretary, an anonymous cleric who helped her write down *The Book* in its final form. As previous critics have noted, *The Book* offers us a unique insight into the process of writing and composition.[2] In the first section of this chapter, 'Authors and secretaries', a discussion of the crucial role of the *secretary*, as opposed to the professional *scribe*, will inform my re-examination of the question of the authorship of *The Book of Margery Kempe*. Both Margery Kempe and those she worked with writing *The Book* are represented as secretaries, but Margery Kempe's greater authority as God's own secretary is clear. Here I am concerned then, not with the contested issue of Margery Kempe's literacy, but rather with the nature of her relationships with both her book and her secretaries.[3] Douglas Gray has suggested that the passage quoted above, describing Margery's healing of the new mother, indicates that the priest may have thought that *The Book* would be used as testimony in Margery Kempe's future beatification.[4] Beatification was often in effect the first step towards canonization, the making of a saint; an individual who was designated *beata* or *beatus* ['blessed'] might have a cult or popular following but no official pronouncement had been made or made yet. Recent studies have emphasized the political and religious contexts of *The Book*, especially the relationship between Margery Kempe's piety and the heretical beliefs and practices associated with the Lollards.[5] In the second section, ' "A holy woman and a blessed woman": *The Book* as saint's life', I will go on to consider *The Book* in relation to orthodox traditions of hagiography and popular religious enthusiasm, looking at evidence within the text indicating it was written to establish Margery Kempe's status as a local, living saint. Following on from this, the final section, ' "For our example and instruction": *The Book* and its readers', examines the possible audiences of *The Book*.

Authors and secretaries

The spiritual climax of *The Book of Margery Kempe* is undoubtedly the description in chapter 28 of Margery Kempe's vision of Christ's Crucifixion. This vision occurred while Margery was taking part in a candlelight ceremony in the Church of the Holy Sepulchre in Jerusalem, during her extended pilgrimages to the Holy Lands and to Rome between 1413 and 1415. It was while Margery was mystically transported that she began her cryings and roarings which continued for many years after she left Jerusalem. These proved to be some of the most disruptive and controversial expressions of her piety, causing her to be excluded from sermons and public places, criticized by her contemporaries and abandoned by her supporters. Chapter 28 describes in considerable and bloody detail Margery's revelation of Christ's Passion, and her emotional and violent physical response to her memory of the Lord's suffering. It then concludes by lamenting that more of us do not remember His sacrifice, and that we do not 'support Our Lord's own secretaries whom He has endued with love, but rather disparage and hinder them as much as we can' (*Book*, 71).

This passage is crucial for our understanding of Margery Kempe's perception of herself as servant of God and as writer. In the context in which the word appears, *secretari(e)* could be used in the modern sense of 'one employed to write for another, a scribe, a secretary'.[6] Jennifer Summit understands the word in this sense when she argues that the passage implies that Margery Kempe 'is merely taking dictation from a divine source'.[7] However, to read the quotation in this way is to misunderstand Margery Kempe's role as a visionary *intimately* involved in the composition of her own text. At the time when *The Book* was written, in the first half of the fifteenth century, *secretari(e)* had the primary meaning of 'one entrusted with private or confidential matters, a confidant; a trusted servant or counselor; one entrusted with the secrets of God'.[8] Margery Kempe, a laywoman and member of the middle classes, lived in a culture that was still predominantly oral rather than literate. For her, to be God's secretary was to be one who communed intimately with God, and whose duty it was to communicate to others her revelations and the story of her pious and sometimes miraculous life, largely, although not entirely, through the spoken word.

As Summit has pointed out, medieval writers like Geoffrey Chaucer or Christine de Pizan did not think of themselves as authors because the title 'author', or *auctor*, was bestowed only on ancient poets, philosophers and theologians: individuals with authority or *auctoritas*.[9] Contemporary authors, male *or* female, were almost inconceivable. It is worth recalling here St Bonaventure's famous analysis of the four different 'ways of making a book'. These were, in addition to the foregrounding of one's own words by the author (*auctor*), the simple copying by the scribe (*scriptor*); the putting together of the words of others by the compilor (*compilator*); and the glossing of the words of others by the commentator (*commentator*).[10] But, as we saw in the Introduction to this study, this model of writing and composition is one that, in a period of limited female literacy, has only partial applicability to women. Furthermore, it does not allow for the distinct and important category of secretary, which, as I have suggested, is to be distinguished from that of the scribe, who was usually a manual labourer working for remuneration alone. As the above definitions indicate, the role of secretary did not necessarily entail the physical process of writing; what it did entail was secrecy, confidentiality and trust. The secretary's position was a privileged one and one that implied a certain status.

If God was the ultimate author, the role of secretary was one that could and indeed might sometimes best be undertaken by a woman. In a key passage in *Ancrene Wisse*, part seven, Love is personified as God's chamberlain (or household attendant) and counsellor, and also, tellingly, as 'his wife, from whom he can keep no secrets, but to whom he confides everything he thinks'.[11] Like this personification of Love, Margery Kempe also portrays herself as God's wife, married to the Father in a mystical ceremony in Rome (*Book*, ch. 35); she also repeatedly represents herself as Christ's lover. Margery's closeness to the Deity is captured when we are told that she understood the 'sweet dalliance' of Christ in her soul 'as clearly as if one friend should speak to another' (*Book*, 214). John Burrow argues that in the Middle Ages 'Men "make books" by writing'.[12] Women, we might add, can do so by listening to *and* talking with and about God.

This extension of the medieval model of 'ways of making a book' to include the activities and responsibilities of the secretary can also encompass the parts played by Margery Kempe's so-called 'scribes' in the writing of *The Book*; thus my preference throughout this chapter, and this book as a whole, for the term 'secretary'. Accounts of the complex genesis of *The Book* are provided in the 'proem' or introduction and the more concise preface that follows it. Margery Kempe's principal secretary wrote both proem and preface in 1436. He explains in the proem that he wrote the preface first, and then 'when he had written a quire, he added a leaf to it, and then wrote this proem to give a more open account' (*Book*, 5). The proem develops what the preface tells us about how Margery Kempe came to have her book written some 'twenty years and more' from the time of her first religious experiences (*Book*, 3; cf. 6). In so doing, it lays great emphasis on Margery Kempe's role as secretary, and thus also on the priest's and his fellows' roles as secretaries to 'God's own secretary'.

The word 'secret' appears twice in the proem to *The Book of Margery Kempe*. It first occurs in a reference to Margery's prophetic abilities: 'She knew and understood many secret and confidential things which would happen afterwards, by inspiration of the Holy Ghost' (*Book*, 2). These abilities are offered as evidence of Margery Kempe's 'dalliance' with the Lord; proof of them is later given by the secretary as an explanation of why he had such faith in her that he agreed to help her write *The Book* (see *Book*, chs 24, 25). 'Secret' next occurs in a passage describing how Margery, fearing that her spiritual experiences might be 'illusions and deceits', confided in clerics and other figures of religious authority:

> And all those to whom she showed her secrets said that she was greatly obliged to love Our Lord because of the grace He showed her, and counselled her to follow her promptings and stirrings and faithfully to believe they were from the Holy Ghost and from no evil spirit.

> [And þei alle þat sche schewed hyr secretys vn-to seyd sche was mech bownde to louen ower Lord for þe grace þat he schewyd vn-to hyr and

cownseld hyr to folwyn hyr meuynggys & steringgys & trustly belevyn it weren of þe Holy Gost & of noon euyl spyryt.] (*Book*, 3)

The proem asserts that some of these pious individuals advised her to record her revelations and make them into a treatise, and that some even offered to write them down for her 'with their own hands' (*Book*, 3). Yet when Margery Kempe was finally directed by God that her work should be made, she was initially unable to find a 'writer who would fulfil her desire nor give credence to her feelings' (*Book*, 4).

The proem emphasizes that those secrets that God has entrusted to Margery Kempe are in turn entrusted by her to those to whom she confesses them and subsequently to those who help in the writing of her *Book*. It gives quite detailed information about Margery Kempe's first secretary (*Book*, 4), who is referred to later as her 'writer' (*Book*, 216, 219), and who was in all probability her son.[13] Certainly what is known of this first secretary, an Englishman living in Germany who, with his wife, came to stay with Margery (*Book*, 4), corresponds fairly closely with the account of the son's life in the second part of *The Book of Margery Kempe* (*Book*, 221–5). Understanding Margery's needs, this man agreed to write her *Book* but died before he had completed his undertaking. The proem emphasizes his closeness to Margery, commenting that he had 'good knowledge' of her (*Book*, 4). The description of the relationship between Margery and her son reinforces this point. The son is portrayed as one of Margery's most intimate lay confidants. In order to encourage his spiritual growth Margery 'opened her heart to him, showing and informing him how Our Lord had drawn her through His mercy and by what means, and also how much grace He had shown her, which he [the son] said he was unworthy to hear' (*Book*, 224). This description of Margery's secular 'confession' sounds remarkably similar to and should perhaps be identified with the process of dictating *The Book* itself.[14]

The proem says little about Margery Kempe's second lay secretary, described simply as a 'good man' whom she agreed to pay well for his task (*Book*, 4). Yet it does remark that this man knew the first secretary, and indeed that he 'had sometimes read letters in the other man's writing, sent from beyond the sea while he was in Germany' (*Book*, 4). This second secretary was sworn to remain silent about the project, urged by Margery 'never to reveal it as long as she lived' (*Book*, 4). How significant is it that Margery Kempe turned to someone whom she may previously have employed to help her reading her son's letters, and who had possibly even written correspondence on her behalf? As we will see in the next chapter, even in the writing of confidential correspondence women and men often relied on secretaries whom they trusted not to reveal their work to others, some of whom would nevertheless have been paid for their services. *The Book of Margery Kempe* mentions other occasions when Margery engaged people to write letters for her. Finding herself in trouble in Leicester, for example, she sent a message to her husband written by one Thomas Marchale, again a layman and a valued friend (*Book*, 111). Yet Margery Kempe's awareness that spiritual matters were secrets between God and herself led her to seek whenever possible the assistance of men of religion in her writing and reading. When she had to communicate certain revelations to a widow who refused to see her, she requested a master of divinity to act as her secretary (*Book*, 45). One unbeneficed priest is described in *The Book* as Margery's 'reader', a role he continued in for seven or eight years (*Book*, 147, 143). Margery believed that God had brought him to her hometown to read to her from the Bible, biblical commentaries, visionary works and books of devotion (*Book*, 143). In this context, it should come as no surprise that the third and final secretary employed by Margery Kempe should be a priest, for whom she 'felt great affection' (*Book*, 4).

Problems of language dogged both the second and third secretary. *The Book* repeatedly stresses that the first to be employed as secretary – Margery Kempe's son – wrote in 'neither good English nor German' (*Book*, 4; cf. 6 and 220). Despite his familiarity with the hand, the second secretary was able only to write a leaf and then had to give up (*Book*, 4). Following the death of the first secretary, Margery Kempe had in fact initially approached the man I label the third or clerical secretary, asking him to read (not *copy*) *The Book* (*Book*, 4). This man had despaired of being able to do so without divine aid, but nevertheless offered to rewrite it for her. However in the face of the hostility of others towards Margery Kempe, he changed his mind and advised her to seek assistance elsewhere, and it was only four years later that he finally embarked on this undertaking.

The first version of *The Book of Margery Kempe* evidently comprised reminiscences dictated by Kempe to her son: the preface warns that the first part does not follow chronological order 'but just as the material back came to [her] mind when it came to be written' (*Book*, 5). When it came to the rewriting, Margery Kempe and her clerical secretary worked together trying to discern the meaning of the matter in front of them. The priest 'read over every word in the presence of [Margery Kempe], and she sometimes helped where there was any difficulty' (*Book*, 4). Their work was time-consuming and, as with her first secretary (*Book*, 216), the two must have remained closeted together for months on end. Margery Kempe's relationship with her clerical secretary was surely, then, an exceptionally close one.[15] The terms used to describe the clerical secretary's activities and Margery Kempe's role are telling. At the end of part 1, the priest says that with the help of God and Margery he 'drew out' the sense of the first version into its new form (*Book*, 220). At the beginning of part 2, he says he only 'copied the same treatise according to his simple knowledge' (*Book*, 221). He seems uncertain of his role, wavering between thinking of himself as scribe, compiler and commentator. At the same time, he is a confessor and a hagiographer, questioning his subject and confirming the accuracy and truth of her story.[16] Margery Kempe, however, *is* his author even if she lacks the requisite authority of the ancient writers because she is the one, after all, who 'experienced all this treatise in feelings and deeds' (*Book*, 220). Margery Kempe testified to the veracity of everything written down in her *Book* (*Book*, 5) and chapters 88 and 89, which describe the spiritual blessings she received from God during the first writing of her *Book*, affirm her status. Gray understands the composition of *The Book* as collaborative, 'somewhere between the two extremes of simple "dictation" and a simple clerical organizing "authorship"'.[17] Yet this collaborative model needs to be nuanced to capture the hierarchical structure of the author–secretary relationship I have explored here, which leaves God at the apex, but positions Margery Kempe above all her secretaries, lay or clerical.

Lynn Staley has characterized the clerical secretary as a narrative trope, a figure created within the text, whose voice functions to render the text authoritative.[18] The problem with such an approach is that it overlooks what the depiction of Margery Kempe's relationship with her secretaries can tell us about the actual process of composition of a medieval book authored by a woman, and about the ideas of authorship and authority that underpin it. Yet it is certainly the case that this secretary's narrative interventions repeatedly testify to Margery's holiness. An example of this occurs in chapter 62, when this secretary recounts how he was driven to doubt Margery by the preaching of a certain famous friar. He regained his faith in her after reading various texts, including *The Life of Mary of Oignies*, *The Prick of Love*, Richard Rolle's *Incendium Amoris* and a treatise attributed to Elizabeth of Hungary. However, aside from offering further evidence of Margery's extraordinary piety, this episode is important for another reason. Two of these texts are also named in the short list of works that Margery had read to her by another priest; given the value and rarity of manuscripts at the time, it is perfectly plausible that he actually read the same copies. Margery Kempe, her clerical secretary and the priest who served her as her reader must all have been part of the same circle of book ownership and exchange. It is telling that the clerical secretary records that he read *The Life of Mary of Oignies* only after 'the prompting of a worthy cleric, a bachelor of divinity' (*Book*, 153). While this man is unlikely to have been Margery Kempe's reader, the mention provides further evidence that the clergy (and lay people) regularly exchanged and discussed books. *The Life of Mary of Oignies* and the other works mentioned all seem to have influenced Margery Kempe's piety and shaped the writing of *The Book* to a greater or lesser extent. Despite her 'illiteracy', Margery Kempe was part of a literate and literary network centred on Lynn. At the same time as we acknowledge Margery Kempe's position as the author of her *Book*, it is vital that we extend our understanding of collaboration to recognize the contribution to its composition of other, often anonymous, members of this reading network, such as her secretaries and reader, and also her confessors and other confidants and supporters.

'A holy woman and a blessed woman': *The Book* as saint's life

Turning now from ideas of the author within *The Book of Margery Kempe* to questions of form, genre and function, the first point to acknowledge is that *The Book* defies narrow categorization. It is an autobiography, a confession, a testament of faith, a book of revelations and a devotional and contemplative work.[19] It starts as a conversion narrative. Indeed this is an element flagged up in the proem and preface, which emphasize the reversals of Margery's fortune as she turned from the world to God. *The Book* then goes on to describe Margery's tribulations, her dalliances with the Lord, her visions, her pilgrimages and, at the very end, it provides us with a series of her prayers. Although certain types of episode are grouped together, Margery's revelations of Christ and His mother, for example, or her journeys to Jerusalem and Rome and her examinations for heresy, the order of the narrative is repeatedly disrupted. Even though *The Book* is a revised text, many irregularities remain. For example, it seems long, yet both parts end abruptly, and a note in the text draws attention to the displacement of the twenty-first chapter, which ought to appear before the seventeenth (*Book*, 38). Indeed overall *The Book* lacks unity and balance: it is made up of an overlapping prologue and preface, two parts of unequal length (the first has eighty-nine chapters, the second only ten), and the short appendix of prayers. The uneven structure of *The Book* reflects the complexities of its composition and production, and its very originality, which results in part from the apparent incoherence of its form and genre, may be explained at least in part by the same factors. Gail McMurray Gibson speaks for many critics, when she suggests that *The Book* 'is also a calculated hagiographical text, a kind of autobiographical saint's life'.[20] Nevertheless, it does not fully conform to hagiographic stereotypes, contains too much personal and local information, and is at times contradictory and ends before Margery Kempe's death. But while this may seem unusual in a saint's life, it is not of course in the life of a living saint (the obvious comparison being *The Life of Christina of Markyate*, discussed in Chapter 1). More significantly, *The Book* is written in English not Latin. For whatever reason, the cumbersome, vernacular *Book of Margery Kempe* failed to metamorphose into a distilled, Latin *vita* of Margery Kempe.

Nevertheless, although in its attention to detail *The Book of Margery Kempe* insists upon its own authenticity, at the same time it makes clear its debts to biblical and religious tradition. Margery venerates and imitates holy women from the New Testament: the Virgin Mary, for example, who figures largely in her revelations, and also Mary Magdalene, a former prostitute according to medieval belief. Margery's identification with the latter saint is particularly marked in her vision of Christ appearing to her as a gardener at His tomb. When Christ says to Mary Magdalen '"Touch me not,"' her reply '"Ah Lord, I see well that you do not wish me to be so homely with you as I have been before"' and Christ's reassuring response (*Book*, 197) closely echo Margery's own conversations with the Lord. Likewise the influence of the legendary martyrs of early Christianity, such as St Katherine of Alexandria who intellectually overcame the emperor Maxentius and his philosophers, is revealed in Margery Kempe's self-representation in *The Book*, especially in her accounts of her examinations for heresy.[21] Indeed one of her fiercest opponents tried to counter this self-fashioning directly when he said '"Saint Katherine told of what kindred she came and yet you are not alike"' (*Book*, 111).

Saints in living memory also provided Margery with models to emulate: most strikingly St Bridget of Sweden, a married woman with children whose death coincided with Margery Kempe's birth, and whose house in Rome Margery visited (*Book*, 95). Indeed, in England at the end of the fourteenth and the first half of the fifteenth centuries, the fervour around the creation and worship of saints increased dramatically. In Yorkshire, for example, John Thweng, a canon of Bridlington, was canonized in 1401, and in addition the cults surrounding the Saxon and Norman bishops, St Cuthbert, St Wilfred and St William of York were revived. Many of these saints seem to have been revered well beyond their own localities. St John of Bridlington enjoyed national devotion and, as we saw in the previous chapter, in chapter 38 of *A Revelation of Love*, Julian of Norwich celebrates the piety of St John of Beverley.[22] Individuals renowned for their piety such as Thomas Arundel, archbishop of Canterbury or the hermit and mystic Richard Rolle were venerated even though their claims for sanctity were never fully recognized by the Church in Rome. The religious enthusiasm fostered in centres of devotion such as pilgrimage sites must have encouraged the proliferation of unofficial cults alongside official ones. John Capgrave (who was born in Lynn in 1393 and lived there most of his life, and who must surely have known Margery Kempe[23]) includes in his life of St John of Bridlington accounts of miracles performed by John's confessor, Canon William Sleightholme.[24] *The Book* reports that Margery visited the shrine of St William in York and also Bridlington where Sleightholme heard her confession (*Book*, 122, 125, 128). In Norwich a posthumous cult surrounded the local priest Richard Caister, who died in 1420.[25] Margery was one of those who venerated Caister. After receiving a revelation about the priest who read to her, who had been seriously ill, she journeyed to Norwich to visit Caister's grave in order to express her thanks for the sick man's recovery (*Book*, 147). As she wept in the churchyard she was overcome by the realization that God had shown 'such special grace' to Caister. Her graveside devotions are described in more detail than her account of her pilgrimage to the Holy Blood at Hailes (*Book*, 110), while her visits to York, Bridlington and one of the most popular sites in England, the shrine of Our Lady of Walsingham (*Book*, 227), are only mentioned in passing. Promotion of the sanctity of Margery Kempe may well have both supported and been supported by Caister's cult.

There is good reason to think that Margery Kempe anticipated being revered as a saint after her death. Before leaving for Jerusalem she received the divine promise, ' "Daughter, I shall make all the world wonder at you, and many men and many women shall speak of me for love of you, and worship me in you" ' (*Book*, 73). Subsequently the Lord extended her plenary remission – the full pardon of temporal punishment granted to penitents who pilgrimaged to the Holy Lands – ' "to all those who believe and to all those who shall believe until the world's end that God loves you, and shall thank God for you" ' (*Book*, 175). Margery also foresaw that she would be honoured in her hometown of Lynn, in the Church of St Margaret. After a vicious attack on her piety by a visiting friar preacher, Christ reassured her with this revelation:

> 'As his name is now, it shall be thrown down and yours shall be raised up. And I shall make as many men love you for my love as have despised

you for my love. Daughter, you shall be in the church when he shall be outside. In this church you have suffered much shame and reproof for the gifts I have given you and for the grace and goodness that I have worked in you, and therefore in this church and in this place I shall be worshipped in you.'

['As hys name is now, it xal ben throwyn down & þin schal ben reysed up. & I xal makyn as many men to lofe þe for my lofe as han despisyd þe for my lofe. Dowtyr, þu xalt be in cherch whan he xal be wyth-owtyn. In þis chirche þu hast suffyrd meche schame & reprefe for þe ʒyftys þat I haue ʒouyn þe & for þe grace & goodnes þat I haue wrowt in þe, and þerfore in þis cherche & in þis place I xal ben worschepyd in þe.'] (*Book*, 156)

Returning then to the suggestion made earlier, it is plausible that *The Book* was written not only to encourage its readers to live a more pious life, but also to encourage a popular cult of Margery Kempe. However unrealistic it may seem to us now (it was certainly extremely difficult to create a case for canonizing a contemporary woman in the later Middle Ages), it was perhaps even written with Margery Kempe's beatification or even canonization in mind.

It is worth remembering that written (Latin) testimonies by and about the candidate were considered crucial evidence in a claim for sanctity. *The Book of Margery Kempe* could well have been intended to provide material for such a testimony: as well as relating the visions and miracles attributed to Margery Kempe, it describes at length her widespread support. The households of the higher clergy and the devout nobility played an important role in local spiritual life by fostering the creation of new saints and patronizing religious institutions and pious individuals. According to *The Book*, Margery approached some of the most important figures in the Church of her day seeking their approval, including Archbishop Arundel (*Book*, 36–7), an active supporter of contemporary contemplatives such as Walter Hilton. *The Book* also records that Margery acted as spiritual adviser to religious figures such as the abbess of Denny, who invited her to come and speak to the nuns in her care (*Book*, 202). Margery was consulted by powerful members of the laity, such as Joan Beaufort Lady Westmorland (daughter of John of Gaunt and Catherine Swynford), who herself had a reputation for piety, read devotional works and was a patron of Yorkshire solitaries (*Book*, 133–4).[26] Margery's clerical friends and sympathizers stood by her during difficult times. She reports that many of them defended her from criticism. When the friar visiting Lynn excluded her from his sermons because of the disturbance she caused, both learned priests and worthy townspeople sought to convince him of his error (*Book*, 148–52). A priest of the Church of St John Lateran in Rome had to give up his office because he supported Margery's tears and crying in the face of the hostility of other English pilgrims (*Book*, 83). *The Book* is then witness to the endorsement of Margery Kempe's piety by those of the higher and middle ranks in society and by members of the clergy.

Quite apart from aristocratic and ecclesiastical support, evidence of a popular following played an important part in establishing a reputation for holiness. One of the arguments put forward during the Process of St Bridget of Sweden in support of her canonization was that her sanctity was already widely recognized.[27] *The Book* represents Margery's fame as widespread. When she was examined for heresy in Leicester, one man defended her, saying that in his hometown of Boston in Lincolnshire, ' "this woman is considered a holy woman and a blessed woman" ' (*Book*, 112). Margery found admirers and followers everywhere. In Jerusalem she enjoyed the companionship of friars who had heard that she was a woman who spoke with God (*Book*, 73). During her stay in Rome a priest who had heard of her reputation while he was still in England sought her out (*Book*, 96). According to her own account, Margery also gained the respect and love of many of the poor by living a life of *imitatio christi* or imitation of Christ, caring for the sick and infirm, even lepers (*Book*, 85–6, 176–7). Her own patient endurance of an illness which lasted for almost eight years would itself have been seen as a sign of holiness (*Book*, 137–9). The dying called for her to be with them in their final hours, to help them prepare for their judgement (*Book*, 172–3). Christ promised Margery that her intercession would save hundreds of thousands of souls (*Book*, 20). Her gift of prophecy gained her many followers and she records a number of events which she correctly foretold, including a prophecy concerning the solution of a controversy over the granting of certain privileges to the Chapel of St Nicholas in Lynn (*Book*, 58–60). Margery was able to discern the physical and spiritual health of certain individuals and to intercede for them (*Book*, 25–7, 53–4), although her revelations of the damnation of souls sometimes drove her to the verge of despair (*Book*, 54–5, 144–6).

Miracle working was of course crucial evidence of sanctity. In addition to Margery's healing of the woman afflicted following childbirth, *The Book* records a number of other supernatural phenomena. Another marvel attributed to Margery occurred when a fire broke out in Lynn (*Book*, 162–4). Flames consumed the Guildhall of the Trinity and St Margaret's Church was itself in danger. Margery's confessor, Robert Spryngolde, put his faith in her prophetic powers. He followed her advice and carried the Sacrament to the fire. In doing so he also placed his trust in the power of the Sacrament as a relic of Christ to save the church. Apparently in response to Margery's prayer, the fire was unexpectedly extinguished by a snowfall. On another occasion, as Margery knelt in prayer in St Margaret's Church, a heavy piece of masonry fell from the vault on top of her, but amazingly she was unhurt by the accident (*Book*, 21–2). Margery's escape from injury has parallels in the life of St John of Bridlington.[28] Furthermore, a stained glass window in York Minster, designed for the edification of non-literate pilgrims like Margery Kempe visiting the Shrine of St William, depicts a stone falling on a monk sleeping during mass; the monk escaped unscathed.[29] In *The Book* we are told that Master Alan, the White Friar or Carmelite (usually identified as Alan of Lynn[30]), 'desiring the work of God to be magnified' examined Margery on 'all the form of this process' and weighed the fallen masonry, declaring her preservation a miracle (*Book*, 22). It is remarkable that here and elsewhere quasi-legal terms and formulations such as 'all the form of this process' are used, providing further evidence that *The Book* may have been intended as the basis of a treatise that would undergo scrutiny by an ecclesiastical inquiry. To give another example, the second part of *The Book* was apparently made at the clerical secretary's suggestion. It is said that he set himself the task of writing it after he had finished copying the first part because 'he [the priest] held it expedient to honour the blessed Trinity that His holy works should *be notified and declared* to the people' (*Book*, 221; my italics). Again the language chosen has legal connotations; the miracle is to be publicly proclaimed and elucidated. The proem was also added as a testimony to a miracle. When this priest, having overcome his earlier doubts, finally came to rewriting *The Book*, he faced yet another setback: his eyesight failed whenever he tried to write or to mend his pen (*Book*, 5). He tried putting on a pair of spectacles, but this made matters worse. He complained to Margery, and she blamed his affliction on the devil: sure enough, when he returned to his task he was cured. In summary, *The Book of Margery Kempe*, or rather a Latin rewriting of it, could have provided some compelling evidence in support of her beatification, should it ever have come to consideration.

'For our example and instruction': *The Book* and its readers

In her influential study, *Margery Kempe's Dissenting Fictions*, Staley sustains a careful distinction between Kempe as author of her *Book* and 'Margery' as its subject or protagonist, akin to the differentiation generally made between Chaucer as the poet who composed *The Canterbury Tales* and Geoffrey the fictional pilgrim.[31] While this discrimination serves as a useful reminder to the modern reader that Kempe's *Book* does not necessarily describe actual events with any accuracy, it is nevertheless problematic. First, it is difficult to maintain given the autobiographical and extra-textual aspects of *The Book*. If we accept *The Book's* authenticity, in other words, if we accept that it does attempt to describe the life and experience of a woman who existed in history, then we have to acknowledge that Kempe and Margery bear a closer relationship to one another than do Chaucer and Geoffrey. Second, and of equal importance, within *The Book* itself 'Margery' is not the name commonly assigned to its protagonist.[32] In fact, she is only referred to as 'Margery' fifteen times, as 'Margerya' once (*Book*, 93), and as 'Mar. Kempe of Lynn' once (*Book*, 243). The term favoured is 'this creature' – a phrase which simultaneously underlines the humility of the post-conversion Margery, and emphasizes the closeness of her relationship to God the Creator. As Nicholas Watson observes, this term, combined with the narration in the third person, 'does so much to conventionalize the narrative into something approximating a saint's life'.[33] In attempting to draw a firm distinction between Kempe and Margery we are therefore following modern conventions in literary criticism – conventions that stress the textuality of a work while questioning its connection with historical reality – rather than responding to distinctions within the work itself.

When we turn to considering the readership of *The Book*, similar caveats have to be made, and any attempts to reconstruct the audiences have to be nuanced. The inscribed audiences of *The Book* – which Paul Strohm explains can be inferred from 'the imagined situations of telling and listening' of a work that are actually described in that work[34] – are embodied in the figures of Margery Kempe's secretaries. Her main secretary's emotional, spiritual and indeed physical responses to reading the first version of *The Book* are described in detail in the proem, and his responses to her piety (including his doubts about its authenticity) and to other religious works are recounted later. Likewise we are told that her first secretary actually wept as he listened to and copied down her narrative (*Book*, 219). In a sense the myriad other lay and religious people who, we are told, witnessed and reacted to Margery's expressions of her spirituality also constitute the inscribed audience of *The Book*. Distinct from the inscribed audience is the implied audience, which is, as Strohm has outlined, the equivalent of the ideal reader, 'a hypothetical construct, the sum of all the author's assumptions about the persons he or she is addressing'.[35] One view, put forward by Sarah Rees Jones, is that *The Book* is more concerned with the Church and with ecclesiastical authority than with Margery Kempe herself. Consequently, Rees Jones concludes that *The Book* is neither by, nor for, nor about Kempe, but rather 'written by clergy, for clergy and about clergy'.[36] It is important in relation to such perspectives which effectively deny Margery Kempe's significance and agency, to reiterate that *The Book* is, as I have suggested, a woman-oriented text. It dwells on the experiences of a woman who identifies herself in both her religious and domestic lives as wife and mother, and who is indebted to a distinctive female visionary and hagiographic tradition. Even if, as has been argued here, it was written with the aim of fostering a local cult and possibly of gaining official Church recognition of Margery Kempe's piety, it must also be intended as a treatise that would aid the devotions of and offer consolation to other women.

Nevertheless, we should also acknowledge that the proem implies an audience of Christians that is much more all embracing and not limited by gender. The opening lines state, 'Here begins a short treatise and a comforting one for sinful wretches, wherein they may have great solace and comfort for themselves and understand the high and unspeakable mercy of our sovereign Saviour Christ Jesus' (*Book*, 1). The proem further outlines the reader competency necessary to understand *The Book*:

> All the works of our Saviour are for our example and instruction, and what grace that He works in any creature is our profit if lack of charity be not our hindrance.
>
> [Alle þe werkys of ower Saviowr ben for ower exampyl & instruccyon, and what grace þat he werkyth in any creatur is ower profyth yf lak of charyte be not ower hynderawnce.] (*Book*, 1)

The proem alludes here to Romans 15. 4, 'whatsoever things were written aforetime were written for our learning', a verse central to medieval literary theory, which emphasizes that all texts are intended to instruct and to edify.[37] Likewise the word charity – *caritas* in Latin – had a very specific meaning when applied to medieval reading processes: it was used to describe the process of allegorical interpretation, by which all texts were understood in terms of the message of the Bible. The implied audience is therefore expected to be able to look below the surface of *The Book* and to locate the truth – the divine moral – that is hidden there.

Later in *The Book*, the Lord tells Margery that her life is intended as a 'mirror'. From it the people 'should take example from you to have some little sorrow in their hearts for their sins, so that they might through that be saved, but they do not love to hear of sorrow or contrition' (*Book*, 186). *The Book of Margery Kempe* is intended as a guide for salvation, but it is revealing that both here, and in the passage from the proem just cited, an alternative response is also envisaged. This is the response of an audience that, although it is still implied by the text, is not ideal, an audience or readership that lacks charity, that is hostile to Margery Kempe and her *Book* and that refuses to be saved. While her piety and faith might convert some (for example, they inspired a young man Margery encountered at Sheen (*Book*, 246)), they by no means converted all. Indeed sometimes quite the opposite seems to be true, when she repeatedly drives a wedge between others (such as clerics or pilgrims) and God. Here we get to the heart of one of the difficulties in reading *The Book of Margery Kempe* as a hagiographic text: the complexity of the representation of Margery herself, and of the effect she has on people. Watson observes, 'The *Book* demands readers believe in Margery Kempe, but it also gives them every opportunity to number themselves among her doubters or opponents . . . Unlike a saint's *vita*, *The Book of Margery Kempe* . . . invites readers to struggle with it in order to be edified by it.'[38] But once again, if we think of *The Book* as a first, vernacular, version of the life of a local, living saint, then the contradictions, ambiguities and ambivalence of the text seem less out of place – the creases have simply not yet been ironed out.

There is, however, a more narrowly defined audience implied in *The Book of Margery Kempe*, an audience that is familiar with the often very local events being described and that will be able to identify the many individuals (including the main secretary himself) who are not referred to by name. This audience must comprise the people of Margery Kempe's hometown of Lynn, the city of Norwich, and their environs.[39] This audience may have been similar to the initial actual audience of Julian of Norwich's *Revelation of Love*. If we assume that the implied audience can overlap with the intended audience of *The Book*, then Margery Kempe and her secretaries may have felt it imperative to acknowledge fully the extent of the controversy surrounding her piety and to give a favourable account of it. This would have especially been the case given that regional authorities would in the first instance undertake on behalf of the Church in Rome any ecclesiastical inquiry that might be initiated. The probability that the implied audience is East Anglian adds support to the suggestion that *The Book* aimed both to encourage and to provide evidence of a local following.

Unlike other more literary works that include paratextual evidence of the intended audience in the form of dedications or addresses to individuals, the intended audience of *The Book of Margery Kempe* is not articulated within *The Book* itself. However our understanding of the function of *The Book* necessarily impacts on our understanding of its intended audience. If *The Book* can be seen as an early version of a treatise aimed at least in part to support the case for the beatification or canonization of Margery Kempe, this may explain why it is not anonymous throughout. Indeed, in the second part, its subject is actually named (albeit within a narrative episode) as 'Mar. Kempe of Lynn' (*Book*, 243). This intervention serves to remove any uncertainty about the identity of the protagonist of this treatise in the minds of a readership that has not witnessed the events described. The title by which *The Book* is now known was first recorded almost seventy years after it was written, which indicates that Margery Kempe's name was indeed preserved. To find out if *The Book* reached its destination we have to consider the evidence of its actual audience.

In conceptualizing the actual audience of a medieval text, Strohm distinguishes between the *primary* and the *secondary* audience – the author's immediate circle and the text's later readership.[40] How applicable is this distinction to *The Book of Margery Kempe*? One point to note is that Margery Kempe expected to be honoured only posthumously. As mentioned above, she did not intend her book to be circulated within her own lifetime, telling her second secretary that he was not to let anyone know about it before she died (*Book*, 4). From what *The Book* itself reveals, its primary audience was limited to Margery Kempe's secretaries and (if we extrapolate slightly), her confessors and other close supporters. The textual history of *The Book* suggests that in fact it was *never* widely circulated: it exists in only one manuscript which would appear to be a direct copy of the original, lost version written down by Margery Kempe's main secretary.[41] As for the secondary audience, all that is known is that the extant manuscript of *The Book of Margery Kempe* was once part of the library at Mountgrace Priory in North Yorkshire. Again parallels can be drawn with Julian of Norwich as her *Vision Showed to a Devout Woman* also found its way into a Carthusian house. The fifteenth- and sixteenth-century annotations on the extant manuscript of *The Book* allow speculation about its early reception. One of the readers of the manuscript, a Carthusian monk, noticed with apparent approval an affinity between Margery's ecstasies and those of Richard Rolle (tellingly identified as a saint: *Book*, 88 n. 3) and two of his contemporaries at Mountgrace, the writers and contemplatives Richard Methley and John Norton.[42] Even though it seems clear that *The Book* was never rewritten in Latin, nor examined as part of an ecclesiastical inquiry into Margery Kempe's sanctity, the survival of this manuscript in one of the spiritual powerhouses of the Carthusian movement in England and the evidence of the annotations prove that it had some impact. This is confirmed by the existence of two sixteenth-century printings of very short extracts from *The Book*, first by Wynkyn de Worde around 1501 and then by Henry Pepwell in 1521. These extracts conceal far more than they reveal of Margery Kempe's controversial life, visions and piety, paradoxically suggesting that only in a highly sanitized form could any part of *The Book* finally reach an actual audience that reflected its implied readership of lay as well as religious men and women. Yet at the same time they indicate that in the century after her death Margery Kempe's reputation for holiness continued.[43]

Conclusion

The evidence of the readership and audiences of *The Book of Margery Kempe* can usefully be compared to that of both versions of Julian of Norwich's showings. However, the fate of *The Book of Margery Kempe* also bears some comparison with the much earlier *Life of Christina of Markyate*. Both works survive in only one extant manuscript which was formerly part of the library of a male religious institution (St Albans in the case of Christina's *Life*; Mount Grace in the case of Kempe's *Book*). At least one other manuscript of each text must have been in existence at one time: Markyate Priory owned a copy of Christina's *Life*; nothing is known about where the other manuscript of Kempe's *Book* was held. Both texts make an appearance in abridged form in the Early Modern period, a synopsis of *The Life of Christina of Markyate* having been written by the recusant Nicholas Roscarrock in the late sixteenth or early seventeenth century. In fact, both texts were known only in these summaries until they were rediscovered by twentieth-century scholars. Hope Emily Allen identified the manuscript of Margery Kempe's *Book* in 1934. C. H. Talbot reconstructed the text of the badly damaged manuscript of Christina's *Life*, which he published in 1959. In both cases, the textual histories are revealing about the afterlives of these devout and dynamic women, whose fame and influence may have been relatively extensive during their lifetimes, were circumscribed around the times of their deaths, but were not fully extinguished.

Our understanding of the form, genre and function of *The Book of Margery Kempe* inevitably impacts on the sense we make of the evidence of its readership. *The Book* is of course a mystical and devotional work, and it was clearly read as such – in so far as it was read at all – in the century after its composition. Yet I have argued in this chapter that it is also at least in part a hagiographic work, written to encourage a local cult and perhaps also to provide evidence of Margery Kempe's sanctity. In this respect it is then also similar to *The Life of Christina of Markyate*. But in this chapter I have also explored Margery Kempe's role in the composition of her *Book* and here the comparisons with Christina of Markyate (whose involvement in the telling of her own life story is far more indirect) are less obvious. Kempe's is a role that I characterize as that of God's secretary; it was one that entailed intimacy and trust. Those men who helped Kempe write her *Book* are in turn described as secretaries to God's secretary: no mere scribes and readers, they were both more and less than collaborators. They listened to Kempe's confidences and revealed them in writing only according to her instructions. Many other members of her spiritual network must also have contributed, if indirectly, to the writing of *The Book*. This model of authorship is one that could readily be applied to other mystical and visionary works by women, but can it also be extended to other types of texts, including secular writing? In the next chapter I return to the role of the secretary and the question of collaboration in relation to late medieval private correspondence by women. I also, crucially, return to a consideration of voice;[44] an issue that I have side-stepped in this chapter in a deliberate attempt to focus, not on Margery Kempe's subjectivity, but on the production of her *Book* as text.

6

The Paston Letters (1440–1489)

Introduction

In this analysis of writing by and for women, I have concentrated so far on religious and imaginative writing, looking at hagiographies, visionary works and other devotional treatises alongside the lais and fables of Marie de France. At this point I turn to the epistolary genre: the women's letters from the collection of documents known as the Paston letters. The letters and papers relating to the Pastons, a fifteenth-century Norfolk family, constitute the largest archive of personal correspondence from medieval England. If, with the exception of some of the poetry of Marie de France, none of the texts considered in the previous chapters can really be described as literary in inception, writing of the sort discussed here is the most overtly functional or pragmatic. Elsewhere I have examined the letters by the Paston women in terms of medieval women's letter writing more generally and in terms of their literary, cultural and social context.[1] Here, at the same time as I highlight some of the most significant themes to emerge from a reading of the women's letters, I think about ways in which a close study of the letters can contribute to *and problematize* our understanding of medieval women's writing more generally. In so doing I discuss letters by women in the Paston collection alongside letters by men.

The chapter is structured in three sections. The first, 'Absent women', focuses on two groups of letters on the topic of women's marriages. In both groups, the voice of the woman at the centre of the affair is to varying extents lost to us, and the exact sequence or nature of events may at times seem unclear. This section is primarily concerned with where and how to locate the voice of the absent women: only by carefully cross-referencing sequences of related letters by different writers can this voice begin to be heard. The second section, 'Reading medieval women's letters', examines the extent to which we can really talk about 'authorship' in relation to these letters given the extent of the collaboration in their composition.[2] Here I argue that the task of the secretary responsible for writing down letters such as these was not a menial one, and that the secretary might play a significant role in the process of composition.[3] This section also addresses the reasons why the letters were written in the first place and then kept, and other distinct features of the letters, and asks what more we can learn from them, especially in terms of female networks and women's lives. The third section, 'Women correspondents and the writing process', looks at what can be gleaned from comparing different drafts of the same letter, or from examining the annotations to a letter made by its recipient. This brings us back, at the end of the section, to another group of letters on the subject of a marriage and, by offering an analysis of ways in which the letters resonate with one another, to the question of collaborative authorship. To distinguish firmly between the different correspondents and secretaries is once more shown to be somewhat artificial. The Paston letters confirm the thesis of this book that authors, secretaries and readers, women and men, worked together in the production of texts and meanings. At the same time, the Paston letters offer us an insight into the actual practice of writing itself that is unique in medieval women's writing in English.

Absent women

Margery Paston Calle was the elder of the two daughters of Margaret Paston and John I. She earned the displeasure of her family in 1469 when, aged around 20, she secretly married Richard Calle, the Paston family bailiff. A letter from her second brother John III to their eldest brother, John II, now (following the death of their father three years earlier) the head of the family, vividly captures their anger.[4] John III vehemently asserts that there is no truth in claims made by Margery and Richard that he has assented to their union. He goes on to relate an exchange he had with a friend whom he suspected to have taken Calle's side. In this conversation he had stated that he would never countenance the wedding, even if his father, had he been alive, his mother and John II all agreed to it. Richard Calle was simply of too low a social status to marry into the family. Not only did he work for the Pastons, but, so John III claims, his family were mere grocers. In the opinion of John III, the marriage would see his sister reduced to selling 'candle and mustard in Framlingham'. There may be a political dimension to this remark: Framlingham was the ancestral home of the Duke of Norfolk and 1469 saw the height of the Paston dispute with Norfolk.[5] John III therefore is expressing his concern that the family will be humiliated before its enemies. He may even be suggesting that a darker plot lay behind the elopement.

Margery's defiance, her opposition to the wishes of her kinsfolk, suggests an independence of spirit that is really quite remarkable. Yet no letters from Margery have survived. Margery's voice is transmitted only indirectly, through the letters of others. It is impossible to know whether this is because Margery did not write any letters, or because her letters were considered either too insignificant or even too contentious to preserve. Perhaps out of sheer anger and frustration the family deliberately destroyed any she may have written. We do, however, have two other vitally important pieces of correspondence from the time of the wedding – one by Margery's mother Margaret, the other by her new husband Richard. There are also a number of scattered references to Margery in letters written before the marriage, which provide snippets of information about her life as a girl and young woman. Immediately prior to the secret wedding, for example, Margaret Paston wrote to her eldest son requesting that he find a suitable situation for Margery (no. 59).[6] Before their marriages, daughters of the wealthier classes were often placed in the service of worthy families as a form of education. However, in this case, it seems likely that Margaret Paston had begun to suspect that some sort of attachment had formed between her daughter and Calle, and wanted to send Margery away to prevent it developing further.

The letter written by Margaret to John II describing her attempts to have the marriage of Margery and Richard invalidated is justifiably well known (no. 60). Here Margaret tells how, accompanied by her mother-in-law Agnes, she tried to persuade Walter Lyhert, bishop of Norwich, to annul the marriage. The bishop was sympathetic to the cause of these formidable women, but insisted that he would need to interview Margery himself. Margaret recounts what happened next:

> On Friday the bishop sent for her by Ashfield and others who are very unhappy about her behaviour. And the bishop spoke to her very plainly and reminded her of her birth, who her relatives and friends were, and how she should have more, if she would be ruled and guided by them. And if she would not, what rebuke and shame and loss it would be to her if she would not be guided by them, and the reason for her being abandoned in terms of the material help or comfort she could have had from them. And he said that he had heard it said that she loved such a one as her friends did not want her to marry, and therefore he commanded her to consider very carefully what she did. And he said he wanted to understand whether the words she had said to him constituted matrimony or not. And she repeated what she had said, and said that if those words did not make it sure, she said boldly she would make it surer still before she

went from there. Because she said she believed in her conscience she was committed, whatever the words were. These foolish words grieve me and her grandmother as much as all the rest.

[On Fryday the Bysschope sent fore here be Asschefeld and othere þat arn ryth sory of here demenyng. And þe Bysschop seyd to here ryth pleynly, and put here in rememberawns how sche was born, wat kyn and frenddys þat sche had, and xuld haue mo yf sche were rulyd and gydyd aftyre them; and yf sche ded not, wat rebuke and schame and los yt xuld be to here yf sche were not gydyd be them, and cause of foresakyng of here fore any good ore helpe ore kownfort þat sche xuld haue of hem; and seyd þat he had hard sey þat sche loued schecheon þat here frend were not plesyd wyth þat sche xuld haue, and there-fore he bad here be ryth wel a-vysyd how sche ded, and seyd þat he woold wndyrstond þe worddys þat sche had seyd to hym, wheythere yt mad matramony ore not. And sche rehersyd wat sche had seyd, and seyd yf thoo worddys mad yt not suhere, sche seyd boldly þat sche wold make yt suerhere ore þan sche went thens; fore sche sayd sche thowthe in here conschens sche was bownd, wat so euere þe worddys wern. Thes leud worddys gereue me and here grandam as myche as alle þe remnawnte.[7]]

Medieval marriages could be legally contracted without a priest or any witnesses present. However, for a marriage to be valid the correct form of words had to have been spoken. Margery refused to be bullied and intimidated. Her determination is evident. She knew what she had said and she had said what she had meant. Calle subsequently confirmed to the bishop Margery's account of where and when the marriage took place and what each party had said. Despite his evident disapproval of the marriage itself, of Margery's disobedience of her family and of her disrespectful behaviour more generally, the bishop ultimately had little choice but to acknowledge that it had actually taken place. He could remonstrate and cajole, but he could not deny the truth.

Margaret's retribution was swift: she refused to admit Margery into her house and later disowned her completely. Her words to her son convey her anger, frustration and pain:

I entreat you and request you not to take this too sadly, because I know very well that it goes very close to your heart, as it does to mine and to others. But remember, as I do, that in losing her we have only lost a wretch, and so take it less to heart. Because if she had been virtuous, whatever she had been, things would not have been as bad as this. Because even if he [Calle] were to fall down dead at this hour, she would never be in my heart as she used to be.

[I pray ʒow and requere ʒow þat ʒe take yt not pensyly, fore I wot wele
yt gothe ryth nere ʒowr hart, and so doth yt to myn and to othere; but
remembyre ʒow, and so do I, þat we haue lost of here but a brethele, and
setyt þe les to hart; fore and sche had be good, wat so euere sche had be
yt xuld not a ben os jt tys, fore and he were ded at thys owyre sche xuld
neuere be at myn hart as sche was.][8]

It appears that Margaret Paston never forgave her daughter. In a later
letter, Margaret tells her eldest son, 'As for your sister, I can send you no
good news about her.'[9] Although Margery's children do figure in her
mother's will (Margery herself seems to have pre-deceased her mother),
they are mentioned only after John II's illegitimate daughter (no. 75).
Richard Calle nevertheless continued to work for the family; while a
daughter was not thought to contribute much to the household and could
be readily disowned, a valuable servant would be difficult to replace and
presumably could not be given up so lightly.

Richard Calle's solitary love letter to Margery provides us with the other
side of the story. Richard describes his anguish at being separated from his
beloved new wife, and complains of the injustice that forces them apart.[10]
He insists on the validity of their marriage, repeating the words of the
marriage service when he prays to God to reunite them because 'we that
ought out of right to be most together are most asunder'. He then omi-
nously alludes to the sentence of excommunication that befalls those who
prevent rightful matrimony. He expresses his concern that Margaret, with
the connivance of her chief confidant, the family's chaplain Sir James
Gloys, is attempting to intercept their letters to one another and conveying
false rumours about him. It seems that a Paston man even brought a
present of a ring, claiming it was from Margery, trying to trick Richard's
go-between into handing over the correspondence from Richard with
which he had been entrusted. Richard writes that he has been informed
that Margery has not told her family the truth about the marriage and
urges her to do so because they refuse to believe him. He also describes
how he is wary of writing to Margery because he has also heard that she
has shown his previous letters to her family. He pleads with her to not let
anyone else see the letter and to get rid of it, something that she evidently
failed to do, given that it remained in the family's collection. The Margery
that appears in this letter is rather different from that depicted by Margaret.
Whereas Margaret sees Margery as headstrong and stubborn, as a selfish
and ungrateful individual who puts her own whims above her duty to her
kin and friends, Richard understands that she may have tried to placate her

family and buckled under the pressure put upon her to deny the marriage. He sympathizes with her unhappiness and acknowledges that she is torn by conflicting loyalties. All he can do is try to strengthen her resolve to hold with her promise to him. This Margery is a far more vulnerable figure than the Margery depicted by her mother.

Margery Paston Calle can be usefully considered alongside her Paston aunt, Elizabeth. Elizabeth differs from Margery in that letters from her have been preserved. Yet these letters post-date her first marriage, and from our point of view they do not cover the most interesting period in which she, like Margery, became engaged in a vicious struggle with her mother over the question of whom she was to marry. Nonetheless, as with Margery, a cluster of letters discussing this matter, written by other family members and friends, does exist. Reconstructed chronologically, the narrative unfolds in such a way that we can once again detect at least two sides to the story. Writing to her eldest son, John Paston I, around 1449, Elizabeth's mother, Agnes Berry Paston asked him to give more encouragement to a prospective suitor, the elderly and apparently somewhat disfigured Sir Stephen Scrope (no. 3). Agnes reported a conversation she had had with her cousin and close friend Elizabeth Clere, who had advised against discouraging Scrope unless a more suitable marriage candidate could be found. Agnes also claimed that Elizabeth Paston herself was more than willing to marry Scrope, just as long as his claims to property were confirmed. A rather different perspective on the same events is however provided by a letter from Elizabeth Clere herself, also to John I (no. 76).

To some extent this letter does confirm Agnes's account of both the events and their discussions. Elizabeth Clere tells of Scrope's meeting with Agnes and her daughter, although according to this version it is Agnes who *first* insists that Scrope's financial situation should be carefully checked out. While this does not actually contradict what Agnes herself says, it does suggest that Agnes may be somewhat misrepresenting her daughter's feelings. That this is the case becomes clear a few lines later. Elizabeth Clere describes the situation in which Agnes keeps her daughter. Elizabeth Paston is a virtual prisoner in her own home, forbidden to speak to any visitors or even her mother's servants. It is only with the co-operation of one Friar Newton (who seems to be conforming to the stereotypical role of the friar as go-between) that she is able to send secret messages out of the house. Her mother also physically mistreats her: 'since Easter she has for the most part been beaten once or twice a week, and sometimes twice in one day, and her head has been broken in two or three places'. Elisabeth

Paston is, quite literally, being beaten into submission. Neither Elizabeth Clere's own advice to John I, nor her account of Elizabeth Paston's thoughts on the matter, give the lie to Agnes's letter, but they do suggest an alternative interpretation of events. Elizabeth Clere does indeed recommend the marriage to Scrope, as Agnes indicated, if it is the only one to be had, but she also urges John I to try to find another suitor in much stronger terms than Agnes acknowledges: 'Cousin, I have been told that there is a pleasant man in your Inn whose father died recently. If you think that he would be better for her than Scrope, it ought to be canvassed.' Likewise, she tells John I that his sister is willing to marry Scrope if the money is there, and if it is with her brother's approval, but this claim is qualified with the words 'even though she [Elizabeth Paston] has been told that his [Scrope's] appearance is unattractive'. Later in the same letter she adds a warning that 'sorrow often causes women to bestow themselves in marriage on someone they should not; and if she were in that situation I know very well that you would regret it'. It is in this context that Elizabeth Clere observes that Scrope is beginning to lose interest (Agnes reports this much herself) but she goes on to explain that this is because he is not allowed to see Elizabeth Paston and suspects that her mother does not really want the match to go ahead. Agnes in contrast does not give any reasons for this loss of interest and in fact claims that she had pleased Scrope with the warmth of her welcome. In other words, there is some contradiction between the two accounts. Elizabeth Clere here adopts the role of ambassador and diplomat. On the one hand she intervenes on Elizabeth Paston's behalf, describing her suffering and emphasizing Elizabeth's willingness to sacrifice her own interests on behalf of those of her family ('if you want her to, she will marry him'). At the same time, she hints that both she *and* Agnes have some doubts about the wisdom of the plan. Yet, on the other hand, she does not challenge the rights of John I, as head of the family, or Agnes as matriarch, to arrange Elizabeth Paston's marriage, and to put financial and social concerns above personal inclination. She acknowledges John I's authority, even as she appeals to his brotherly feelings. Elizabeth Clere knew that she was taking a risk here – she asked John I to burn the letter because if Agnes read it she would want nothing more to do with her – but she clearly felt her intervention to be necessary.

Whatever John I thought of this letter, the projected marriage did not take place (even Elizabeth's younger brother, William II, later advised against it[11]). It was not until several years, and a series of other potential husbands, later and after a great deal more mother–daughter friction, that Elizabeth, by now aged 30, finally did marry. It may well have been the

case that one factor in her remaining single for so long was the unwilling-
ness of her family to provide sufficient financial incentives to lure a potential husband. The earliest surviving letter from Elizabeth is dated shortly
after she wedded Sir Robert Poynings in 1458 (no. 18). This is a curious
letter, written in what seems to be an excessively formal style even for a
time when most letters were formulaic.[12] It is addressed to Agnes, 'very
honourable and my most dearly beloved mother', and adopts a deferential
tone, commending the writer to the recipient, requesting Agnes's blessing,
asking about her health and informing her of her own 'if it pleased your
good motherhood to hear of me'. Yet, once these greetings and enquiries
have been disposed of, the direction of the letter takes a curious twist as
Elizabeth turns from describing the physical well-being of her new husband,
'my most loved one as you call him, and I shall call him now', to praising
his generosity. This leads her to the real subject of the letter: money owed
by Agnes to Robert Poynings for Elizabeth's dowry, and to Lady Pole, with
whom Elizabeth had been in service before her marriage. In summary,
Elizabeth asks her mother to pay her outstanding debts. This letter poses
the reader with some difficulties in interpretation. What exactly should we
make of what might be described as the cold formality of the opening lines?
How does this square with the contents of the letter proper? Is the tone of
the letter simply governed by convention, or can we detect some irony in
Elizabeth's humility and self-depreciation? Given what we know from the
earlier correspondence of Agnes's difficult relationship with her daughter,
and of her despair at finding her a suitable moneyed husband, it may not
be unreasonable to read into Elizabeth's request that the family should
honour its debts an element of black or bleak humour. Following the premature death (in battle) of Robert Poynings, Elizabeth married again a
younger man, and, following *his* execution, became a wealthy widow. In
her own will, she made no mention whatsoever of her Paston relatives,
but did make some provision for her own daughter Mary, with the express
wish that it should help her find herself a husband (no. 20). Elizabeth, it
seems, did not want her daughter to suffer as she had done. This group of
letters provides a sense both of the financial issues at stake in negotiating
a marriage, and also of Elizabeth's own feelings towards her family after
she married, and perhaps also at the time of the earlier discussions.

   The letters relating to the marriages or proposed marriages of Elizabeth
and her niece Margery, while fascinating in themselves, highlight just some
of the problems inherent in reading medieval women's letters. Two
obvious difficulties are first, that of trying to detect in the letters of others
or perhaps to reconstruct from them the 'authentic' voice of the medieval

women, and second, that of trying to reconstruct something akin to a chronological narrative out of an incomplete collection. The circumstances in which medieval letters, especially private personal correspondence such as the Paston letters, were written, received and preserved means that they cannot be read in exactly the same ways as literary texts are.[13] Medieval letters require their own analytical frameworks, which take into account questions of context, authorship, form, function and content. It is the purpose of the next section of the chapter to outline these frameworks in more detail.

Reading medieval women's letters

In thinking about how to analyse these writings, we need to begin by considering who are the authors of the Paston letters, and indeed whether the term 'author' is any more or less appropriate in this context than in the others discussed already in this study. As Jennifer Summit observes, 'if letters do not have authors, as Foucault insists, they offer an opportunity to challenge the assumptions that underlie modern theories of authorship, which erect divisions between creative authors and passive readers, as well as between the authorship of literary and non-literary texts.'[14] The surviving letters in the collection were largely written by members of the immediate family, women as well as men, or by more distant family members, aristocratic patrons and social superiors, neighbours, friends and associates, some enemies, tenants and servants. Norman Davis, in editing the collection, divided the letters into two categories, letters by family members, and letters to them. However this division seems somewhat arbitrary, separating as it does biological mothers who were not Pastons from their daughters who married into the family, and friends who sometimes proved closer than kinsfolk.

By far the most letters from a single correspondent are by Margaret Mautby Paston, sister-in-law of Elizabeth, mother of Margery.[15] Margaret wrote mainly to her husband and her two eldest sons, and in fact few of the letters by the main women in the collection are to non-family members and hardly any are to other women. Many of the letters, especially those by men in the family, were penned in the writers' own hands. Most of those by women were not.[16] It is important not to overstate the significance of this. Margaret was, it seems, illiterate, or at any rate if she could read she does not seem to have been able to write, and she relied on secretaries for the physical act of writing.[17] But this did not prevent her composing letters at all hours of the day, occasionally taking several days to complete one long letter, and sometimes going to the other extreme of producing several in a single day. In all Margaret seems to have had almost thirty different secretaries (perhaps more). These included her sons, the bailiff Richard Calle (even after his marriage to Margery), and other family servants and associates, one favourite being the priest Sir James Gloys; her dependence on this last as an adviser and friend was a source of jealousy amongst her sons. Sometimes the hands of several secretaries appear in one letter. One secretary whom she used many times has proved impossible to identify. Whoever this person was, it is nonetheless clear that Margaret Paston preferred to rely on people close to her, people she could put her faith in, to act as her secretaries. When Agnes Paston, in a letter written in a neat hand that must be her own in which she describes to her husband the introduction of her eldest son to his future bride, laments the 'absence of a good secretary' (no. 1), she may mean that she lacks a confidant or reliable servant rather than a competent scribe. As is the case with Margery Kempe's *Book*, it would surely be a mistake to deduce from her dependence on secretaries that Margaret was not in some way the author of her own letters. Nevertheless, and again the comparison with Margery Kempe holds good, it is important not to overlook the impact the collaborative process may have had on the texts we are reading.

Letter writers often requested the help of others. Thus one letter from Margaret Paston to James Gloys includes the instruction that he 'write a letter in my name to Walter [Margaret's favourite son, who studied at Oxford University] considering you already know my intentions for him' (no. 69). In this case, the actual letter to Walter either was not written or, more likely, was lost following Walter's premature death from plague. Sometimes an individual sought permission to write a letter in someone else's name. Margaret's second son John Paston III wrote three such letters in women's names on matters relating to his own business. Two of these I will discuss later, so a single example, linked to John III's disputes with his uncle, will suffice here. According to the endorsement of the letter, this is a copy of an original written by his father's sister, Elizabeth.[18] It is, nevertheless, more likely (as Davis suggests) that John III wrote a letter as if it were from his aunt, with the expectation that she would either copy it herself or have a fair copy made which she would then sign. In this case, we have enough contextual information (in the nature of the corrections) for the attribution of the letter to John III rather than to Elizabeth Poynings Browne to be uncontroversial. Therefore, it should be clear that just because an individual signs a letter in his or her own name, we cannot always be certain that that person composed it. As we will see later, judgements based simply on style or content may prove deceptive. Furthermore, as with other authors or writers, correspondents' styles evolve and vary over time.

If the notion of authorship remains problematic when applied to late medieval women's letters, so too is the inclusion of letters such as these alongside other more imaginative forms of textual production. The Paston letters, taken as a whole, are manifestly not literary letters, by which I mean letters written according to standards of formal composition and rhetorical principles (although these models do underlie them), which deliberately aim to have artistic merit and which are written for public dissemination. Rather, they were written for a range of practical and often urgent reasons, and are largely concerned with domestic and business matters. As the examples above illustrate, many of the letters carry with them instructions that they are only to be read by the intended recipient, and to be disposed of on receipt. But while many pieces of correspondence carrying such instructions may well have been destroyed, others clearly survived. Why was this the case? The answer is revealed in a key letter from Margaret Paston to John II, in which she warns him to take care to guard his documents carefully:

> Your father, may God absolve him, in his troubled period set greater store by his documents and deeds than he did by any of his moveable goods. Remember that if those were taken from you, you could never get any more that would be of such help to you as those are. (no. 57)

> [Youre fadere, wham God assole, in hys trobyll seson set more by hys wrytyngys and evydens than he dede by any of his moveabell godys. Remembere that yf tho were had from you ye kowd neuer gyte no moo such as tho be for youre parte.][19]

Certainly many of the writers may have had an eye to posterity, but as this quotation reveals it was not a literary afterlife that they had in mind. Although Margaret Paston is talking here about legal documents, letters served as important written records. The survival of the letters is a by-product of the relatively sudden rise to prominence of and the rapid accumulation of wealth by the Paston family in the fifteenth century.[20] It is helpful to remember that Agnes Paston's husband William, although himself a judge, seems to have had rather humble origins. Education, professional success, property purchases and, last but by no means least, marriage to an heiress all contributed to William I's social and economic elevation. In marrying Margaret, the eldest son John I accumulated even more land, money and connections, but he also brought a great deal of trouble to his wife and children when he named himself principal heir of a distant relative of his wife, Sir John Fastolf. The Paston family, women as well as men, faced a seemingly endless stream of legal claims against them, and a number of physical battles (such as the siege of Caister in 1469) as well. Most correspondence must have been preserved as a matter of course in anticipation of the possibility that it might be used as evidence for future disputes and court cases. Even seemingly private letters, such as the love letters discussed in this chapter, are unlikely to have been held on to primarily for sentimental reasons.

All letters, with the possible exception of those written with publication in mind, are fragments; parts of a dialogue of which we may only be able to hear one side or of a conversation of which we only catch snatches of what is being said. Even in the case of a large collection such as the Paston letters, many pieces of correspondence must have vanished (such as letters to Margaret's son Walter), and much of the context has disappeared. To reiterate, these letters are semi-private documents, usually written for a specific recipient, albeit with the knowledge that they might be shared with others and stored away in case they might prove useful in the future. One consequence of the specific circumstances of their composition – during a period of exceptional social and political upheaval – is that there is often an irretrievable oral element to them. The letter writer might well choose to withhold confidential news until she could speak with the recipient or she might entrust further highly sensitive information to the bearers of the letters to be imparted by word of mouth.

How then should we read women's letters? The focus of this book is of course on medieval writing by and for women, and the approach to reading is broadly literary-historical, focusing on issues of gender, composition and readership. Letters such as those found in the Paston collection provide us with tremendous insight into the real lived experiences of a certain class of women in a small corner of late medieval England, but they also tell us about female networks and relationships. Whereas Davis organized his edition of the collected Paston letters around a male genealogy, considering the matriarchal line enables us to tease out connections between women. The main female figures in the Paston family are well known: Agnes, her daughter Elizabeth and daughter-in-law Margaret, Margaret's daughters Margery and Anne, and Margaret's daughter-in-law Margery Brews. However, we can take the matriarchal line back further if we include Eleanor Chamber, who was Margaret Brews Paston's paternal grandmother and who wrote a letter to Agnes's husband William in around

1442.[21] By the same token, Elizabeth Mundford, Margaret's maternal aunt, is also represented in the collection.[22] We can also bring the matriarchal line further forward in time if we include the wills of Margaret, widow of Agnes's grandson Edmund II, and Agnes, second wife of John III.[23]

This female genealogy can also be extended to include at least three other types of correspondents. First, there are two separate surviving letters by mistresses of John II: Cecily Daune (no. 85) and Constance Reynyforth (no. 86), the latter being the mother of John II's illegitimate daughter, also called Constance. Second, there are letters by (and in one case also to) female friends of the family. The most important of these women is Elizabeth Clere, a relative and close companion of both Agnes and Margaret, from whom four letters survive (nos 76–9). But under this heading should also be included Elizabeth Brews, mother-in-law of John III, the only female recipient of a letter from Margaret in the entire collection (no. 73) and from whom five letters survive (nos 80–4), and one Alice Crane, from whom only one letter (to Margaret) survives,[24] but who is mentioned elsewhere in the women's correspondence. The third and final category encompasses letters from and to female members of the aristocracy and religious women, such as Eleanor, duchess of Norfolk[25] and Joan Keteryche, abbess of Denny.[26]

Many of the letters directly concern themselves with issues relating to women's interests, such as women's upbringing and education, women's activities in business and in the running of the household and estates, women's engagement with politics and patronage, female piety, women and health, and female book ownership and literacy. As part of an ongoing dialogue or conversation between writers and recipient(s), the late medieval letter can also provide us with an insight into women's relationships with their families, their patrons, their servants, their lovers and their close and distant associates. Marriage and love, children and friendships are all topics that can be explored. And, as we have seen in the example of Elizabeth Paston Poynings' letter to her mother Agnes, while the letters are often highly formulaic, one can nevertheless sometimes detect that all-too-elusive expression of individuality and personal experience and emotion.

Women correspondents and the writing process

One point to emerge clearly from this discussion of women's letters is the importance of not isolating them from the correspondence as a whole, but of locating them alongside other letters not only by women, but by men as well. In this final section I provide more examples of reading the letters in context, in order to draw out further my discussion of collaboration and voice. Before doing so, however, I examine further the question of how letters were actually composed. The unique bonus of extending our definition of women's writing to include personal correspondence is that a collection such as the Paston letters, which includes drafts of letters sent as well as final copies of letters received, allows us some insight into the actual processes of writing. This may in turn force us to reconsider our assumptions about the processes of composition of other forms of writing.

It is even possible in one case to compare a draft of a letter from Margaret with the final copy of the same letter.[27] The same secretary wrote both versions, but as we might expect, the second version is more neatly executed. All of the changes are fairly minor. Emendations are incorporated into the final copy and new slips are inevitably introduced. Some additions serve to make the meaning clearer, or to add emphasis. For example, a major concern of the letter, which is addressed to Margaret's second son, is the necessity of repaying urgently a debt to Elizabeth Clere. Margaret paints a bleak picture of her own financial situation: she could not find the money even if she had to go to prison for it. Margaret blames her eldest son, and his profligacy for the situation in which she finds herself, and tells John III to pass on the warning that she may have to sell her woods at a considerable loss. In the draft she states that she had been keeping the woods for John II's profit; in the final version she adds that she had been keeping the woods for his profit *in the future*.

Later in the letter Margaret discusses the necessity of moving John Pamping, a gentleman in service to the family, to London. Margaret only hints darkly at her reasons, but it is apparent from later correspondence that her second daughter Anne, following the example of her sister, had made an unfortunate choice in falling in love with a social inferior (in this case, the prompt action seems to have worked and no marriage resulted). In the final copy, Margaret adds that to find Pamping a suitable situation would reflect well on the family, and promises to give more information later. Margaret also tones down a reprimand concerning a lost key: from telling her son to 'remember where you have put the key' she simply asks him to 'remember where the key is'. Margaret rephrases a reassurance about the health of family and friends amidst news of a series of deaths from the plague ('all this household and parish is as you left it' becomes 'all this household and parish are safe'). She also inserts more specific instructions relating to the purchase of sugar and dates. Another telling addition is the final sentence: 'I warn you to keep this letter confidential and rather burn it than lose it.' Although, as I have said, these changes are all fairly minor in themselves, what they do reveal is that the process of letter writing, the composition as well as the copying down and copying out of the letter, was taken very seriously. Even though Margaret sometimes wrote several letters in one day, these were rarely rushed productions, but carefully constructed and phrased.

Another, earlier group of letters indicates something of the stages involved in planning and structuring a letter. One reason so many letters from Margaret survive is that she spent such long periods of time apart from her husband and sons. As a result of his property disputes and court cases, John Paston I spent much of his time in London, and some of this time was even spent in jail. In 1465, in the year before his early death, John I was imprisoned in the Fleet once again. A particularly poignant exchange of letters between Margaret and John I has survived from this date. Margaret wrote twice to John I determining to visit him, and reassuring him that their affairs would be safe enough until she returned (nos 51, 52). During her time in London her second son sent her a letter affectionately referring to her as 'my fair mistress of the Fleet'.[28] A letter written by John I after Margaret's return home rather uncharacteristically combines affection and jocularity with more practical matters and business. John I begins with a formal courtly and romantic address to 'My own dear sovereign lady', thanking Margaret for the welcome she gave him. He ends with a piece of doggerel about borrowing some money to repay a debt owed by Richard Calle, signing off as 'your true and trusty husband'.[29]

Margaret's letter in reply to this (no. 53) is particularly interesting for three reasons. First, Margaret begins her letter by echoing the opening lines of the original: 'Most honourable husband, I commend myself to you, wishing with all my heart to hear of your health and happiness, thanking you for the warm welcome you gave me and for the amount you spent on me.' However, uncertain perhaps about how to interpret John I's comment that the visit was to his 'great cost and expense and labour', she adds: 'You spent more than I wished you to, unless it pleased you to do so.' Here we can see how the tenor of one letter impacts on the tone and even the language of the response. Second, this letter is closely related to another much shorter one written to John I on the same day by Margaret, and which seems to serve as a postscript.[30] Indeed judging from the fact that they are numbered in the corner 'iiii' and 'v' in John I's hand, they seem to be part of a sequence of which the first three letters have been lost.[31] This indicates something of the complexity of the relationships between different letters and the fragmentary nature of the surviving evidence. Third, the manuscript of Margaret's first letter includes a fairly large number of marginal annotations in Latin and English in the hands of both John I himself and his secretary, John Pamping. These include sentences such as 'I thank you for your conduct at Cotton', referring to Margaret's defence of the manor, as well as instructions for further actions. They indicate that John I, with the help of his secretary, must have used the original letter as the basis for framing a reply. While this is not in itself surprising, it does again indicate the extent to which letters are interdependent on one another, and the extent to which letter writers (whether men or women) and their secretaries must have co-operated and worked together at their task.

This chapter began by looking at the examples of Margaret Paston's daughter Margery and Agnes Paston's daughter Elizabeth: two women who proved to be disappointments to their mothers. The one resisted the pressure put upon her in the matter of her marriage by choosing her own husband despite the disapproval of her family; the other, for whatever reasons, seems to have defied her relatives by remaining single for what seemed like a very long time. The chapter will end by considering the case of the letters relating to the betrothal of Margery Brews to John Paston III. The engagement of Margery Brews and John III, one very much approved of by the families on both sides, was based on mutual respect and affection, even love. Nevertheless, as always, money became a sticking point: John III felt that Margery's father, Sir Thomas Brews, was not settling enough money on them for it to go ahead. For his part, Sir Thomas felt the Pastons were asking for too much, and argued that he had to keep sufficient back to provide for his other daughters. He wrote to John II, who seems to have been behind the family's stance, 'I would be very loath to bestow so much on one daughter that her other sisters would do worse.'[32] After considerable negotiation the marriage did go ahead, but it took the generous intervention of Margaret Paston for it to do so. Rather against the wishes of her eldest son, she bestowed a manor on the couple, and thus the problem was eventually circumvented.

Unlike her sisters-in-law Margery and Anne, and their aunt Elizabeth, Margery Brews was a daughter of whom her mother was proud. In a letter to John III, encouraging him in the match, despite the obstacles, Dame Elizabeth Brews promised him that he would gain 'a greater treasure' than any financial settlement: 'that is an intelligent gentlewoman, and even though I say it myself, a good and a virtuous one' (no. 81). Yet, while the evidence of the Paston letters suggests that relations between mothers and daughters were often extremely difficult and much more troubled than those between mothers and their sons, this rare example of maternal praise is not so exceptional as it may seem on first glance. There is in fact quite striking evidence in the letters of strong and enduring friendships between women: the closeness of Agnes, Margaret and Elizabeth Clere only being the most obvious example. Furthermore, in this case Margery Brews hopes to marry according to rather than against the wishes of her family. Finally, Elizabeth Brews clearly has an agenda in this letter: she wants to convince the prospective husband that he is getting a bargain. The financial basis of the transaction is made clear in the next sentence: 'Because if I was to take money for her, I would not give her away for £1000.'

The cluster of letters written by various parties interested in the marriage – the betrothed couple, Margery Brews's parents, John III's mother Margaret and his elder brother, even a Brews family servant – make fascinating reading. They also reinforce the point that the questions of authorship and voice are particularly complicated in relation to letters.[33] Margery Brews wrote two letters to John III before their marriage took place (nos 87 and 88). Both are Valentines, written in February 1477. It is impossible to say with any certainty which letter came first, but one is clearly more formal than the other. In the more formal of the two, Margery thanks John III for a letter he has sent her and tells him she will be the 'happiest one alive' if the marriage comes off and very sad indeed if it does not (no. 88). She refers to the particularities of the financial aspect of the marriage, and says that she hopes John III will accept her father's terms, but expresses her willingness to accept his decision, whatever it may be. The other letter seems more intimate, even sentimental (no. 87). Written partly in rhyming prose, it describes in conventional terms her suffering in love, states that however poor they may be she will remain faithful to him, and promises that she will love him for ever, no matter what happens and what her friends may think. One remarkable feature of these love letters is that both are written in the hand of Thomas Kela, a Brews family servant.[34] Limited literacy skills and the necessity of relying on a secretary were no barriers to the composition of love letters.

Nevertheless, while it seems reasonable to assume that Margery did compose her own love letters, even if she did not actually write them herself, it would be wrong to see these very personal pieces of correspondence as intensely private. This is because they are clearly closely related to two other letters in the collection, both also addressed to John III, one by Dame Elizabeth Brews, and the other by Thomas Kela himself. The first of these, written around 9 February 1477, begins by thanking John

III for his kindness when they recently met, but reproaching him for breaching his promise not to speak to Margery until some sort of agreement had been reached (no. 82). Dame Elizabeth complains: 'But you have made her such an advocate for you that I can never have rest night nor day because of her entreating and appealing to bring the said business to its accomplishment.' The next paragraph is particularly noteworthy. Dame Elizabeth reminds John III that Valentine's Day approaches, and suggests that he should visit the family in order to have further discussions with Sir Thomas. She then finishes on an encouraging note, with the proverb, 'it is only a feeble oak that is cut down at a first stroke', and signs off: 'By your cousin . . . who with God's grace will be called otherwise'. Although Dame Elizabeth may have been able to write,[35] this letter, like the letters by her daughter, was dictated to or copied down by Kela. Although this is not in itself particularly noteworthy, what is remarkable is the fact that it is closely echoed in tenor and even in language by a contemporaneous letter to the same recipient on the same topic in the same hand, signed by Kela himself.[36] Like Margery in her love letter, Kela refers directly to the difficulties over money, and tries to suggest some sort of compromise might be possible. Like Dame Elizabeth, he praises 'the young gentlewoman' and makes the point that she has spoken strongly on John III's behalf. He even goes so far as quoting Dame Elizabeth's own arguments, 'And I heard my lady say that it was a feeble oak that was cut down at the first stroke', thus acknowledging her authority over himself as secretary and servant. That another member of the household, a servant, should speak on behalf of the family, urging on the marriage, is in itself surprising. That he should do so using identical words is more so. This begs the question, was Kela writing on his own initiative, or was he writing at the instigation of his mistress, or of her daughter? Whatever was the case, it is clear from this that letter writers and their secretaries often spoke in the same voice.

The letters of Dame Elizabeth Brews and Thomas Kela throw a new light on Margery's love letters, and especially what I will refer to as her Valentine verses for lack of a better term. They suggest that these letters were not spontaneous outpourings, but were carefully constructed, possibly even at the suggestion of Dame Elizabeth (who, if she could remind John III of the coming of St Valentine's Day, could just as easily remind her daughter). They reinforce the point that secretaries were the intimates of their mistresses and masters, that they were trusted friends as well as servants. Such secretaries are therefore likely to have been at least consulted about matters of content and phrasing as part of the process of the dictation, no matter how confidential the letters. And they reinforce the extent to which letters are interconnected with one another. We should not forget that letters were often read by people other than the recipients: Dame Elizabeth's own form of signing off is echoed some months afterwards not by John III, but by his mother (no. 73). At a stage when it looked like the marriage plans really had floundered, Margaret invited Dame Elizabeth and her husband to meet with her in person to try to resolve matters. She finishes by commending herself to her 'cousin' Margery 'to whom I expected I could have given another name before now'. Margaret, presumably recalling Dame Elizabeth's letters to her son, and attempting to bring about reconciliation between the two families, deliberately reminded Dame Elizabeth of her previous aspirations.

A slightly later letter, written by John III to his mother on the subject of the same marriage negotiations, reinforces the argument in this chapter, and in this book as a whole, about the fluidity of the authorial voice.[37] In this letter, John III, writing from a Brews family residence, sketches out a rough draft of a letter his mother should send on his behalf in her own name to Dame Elizabeth. He even specifies that she should follow his wording, but have the letter copied 'in some other man's hand', presumably to disguise the identity of the actual author. Margaret is to express her sympathy on hearing that Dame Elizabeth and Sir Thomas are unwell, before reminding her of their own discussions and of promises made to John III, and interceding on his behalf. In this fascinating letter, the elder brother John II is made the villain of the piece, and John III something of the victim. John III reveals himself to be skilled at ventriloquizing or inhabiting a woman's voice, appealing to the women's shared maternal experience: 'But, madam, you are a mother as well as I.' At the same time, he reflects Sir Thomas's earlier sentiments, when he has Margaret say, 'I have to provide for more of my children than him', and that her offspring complain that she deals with them unfairly by giving John III 'so much and them so little'. John III then follows this with a draft of a letter on the same matter to be sent by his mother to himself at the Brewses' residence. In this, Margaret is to advise him not to marry if the financial promises made to him are not to be kept, to sympathize with the predicament of Margery Brews and to urge him to return home quickly. The purpose of this second composition, which carries with it a threat that Margaret will not support him in the future if he marries against her recommendation, was that he could then present it to the Brews family in order to strengthen his own position. The authorship and content of letters could be and clearly were manipulated by other interested parties. Voice could be convincingly imitated. Of course, ultimately it was Margaret Paston's decision whether or not to send these letters written in her name, whether to claim the voice as her own. Ultimately, then, women's voices, like women's writing, should perhaps be seen, not as a transparent expression of female subjectivity or consciousness, but as a product of negotiation, as collaborative, as dialogic and as textual and intertextual.

Conclusion

Scholars who have studied the Paston women have tended to focus on the most prolific letter writers: Margaret Paston, her mother-in-law Agnes and her daughter-in-law Margery. The advantage of this approach from a literary-critical point of view is that a strong and defined voice tends to emerge from the longer sequences of apparently 'single-authored' letters, and that these sequences can themselves be read as a narrative (if an incomplete one). Yet, as I have shown, in the case of letter writing, the very notion of *an* author is problematic. When the letter is part of a collection such as the Paston correspondence, it is, as I have suggested, really part of a dialogue or perhaps more accurately a conversation. We can in fact hear many people speaking: the letter writer, the secretary, the respondent, the voices behind relayed messages and so on. Sometimes these voices are very hard to distinguish from one another, or even to identify, as is the case when the identity of writer, or secretary, or even addressee is unknown or in doubt, or when one writer or secretary deliberately echoes or imitates another. Sometimes it is almost impossible to trace a clear narrative through the letters, or to understand the nature of events being referred to or other allusions, especially when only one side of the correspondence and thus the conversation has been preserved. Such letters lack a context and thus prove especially difficult to interpret. However, even more problematic is the complete loss of the letters themselves, and thus the loss of the voice of the letter writer. Sometimes we know certain voices have been silenced. This chapter began with a discussion of Margery Paston Calle, from whom no letters survive. Her unmediated voice is unrecoverable. Nevertheless, I hope that I have shown that it is possible to discern at least something of Margery's character, experiences and words in the nexus of accounts of the same events written by others (albeit potentially distorted by rumour or gossip or deliberate misrepresentation). At the same time it is possible to hear echoes of her voice filtered through reported speech. Yet the evidence of the texts discussed in this study (from *The Life of Christina of Markyate* to *The Book of Margery Kempe* and the letters of the Paston women) suggests that the notion of an unmediated female voice is something of a fiction. All medieval English writing emerges out of complex processes of composition and is to a greater or lesser extent the result of writers and their subjects, patrons, secretaries and readers working together. Nowhere is this more the case than in women's letters.

Afterword

But, madam, you are a mother as well as I. With these words of John Paston III, written in a letter for his mother, Margaret, to have copied and sent to his future mother-in-law, in order to achieve his own ends and their shared ambitions, I brought my final chapter to its end. The words are movingly maternal, 'essentially' feminine, and hauntingly 'authentic'. If the context of these words were lost, if only the final copy of the letter John III wanted his mother to send survived, would we be able to distinguish the 'voice' of this letter from that we can hear elsewhere in Margaret Paston's corre-spondence? The answer surely is 'no'. And what of the letter that follows it, also written by John III 'for' his mother but to be copied and sent by her to himself? The register is quite different, but equally convincing. John Paston III, who often acted as his mother's secretary, was clearly familiar enough with the style and typical content of her letters to be able to write *as* his mother.

This realization has enormous implications for how we regard the rest of Margaret Paston's correspondence, and indeed the letters of other writers in the collection, male and female. At the very least it raises the question of how many of the Paston letters that have come down to us might not have been composed by the person in whose name they were sent. More fundamentally, in so far as men can and do write credibly as women, it raises the question of whether it is appropriate to try to distin-guish women's letters from those by men, or indeed to attempt to identify a woman's voice, whatever the form of writing. But this realization, and its implications, is also enabling, in so far as it allows us to rethink con-structively the processes of writing and the idea of the author or writer. Because these letters by John Paston III can also be attributed to Margaret Paston, in so far as the decision whether to copy them, emend them, send them, disregard them or write something else entirely ultimately lay with her (as I suggested in the previous chapter). In the end, John Paston III, out of necessity, had to defer to his mother's judgement on this issue. I have suggested in this book that secretaries and writers have particularly close relationships with one another, and that secretaries (who may be kin, servants, spiritual guides or friends) as confidants are privy to the thoughts and wishes of those for whom they write. A good secretary, like John Paston III, can anticipate needs and intentions even before receiving instruction; can, in other words, write not only for another but also on another's behalf. *The absence of a good secretary*, a helpful adviser, can make the work of writing so much harder, as Agnes Paston acknowledges, in passing, in a letter to her husband, written in haste, on the Wednesday after the third Sunday after Easter in or around 1440. It is perhaps wrong then to suggest, as I did earlier in this book, that, in writing in the person of his mother, John III impersonates or ventriloquizes his mother's voice; rather he speaks with it, or Margaret speaks through him.

Why do I finish this book on medieval women's writing with such problematic examples as these letters of John Paston III, written in his mother's name and voice? I do so precisely *because* they problematize the very categories of writing with which I am working, and the opposition between women's and men's writing. Medieval women's writing, I have argued in this book, is the product of collaboration between authors or writers, secretaries, subjects, patrons, recipients, readers and audience. Voice too is dialogic, and in some sense communal. Seen as the product of collaboration, women's writing can seem an inherently unstable category and, as I have suggested, we might therefore challenge its validity. Certainly women's writing does not exist in isolation, and any distinction between women's and men's writing is necessarily blurred. Yet the need for a specific category of women's writing remains a feminist and critical imperative. Conventional literary histories, often structured according to masculinist notions of patrilineage, genealogy, tradition, influence and authorship, typically do not question their framing principles which privilege men's writing over women's, even if some attempt is made to include female writers and to pay attention to issues of gender.[1] Yet as long as we continue to exclude women's literary history, and thus women's writing, in the broadest sense of the term, from our teleologies, we cannot hope to understand fully how texts were conceived, produced, circulated or received; nor can we understand fully the range of forms, genres or subject matters. And we cannot understand fully how and why they are gendered. In other words, we cannot learn from them and our perspective will be distorted and inaccurate. Conventional literary history could, therefore, learn a great deal from medieval women's writing.

Yet in some respects the premises of this book are themselves highly conventional, as are the structures according to which it is organized.

Medieval Women's Writing concentrates on named figures and works, with the exception of the third chapter, which focuses on the genre of the saint's life, but even here the internal organization concentrates on individual writers or texts. The book does so for two main reasons. First, as I explain in the Introduction, women's literary history still needs its authors because it is crucial that agency should be ascribed to women who for so long have been denied it. Furthermore, as I also suggest in the Introduction, it is still possible to trace a 'tradition' of women writers albeit not along the continuous vertical masculinist lines of influence and anxiety of influence, but along broken and sometimes horizontal lines of congruence and commonality in relation to production and reception. Second, attempts from the 1970s onwards to overthrow the idea of a 'canon' of literature in the context of teaching English in secondary and tertiary education have not fully succeeded, partly because author-based courses lend themselves more readily to the curriculum, and partly because, in marketing terms, authors sell. As Margaret J. M. Ezell puts it:

> Many have argued, and I agree, that canons are a feature of modern education structures. Unless we somehow ban all textbooks, burn all anthologies, and forbid teaching standard syllabi, a canon of most frequently taught works will remain with us. To say we have no canon is to ignore what actually happens in the classroom and examination hall.[2]

As long as a canon remains, and as long as it is constructed along masculinist lines, the need for a female canon and for courses on women writers remains, as indeed does the need for scholarly work in this still underresearched field. And as long as a female canon remains any study of women writers will be framed, and perhaps constrained, by it. Julian of Norwich and Margery Kempe are key figures in this 'English' tradition, not least because their work is easily available in accessible (and inexpensive) editions and translations and is therefore widely read. But I hope that in these chapters I have sufficiently complicated the notion of single authorship for my readers to understand that the roll-call of names in this book – from Christina of Markyate to the Paston women – remains just that. These names allow us to think about larger questions relating to the production, circulation and reception of books, poems and letters; to think about authorship, literacy and patronage, readership and audience. They enable us to think about collaboration in its fullest senses. An understanding of medieval women's writing as collaborative enables us to include a wider range of texts and forms under this heading: not only works by and for women, but also, in some cases, works about women. Critics working with literature from earlier or later periods might also learn from this.

This book has been begun by God's gift and His grace, but it has still not been perfected, in my view. With these lines, Julian of Norwich opens the final chapter of *A Revelation of Love*. When Julian of Norwich passes her book into the hands of her community of readers, which she invites to join her in prayer *for charity*, she acknowledges their ownership of her showings, which can be performed only with their engagement. Let me, for a moment, speak in or through Julian's voice. *Medieval Women's Writing* is not yet perfected, not yet performed, in my view. This conclusion marks not an ending, but a beginning. It invites the readers of this book to think about, think through, rethink, apply, adapt, reformulate or reconfigure its arguments and suggestions, not only in relation to later medieval women's writing in England, and to women and works not discussed in this book, but to writing more generally, from the early medieval period to the present day.

Notes

Introduction

1 Virginia Woolf, *A Room of One's Own* (Harmondsworth, Penguin, 1945).

2 Kate Millett, *Sexual Politics* (London, Virago, 1977); Ellen Moers, *Literary Women: The Great Writers* (London, W. H. Allen, 1977); Elaine Showalter, *A Literature of their Own: From Charlotte Brontë to Doris Lessing* (Princeton, Princeton University Press, 1977); and Sandra M. Gilbert and Susan Gubar, *The Madwoman in the Attic: The Woman Writer and the Nineteenth-Century Literary Imagination* (New Haven, Yale University Press, 1979).

3 Janet Todd, *Feminist Literary History: A Defence* (Cambridge, Polity, 1988); Margaret J. M. Ezell, *Writing Women's Literary History* (Baltimore, Johns Hopkins University Press, 1993); Joan M. Ferrante, *To the Glory of her Sex: Women's Roles in the Composition of Medieval Texts* (Bloomington, Indiana University Press, 1997); Laurie A. Finke, *Women's Writing in English: Medieval England* (London, Longman, 1999); and Jennifer Summit, *Lost Property: The Woman Writer and English Literary History, 1380–1589* (Chicago, University of Chicago Press, 2000).

4 *The Norton Anthology of Literature by Women: The Tradition in English*, ed. Sandra M. Gilbert and Susan Gubar, 1st edn (New York, W. W. Norton, 1985). The second edition was published in 1996 and the third edition in 2007.

5 *The Norton Anthology of Literature by Women*, ed. Gilbert and Gubar, 1st edn, 15.

6 See, for example, the online database *Orlando: Women's Writing in the British Isles, from the Beginnings to the Present* <http://www.cambridge.org/orlandoonline> [accessed 23 August 2006]. Despite the claims to inclusivity inherent in its title, this database provides only very limited coverage of texts not written in English or in England. Finke discusses the Anglo-Saxon period in *Women's Writing in English*.

7 Summit, *Lost Property*, 5.

8 Clare A. Lees and Gillian R. Overing, 'Birthing Bishops and Fathering Poets: Bede, Hild, and the Relations of Cultural Production', *Exemplaria* 6 (1994), 35–65; reprinted in slightly revised form as the first chapter of their *Double Agents: Women and Clerical Culture in Anglo-Saxon England* (Philadelphia, University of Pennsylvania Press, 2001), 15–39.

9 Sheila Delaney, ' "Mothers to Think Back Through": Who are They? The Ambiguous Example of Christine de Pizan', in *Medieval Texts and Contemporary Readers*, ed. Laurie A. Finke and Martin B. Shichtman (Ithaca, NY, Cornell University Press, 1987), 177–97. De Pizan is idealized in the *Norton Anthology of Literature by Women*, ed. Gilbert and Gubar, 1st edn, 13–14. For critiques of Delaney's argument, see Maureen Quilligan, *The Allegory of Female Authority: Christine de Pizan's 'Cité des dames'* (Ithaca, NY, Cornell University Press, 1991), 7–10, and Nicholas Watson, ' "Yf wommen be double naturelly": Remaking "Woman" in Julian of Norwich's *Revelation of Love*', *Exemplaria* 8 (1996), 8–11.

10 For these stereotypes, see the discussion of women's writing in the Middle Ages and Renaissance in *The Norton Anthology of Literature By Women*, ed. Gilbert and Gubar, 1st edn, 1–15.

11 See Alexandra Barratt, 'Introduction', in *Women's Writing in Middle English*, ed. Alexandra Barratt (London, Longman, 1992), 1–23; Julia Boffey, 'Women Authors and Women's Literacy in Fourteenth- and Fifteenth-Century England', in *Women and Literature in Britain, 1150–1500*, ed. Carol M. Meale (Cambridge, Cambridge University Press, 1993), 159–82; Finke, *Women's Writing in English*.

12 *Women and Literature in Britain*, ed. Meale.

13 See Diane Watt, *Secretaries of God: Women Prophets in Late Medieval and Early Modern England* (Cambridge, D. S. Brewer, 1997).

14 *Norton Anthology of Literature by Women*, ed. Gilbert and Gubar, 1st edn, 1; Lees and Overing, *Double Agents*, 36.

15 Summit, *Lost Property*, 14, 61–107.

16 See the editors' introduction to *The Lais of Marie de France*, trans. Glyn S. Burgess and Keith Busby, 2nd edn (Harmondsworth, Penguin, 1999), 11; Howard R. Bloch, *The Anonymous Marie de France* (Chicago, University of Chicago Press, 2003), 12–13; see also Miranda Griffin, 'Gender and Authority in the Medieval French Lai', *Forum for Modern Language Studies* 35 (1991), 42–56.

17 But see June Hall McCash, '*La vie seinte Audree*: A Fourth Text by Marie de France?' *Speculum* 77 (2002), 744–77.

18 Michel Foucault, 'What is an Author?' reprinted in *Medieval Criticism and Theory: A Reader*, ed. David Lodge (London, Longman, 1988), 201.

19 Bloch, *The Anonymous Marie de France*, 2–3.

20 Nancy Miller, 'Changing the Subject: Authorship, Writing and the Reader', in *What is an Author?* ed. Maurice Biriotti and Nicola Miller (Manchester, Manchester University Press, 1993), 23.

21 Miller, 'Changing the Subject', 23.

22 Jennifer Summit, 'Women and Authorship', in *The Cambridge Companion to Medieval Women's Writing*, ed. Carolyn Dinshaw and David Wallace (Cambridge, Cambridge University Press, 2003), 91.

23 Foucault, 'What is an Author?' 202.

24 A. J. Minnis, *Medieval Theory of Authorship: Scholastic Literary Attitudes in the Later Middle Ages*, 2nd edn (Aldershot, Hants, Scholar Press, 1988), 10–12; Barratt, 'Introduction', in *Women's Writing in Middle English*, ed. Barratt, 6; Summit, 'Women and Authorship', 92–3.

25 *The Writings of Julian of Norwich: A Vision Showed to a Devout Woman and A Revelation of Love*, ed. Nicholas Watson and Jacqueline Jenkins (Turnhout, Brepols, 2006), 75. Translation from the Middle English is my own.

26 J. A. Burrow, *Medieval Writers and their Work: Middle English Literature and its Background 1100–1500* (Oxford, Oxford University Press, 1982), 29–30; Minnis, *Medieval Theory of Authorship*, 94–5.

27 *Lais of Marie de France*, trans. Burgess and Busby, 41.

28 See especially *Women and Literature in Britain*, ed. Meale; Mary C. Erler, *Women, Reading, and Piety in Late Medieval England* (Cambridge, Cambridge University Press, 2002); Rebecca Krug, *Reading Families: Women's Literate Practice in Late Medieval England* (Ithaca, NY, Cornell University Press, 2002); and Jocelyn Wogan-Browne, 'Analytical Survey 5: "Reading is Good Prayer": Recent Research on Female Reading Communities', in *New Medieval Literatures 5*, ed. Rita Copeland, David Lawton and Wendy Scase (Oxford, Oxford University Press, 2002), 229–97.

29 *The Book of Margery Kempe*, ed. Sanford Brown Meech and Hope Emily Allen, Early English Text Society original series 212 (Oxford, Oxford University Press, 1940), 21.

30 Summit, 'Women and Authorship', 93.

31 *The Book of Margery Kempe*, ed. Meech and Allen, 71. Translation from the Middle English is my own.

32 Summit, 'Women and Authorship', 99.
33 See, for a recent example, Lees and Overing, *Double Agents*; for the argument against, see Summit, *Lost Property*, 8.
34 Summit, *Lost Property*, 8.
35 See Mikhail Bakhtin's discussion of the 'speaking collective' in his *Problems of Dostoevsky's Poetics*, ed. and trans. Caryl Emerson, intro. Wayne C. Booth (Minneapolis, University of Minnesota Press, 1984), 202.
36 See also Ferrante, *To the Glory of her Sex*, 39 and *passim*.
37 Mary Carruthers, *The Book of Memory: A Study of Memory in Medieval Culture* (Cambridge, Cambridge University Press, 1990), 182, 179.
38 Paul Strohm, 'Chaucer's Audience(s): Fictional, Implied, Actual', *Chaucer Review* 18 (1983), 137–45.

1   Christina of Markyate (*c.*1096–after 1155)

1 All references to *The Life of Christina of Markyate* are to *The Life of Christina of Markyate: A Twelfth Century Recluse*, ed. and trans. C. H. Talbot (Oxford, Clarendon Press, 1959; reprinted Toronto, Toronto University Press/Medieval Academy of America, 1998); hereafter cited in the text as *Life*. All translations are taken from this edition.
2 All references are to the digitized text of the St Albans Psalter, <http://www.abdn.ac.uk/stalbanspsalter> [accessed 31 August 2006]; hereafter cited in the text as Psalter.
3 Jane   Geddes   at   <http://www.abdn.ac.uk/stalbanspsalter/english/essays/calendar.shtml#laterobits>.
4 Geddes, 'The St Albans Psalter: The Abbot and the Anchoress', in *Christina of Markyate: A Twelfth-Century Holy Woman*, ed. Samuel Fanous and Henrietta Leyser (London, Routledge, 2005), 204.
5 *The Life of Christina of Markyate*, ed. and trans. Talbot, 9.
6 Bella Millett, 'Women in No Man's Land: English Recluses and the Development of Vernacular Literature in the Twelfth and Thirteenth Centuries', in *Women and Literature in Britain, 1150–1500*, ed. Carol M. Meale (Cambridge, Cambridge University Press, 1993), 92.
7 Sue   Niebrzydowski   at   <http://www.abdn.ac.uk/stalbanspsalter/english/essays/calendar.shtml#textcanticles> and at <http://www.abdn.ac.uk/stalbanspsalter/english/essays/calendar.shtml#textlitany>   and   at   <http://www.abdn.ac.uk/stalbanspsalter/english/essays/calendar.shtml#collects>   and   Geddes   at   <http://www.abdn.ac.uk/stalbanspsalter/english/essays/calendar.shtml#signifilitany>.
8 Geddes, 'Abbot and Anchoress', 205.
9 Geddes, 'Abbot and Anchoress', 207 and 215 n. 47.
10 Transcribed with translation by Margaret Jubb at <http://www.abdn.ac.uk/stalbanspsalter/english/translation/trans057.shtml>.
11 Transcribed with translation by Patrick Edwards at <http://www.abdn.ac.uk/stalbanspsalter/english/translation/trans068.shtml>.
12 Geddes at <http://www.abdn.ac.uk/stalbanspsalter/english/essays/alexisquire.shtml#spiritual>.
13 Translated by Edwards at <http://www.abdn.ac.uk/stalbanspsalter/english/translation/trans071.shtml>.
14 Translated by Edwards at <http://www.abdn.ac.uk/stalbanspsalter/english/translation/trans071.shtml>.
15 Translated by Edwards at <http://www.abdn.ac.uk/stalbanspsalter/english/translation/trans072.shtml>.
16 Translated by Edwards at <http://www.abdn.ac.uk/stalbanspsalter/english/translation/trans072.shtml>.

17 Translated by Edwards at <http://www.abdn.ac.uk/stalbanspsalter/english/translation/trans071.shtml>.

18 Translated by Edwards at <http://www.abdn.ac.uk/stalbanspsalter/english/translation/trans072.shtml>.

19 Geddes, 'The St Albans Psalter', 209.

20 Transcribed with translation by Edwards at <http://www.abdn.ac.uk/stalbanspsalter/english/translation/trans072.shtml>.

21 Quoted and translated by Geddes at <http://www.abdn.ac.uk/stalbanspsalter/english/essays/alexisquire.shtml#dialogue>.

22 Transcribed with translation by Edwards at <http://www.abdn.ac.uk/stalbanspsalter/english/translation/trans072.shtml>.

23 *Bede's Ecclesiastical History of the English People*, ed. Bertram Colgrave and R. A. B. Mynors (Oxford, Clarendon Press, 1969), 405–15.

24 Christine E. Fell, 'Hild, Abbess of Streonæshalch', in *Hagiography and Medieval Literature: A Symposium*, ed. Hans Bekker-Nielsen, Peter Foote, Jørgen Højgaard Jørgensen and Tore Nyberg (Odense, Odense University Press, 1981), 90.

25 Geddes at <http://www.abdn.ac.uk/stalbanspsalter/english/essays/calendar.shtml#remainingsaints>.

26 Stephanie Hollis and Jocelyn Wogan-Browne, 'St Albans and Women's Monasticism: Lives and their Foundations in Christina's World', in *Christina of Markyate*, ed. Fanous and Leyser, esp. 39.

27 *Bede's Ecclesiastical History*, ed. Colgrave and Mynors, 410–11.

28 For another example, see Wulfstan of Winchester, *The Life of St Æthelwold*, ed. Michael Lapidge and Michael Winterbottom (Oxford, Clarendon Press, 1991), 3–9. I am grateful to Clare A. Lees for providing me with this reference.

29 Mary Clayton, *The Cult of the Virgin Mary in Anglo-Saxon England* (Cambridge, Cambridge University Press, 1990).

30 Clare A. Lees and Gillian R. Overing, *Double Agents: Women and Clerical Culture in Anglo-Saxon England* (Philadelphia, University of Pennsylvania Press, 2001), 23–6.

31 Lees and Overing, *Double Agents*, 23.

32 Lees and Overing, *Double Agents*, 24.

33 *Bede's Ecclesiastical History*, ed. Colgrave and Mynors, 407.

34 *Bede's Ecclesiastical History*, ed. Colgrave and Mynors, 411–13.

35 Rachel M. Koopmans, 'The Conclusion of Christina of Markyate's Vita', *Journal of Ecclesiastical History* 51 (2000), 663–98.

36 *The Life of Christina of Markyate*, ed. and trans. Talbot, 12.

37 *The Life of Christina of Markyate*, ed. and trans. Talbot, 12.

38 See Koopmans, 'Dining at Markyate with Lady Christina', in *Christina of Markyate*, ed. Fanous and Leyser, 144–5.

39 Here I disagree with Douglas Gray, 'Christina of Markyate: The Literary Background', in *Christina of Markyate*, ed. Fanous and Leyser, 12–24.

40 Thomas Head, 'The Marriages of Christina of Markyate', *Viator* 21 (1990), 76.

41 Head, 'Marriages', 81.

42 Hollis and Wogan-Browne, 'St Albans and Women's Monasticism', 50 n. 100.

43 See *Women's Saints Lives in Old English Prose*, ed. and trans. Leslie A. Donovan (Cambridge, D. S. Brewer, 1999), 47 and n. 12.

44 Elizabeth Alvida Petroff, *Body and Soul: Essays on Medieval Women and Mysticism* (Oxford, Oxford University Press, 1994), 144.

45 Christopher J. Holdsworth, 'Christina of Markyate', in *Medieval Women: Dedicated and Presented to Professor Rosalind M. T. Hill on the Occasion of her Seventieth Birthday*, ed. Derek Baker (Oxford, Basil Blackwell, 1978), 203–4.

46 Henrietta Leyser, 'Christina of Markyate: The Introduction', in *Christina of Markyate*, ed. Fanous and Leyser, 1.
47 Michael Camille, 'Philological Iconoclasm: Edition and Image in the *Vie de Saint Alexis*', in *Medievalism and the Modern Temper*, ed. R. Howard Bloch and Stephen G. Nichols (Baltimore, Johns Hopkins University Press, 1996), 388. Camille is referring to an illustration (Psalter, 57).
48 Leyser, 'The Introduction', 1; *The Life of Christina of Markyate*, ed. and trans. Talbot, 12.
49 E. A. Jones, 'Christina of Markyate and *The Hermits and Anchorites of England*', in *Christina of Markyate*, ed. Fanous and Leyser, 233.
50 Dyan Elliott, 'Alternative Intimacies: Men, Women and Spiritual Direction in the Twelfth Century', in *Christina of Markyate*, ed. Fanous and Leyser, 178.

2   Marie de France (*fl.* 1180)

1 Caroline Walker Bynum, *Metamorphosis and Identity* (New York, Zone Books, 2001), 15–36.
2 See Susan Crane, 'Anglo-Norman Cultures', in *The Cambridge History of Medieval English Literature*, ed. David Wallace (Cambridge, Cambridge University Press, 1999), 43.
3 According to John Davies, 'Arthur was received into the Valhalla of his enemies': *A History of Wales* (Harmondsworth, Penguin / Allen Lane, 1993), 133.
4 All in-text references are to *The Lais of Marie de France*, trans. Glyn S. Burgess and Keith Busby, 2nd edn (Harmondsworth, Penguin, 1999). References to the English translation are by page rather than line number.
5 Marie de France, *Lais*, ed. Alfred Ewert, with an introduction and bibliography by Glyn S. Burgess (Oxford, Basil Blackwell, 1944; republished London, Bristol Classics, 1995), Prologue, l. 16. All in-text quotations from the original French text are by line number from this edition.
6 In this context, see Michelle A. Freeman, 'Marie de France's Poetics of Silence: The Implications for a Feminine *Translatio*', PMLA 99 (1984), 860–83.
7 Crane, 'Anglo-Norman Cultures', 47.
8 The essays in *Fama: The Politics of Talk and Reputation in Medieval Europe*, ed. Thelma Fenster and Daniel Lord Smail (Ithaca, NY, Cornell University Press, 2003), offer insights into medieval uses of gossip, slander and reputation.
9 Pickens takes the view that Marie *is* responding to the fear of 'the scandal of the woman who appropriates a male poetics': Rupert T. Pickens, 'The Poetics of Androgyny in the *Lais* of Marie de France: *Yonec, Milun*, and the General Prologue', in *Literary Aspects of Courtly Culture: Selected Papers from the Seventh Triennial Congress of the International Courtly Literature Society*, ed. Donald Maddox and Sara Sturm-Maddox (Cambridge, D. S. Brewer, 1994), 219.
10 For the problematic etymology of 'Bisclavret' see Howard R. Bloch, *The Anonymous Marie de France* (Chicago, University of Chicago Press, 2003), 82.
11 *Lais*, ed. Ewert, 'Bisclavret', l. 9.
12 See William E. Burgwinkle, *Sodomy, Masculinity, and Law in Medieval England: France and England, 1050–1230* (Cambridge, Cambridge University Press, 2004), esp. 167–8.
13 Sharon Kinoshita, 'Cherchez La Femme: Feminist Criticism and Marie de France's *Lai de Lanval*', Romance Notes 34 (1994), 269, 272.
14 See especially Robert Sturges, 'Texts and Readers in Marie de France's *Lais*', Romanic Review 71 (1980), 260–2.
15 See Burgwinkle, *Sodomy, Masculinity, and Law*, 151–2.
16 Matilda Tomaryn Bruckner, *Shaping Romance: Interpretation, Truth, and Closure in Twelfth-Century French Fictions* (Philadelphia, University of Pennsylvania Press, 1993), 183.

17 Bruckner, *Shaping Romance*, 174.
18 See Jane Gilbert, who, following Eve Kosofsky Sedgwick, argues that what we now think of lesbian sexuality simply does not count in medieval literature: 'Boys Will Be . . . What? Gender, Sexuality, and Childhood in *Floire et Blancheflor* and *Floris et Lyriope*', *Exemplaria* 9 (1997), 45 and n. 15.
19 Bruckner, *Shaping Romance*, 176.
20 Roberta L. Krueger, 'Marie de France', in *The Cambridge Companion to Medieval Women's Writing*, ed. Carolyn Dinshaw and David Wallace (Cambridge, Cambridge University Press, 2003), 181.
21 All in-text references are to Marie de France, *Fables*, ed. and trans. Harriet Spiegel (Toronto, University of Toronto Press, 1994; reprinted Toronto, University of Toronto Press / Medieval Academy of America, 2000). References are by fable number and line number. All quotations from the original French and in translation are taken from this edition.
22 *The Canterbury Tales*, III (D) l. 692. References to Chaucer's works are to *The Riverside Chaucer*, 3rd edn, gen. ed. Larry D. Benson (Boston, Mass., Houghton Mifflin, 1987). Modernizations are my own.
23 *The Canterbury Tales*, III (D) ll. 693–6.
24 Karen K. Jambeck, 'The *Fables* of Marie de France: A Mirror of Princes', in *In Quest of Marie de France: A Twelfth-Century Poet*, ed. Chantal A. Maréchal (Lewiston, Edwin Mellen Press, 1992), 59–106; see also Bloch, *Anonymous Marie de France*, 111–38, 139–74.
25 Jambeck, 'Mirror of Princes', 90.
26 For the view that the *Fables* specifically address the women in a mixed audience, see Harriet Spiegel, 'The Woman's Voice in the *Fables* of Marie de France', in *In Quest of Marie de France*, ed. Maréchal, 45, 50, 57.
27 For a subtle reading of no. 70, see Spiegel, 'Woman's Voice', 51–4.
28 All in-text references are by line numbers to *Saint Patrick's Purgatory: A Poem by Marie de France*, trans. Michael J. Curley (Binghamton, NY, Medieval and Renaissance Texts and Studies, 1993). All quotations from the original French and in translation are from this edition.
29 Bloch, *Anonymous Marie de France*, esp. 229–40.
30 Bloch, *Anonymous Marie de France*, 266, 267–310.
31 *Saint Patrick's Purgatory*, trans. Curley, 21–6.
32 *Saint Patrick's Purgatory*, trans. Curley, 24.
33 See Jacques Le Goff, *The Birth of Purgatory*, trans. Arthur Goldhammer (London, Scolar Press, 1984).
34 Julia Kristeva, *Powers of Horror: An Essay on Abjection*, trans. Leon S. Roudiez (New York, Columbia University Press, 1982), 4.
35 For extracts of this text see *Women's Writing in Middle English*, ed. Alexandra Barratt (London, Longman, 1992), 163–76. Mary Erler has an important essay on this text forthcoming in *Viator*. See also Takami Matsuda, *Death and Purgatory in Middle English Didactic Poetry* (Cambridge, D. S. Brewer, 1997), 67–72.
36 *Saint Patrick's Purgatory*, trans. Curley, 32.

3   Legends and Lives of Women Saints (Late Tenth to Mid-Fifteenth Centuries)

1 See Joyce Hill, 'The Dissemination of Ælfric's *Lives of Saints*: A Preliminary Survey', in *Holy Men and Holy Women: Old English Prose Saints' Lives and their Contexts*, ed. Paul E. Szarmach (Albany, NY, SUNY Press, 1996), 235–59, and also Mary Swan and Elaine Treharne, eds, *Rewriting Old English in the Twelfth Century* (Cambridge, Cambridge University Press, 2000).
2 All references to lives in this collection are to the selection in *Women's Saints' Lives in Old English Prose*, ed. and trans. Leslie A. Donovan (Cambridge, D. S. Brewer, 1999); hereafter

cited in the text as *Women Saints' Lives*. For the Old English texts, see *Ælfric's Lives of Saints*, ed. Walter W. Skeat, Early English Text Society 76, 82, 94, 114, 2 vols (London and Oxford, Trübner and Kegan Paul, Trench and Trübner, 1881–1900). For the argument that Christina of Markyate's *Life* is indebted to Anglo-Saxon saints' lives, including Ælfric's *Lives of Saints*, see also Shari Horner, *The Discourse of Enclosure: Representing Women in Old English Literature* (Albany, NY, SUNY Press, 2001), 173–85. All references to *The Life of Christina of Markyate* are to *The Life of Christina of Markyate: A Twelfth Century Recluse*, ed. and trans. C. H. Talbot (Oxford, Clarendon Press, 1959; reprinted Toronto, Toronto University Press / Medieval Academy of America, 1998); hereafter cited in the text as *Life*. All translations and quotations from the original Latin are taken from this edition.

3 Catherine Cubitt, 'Virginity and Misogyny in Tenth- and Eleventh-Century England', *Gender and History* 12 (2000), 15–16. On the complexity of the gendering of virginity, see Maud Burnett McInerney, 'Like a Virgin: The Problem of Male Virginity in the *Symphonia*', in *Hildegard of Bingen: A Book of Essays*, ed. Maud Burnett McInerney (New York, Garland, 1998), 133–54.

4 Clare A. Lees, *Tradition and Belief: Religious Writing in Late Anglo-Saxon England* (Minneapolis, University of Minnesota Press, 1999), 148.

5 Indeed the primary readership of Ælfric's *Lives* may have included women in the households of Æthelweard and Æthelmær, as Mary Swan has pointed out to me.

6 'St Mary of Egypt', ll. 221–6, in *Ælfric's Lives of Saints*, ed. Skeat, vol. 2, 14–15.

7 Clare A. Lees and Gillian R. Overing, *Double Agents: Women and Clerical Culture in Anglo-Saxon England* (Philadelphia, University of Pennsylvania Press, 2001), 133.

8 Lees and Overing, *Double Agents*, 133, 135.

9 *Women Saints' Lives*, ed. and trans. Donovan, 57.

10 Karen A. Winstead, *Virgin Martyrs: Legends of Sainthood in Late Medieval England* (Ithaca, NY, Cornell University Press, 1997), 20.

11 Dyan Elliott, *Spiritual Marriage: Sexual Abstinence in Medieval Wedlock* (Princeton, Princeton University Press, 1993), 74.

12 Jocelyn Wogan-Browne, *Saints' Lives and Women's Literary Culture c.1150–1300: Virginity and its Authorizations* (Oxford, Oxford University Press, 2001), 115.

13 Wogan-Browne, *Saints' Lives*, 96.

14 For a comparison with *Eugenia*, see Horner, *Discourse of Enclosure*, 176–8.

15 *Medieval Women's Visionary Literature*, ed. Elizabeth Alvilda Petroff (Oxford, Oxford University Press, 1986), 47–8.

16 See Jocelyn Wogan-Browne, ' "Clerc u lai, muïne u dame": Women and Anglo-Norman Hagiography in the Twelfth and Thirteenth Centuries', in *Women and Literature in Britain, 1150–1500*, ed. Carol M. Meale (Cambridge, Cambridge University Press, 1993), 61–85; and Wogan-Browne, *Saints' Lives*, 207–12, 227–45, 249–56.

17 See June Hall McCash, '*La vie seinte Audree*: A Fourth Text by Marie de France?' *Speculum* 77 (2002), 744–77. McCash sees a connection between the saint's life and Marie de France's 'interest in the growing phenomenon of spiritual marriage' (776).

18 See William MacBain, 'Anglo-Norman Women Hagiographers', in *Anglo-Norman Anniversary Essays*, ed. Ian Short (London, Anglo-Norman Text Society, 1993), 235–50.

19 All in-text references to the modern English translation of *The Life of St Catherine* are to *Virgin Lives and Holy Deaths: Two Exemplary Biographies for Anglo-Norman Women*, trans. Jocelyn Wogan-Browne and Glyn S. Burgess (London, Everyman, 1996). References to the English translation are by page rather than line number. All in-text references to the original French version are by line number to Clemence of Barking, *The Life of St Catherine*, ed. William MacBain, Anglo-Norman Text Society 18 (Oxford, Blackwell, 1964).

20 See Catherine Batt, 'Clemence of Barking's Transformations of *Courtoisie* in *La Vie de Sainte Catherine d'Alexandrie*', *New Comparison* 12 (1991), 104–5; and Jocelyn Wogan-Browne, 'Wreaths of Thyme: The Female Translator in Anglo-Norman Hagiography', in

The Medieval Translator 4, ed. Roger Ellis and Ruth Evans (Binghamton, NY, Medieval and Renaissance Texts and Studies, 1994), 56–7.

21 In-text references are to *The Lais of Marie de France*, trans. Glyn S. Burgess and Keith Busby, 2nd edn (Harmondsworth, Penguin, 1999). References are by page rather than line number.

22 Batt, 'Clemence of Barking', 105.

23 See Tara Foster, 'Clemence of Barking: Reshaping the Legend of Saint Catherine of Alexandria', *Women's Writing* 12 (2005), 13–27.

24 *Virgin Lives*, trans. Wogan-Browne and Burgess, 65–6 n. 21.

25 Here I follow the version of line 705 in *Virgin Lives*, trans. Wogan-Browne and Burgess, 68 n. 33, rather than that in the *Life of St Catherine*, ed. MacBain.

26 Wogan-Browne, *Saints' Lives*, 242–3.

27 Simon Gaunt, *Gender and Genre in Medieval French Literature* (Cambridge, Cambridge University Press, 1995), 231–2.

28 The translated text is from *St Katherine* in *Anchoritic Spirituality: Ancrene Wisse and Associated Works*, trans. Anne Savage and Nicholas Watson (New York, Paulist Press, 1991), 274. The Middle English is based on the diplomatic edition of the text of *St Katherine* found in London, British Library, MS Cotton Titus D.XVIII (on which Savage and Watson base their edition) in *Seinte Katerine*, ed. S. R. T. O. d'Ardenne and E. J. Dobson, Early English Text Society supplementary series 7 (Oxford, Oxford University Press, 1981), ll. 1045–53. I have not followed the manuscript line breaks.

29 *Virgin Lives*, trans. Wogan-Browne and Burgess, p. xxxiii.

30 Paul Strohm, 'Chaucer's Audience(s): Fictional, Implied, Actual', *Chaucer Review* 18 (1983), 138.

31 Batt, 'Clemence of Barking', 102.

32 See Savage and Watson, trans., *Anchoritic Spirituality*, 428 n. 38.

33 Gaunt, *Gender and Genre*, 232.

34 MacBain, 'Anglo-Norman Women Hagiographers', 249.

35 Wogan-Browne, *Saints' Lives*, 227; my italics.

36 See Wogan-Browne, *Saints' Lives*, 6–12 and *passim*.

37 Wogan-Browne, *Saints' Lives*, 243.

38 In-text references to the modern English translation of Osbern Bokenham's *Legends of Holy Women* are to *A Legend of Holy Women*, trans. Sheila Delaney (Notre Dame, University of Notre Dame Press, 1992). References to the translation are by page number.

39 A. S. G. Edwards, 'The Transmission and Audience of Osbern Bokenham's *Legendys of Hooly Wummen*', in *Late-Medieval Religious Texts and their Transmission: Essays in Honour of A. I. Doyle*, ed. A. J. Minnis (Cambridge, D. S. Brewer, 1994), 157–67.

40 Sheila Delaney, *Impolitic Bodies: Poetry, Saints, and Society in Fifteenth-Century England: The Work of Osbern Bokenham* (Oxford, Oxford University Press, 1998); Simon Horobin, 'The Angle of Oblivion: A Lost Medieval Manuscript Discovered in Walter Scott's Collection', *TLS* (11 November 2005), 12–13.

41 See the Middle English text: Osbern Bokenham, *Legendys of Hooly Wummen*, ed. Mary S. Serjeantson, Early English Text Society original series 206 (London, Oxford University Press, 1938), l. 1. All in-text quotations from the Middle English are by line number to this edition.

42 See Ian Johnson, 'Tales of a True Translator: Medieval Literary Theory, Anecdote and Autobiography in Osbern Bokenham's *Legendys of Hooly Wummen*', in *The Medieval Translator* 4, ed. Roger Ellis and Ruth Evans (Binghamton, NY, Medieval and Renaissance Texts and Studies, 1994), 104–24.

43 For information about these women, see Delaney, *Impolitic Bodies*, 15–22.

44 Delaney, in *Impolitic Bodies*, 17, confuses this Katherine Howard with another of the same name, who was mother of Elizabeth de Vere. Either woman could be the Katherine Howard mentioned by Bokenham.

45 See Margaret Bridges, 'Uncertain Peregrinations of the Living and the Dead: Writing (Hagiography) as Translating (Relics) in Osbern Bokenham's Legend of St Margaret', in *Chaucer and the Challenges of Medievalism: Studies in Honor of H. A. Kelly*, ed. Donka Minkova and Theresa Tinkle (Frankfurt am Main, Peter Lang, 2003), 275–87.

46 Delaney, *Impolitic Bodies*, 54–69, 69. See also Nancy Bradley Warren, *Spiritual Economies: Female Monasticism in Later Medieval England* (Philadelphia, University of Pennsylvania Press, 2001), 147–62. Warren's analysis touches on a number of the same points as my own but comes to rather different conclusions about Bokenham's relationship to his fellow poets and to female authority.

47 John Gower, *Vox Clamantis*, 52, in *The Major Latin Works of John Gower*, trans. Eric W. Stockton (Seattle, University of Washington Press, 1962).

48 John Gower, *Confessio Amantis*, viii. 3127, in *The English Works of John Gower*, ed. G. C. Macaulay, Early English Text Society early series 81, 82 (London, Kegan Paul, Trench, Trübner, 1900–1). Modernizations are my own.

49 Cf. *Confessio Amantis*, viii. 3106–28. Gower, like Bokenham, is concerned that his work will be rejected by 'learned men' (l. 3113).

50 *Confessio Amantis*, *Prol. 51.

51 Delaney, ed., *A Legend of Holy Women*, p. xiii; and Delaney, *Impolitic Bodies*, 130–3 and *passim*.

52 Horobin, 'The Angle of Oblivion', 13.

53 *The Writings of Julian of Norwich: A Vision Showed to a Devout Woman and A Revelation of Love*, ed. Nicholas Watson and Jacqueline Jenkins (Turnhout, Brepols, 2006), 65–7.

54 Felicity Riddy, ' "Women Talking about the Things of God": A Late Medieval Sub-Culture', in *Women and Literature in Britain, 1150–1500*, ed. Meale, 105.

55 Alexandra Barratt, 'Margery Kempe and the King's Daughter of Hungary', in *Margery Kempe: A Book of Essays*, ed. Sandra J. McEntire (New York, Garland, 1992), 189–201. In-text page references are to *The Book of Margery Kempe*, ed. Sanford Brown Meech and Hope Emily Allen, Early English Text Society original series 212 (Oxford, Oxford University Press, 1940). Translations are my own.

56 *Jacobus de Voragine: The Golden Legend: Readings on the Saints*, trans. William Granger Ryan (Princeton, Princeton University Press, 1993), vol. 2, 309.

57 *The Golden Legend* simply alludes to those ' "who looked gloomy when they wept" ': *The Golden Legend*, ed. Ryan, vol. 2, 310.

58 Jacqueline Jenkins and Katharine J. Lewis, eds, *St Katherine of Alexandria: Texts and Contexts in Western Medieval Europe* (Turnhout, Brepols, 2003), 14; Paul Price, 'Trumping Chaucer: Osbern Bokenham's *Katherine*', *Chaucer Review* 36 (2001), 158–83.

59 Price, 'Trumping Chaucer', 168. For the opposing view, that Bokenham encourages the 'unruly' piety of individuals such as Margery Kempe, see Winstead, *Virgin Martyrs*, 140.

60 *The Paston Letters and Papers of the Fifteenth Century*, ed. Norman Davis (Oxford, Clarendon Press, 1971, 1976), nos 501–3.

61 *Paston Letters*, ed. Davis, no. 27.

62 *Paston Letters*, ed. Davis, no. 352.

63 See further Diane Watt, ed. and trans., *The Paston Women: Selected Letters* (London, D. S. Brewer, 2004), 145–6.

4 Julian of Norwich (1342/3–after 1416)

1 Nicholas Watson, 'The Composition of Julian of Norwich's *Revelation of Love*', *Speculum* 68 (1993), 637–83. Here I use the titles given in *The Writings of Julian of Norwich: A Vision Showed to a Devout Woman and A Revelation of Love*, ed. Nicholas Watson and Jacqueline Jenkins (Turnhout, Brepols, 2006). All in-text page references to and quotations

from the *Vision* or the *Revelation* are to and from this edition. Translations from the Middle English are my own.

2 For the descriptions of the manuscripts and printed text, see *A Book of Showings to the Anchoress Julian of Norwich*, ed. Edmund Colledge and James Walsh, 2 parts, (Toronto, Pontifical Institute of Mediæval Studies, 1978), 1–10.

3 See Amy Appleford, 'The "Comene Course of Prayers": Julian of Norwich and Late Medieval Death Culture', forthcoming in the *Journal of English and Germanic Philology*. I am grateful to Dr Appleford for allowing me to read this article prior to publication.

4 *Writings*, ed. Watson and Jenkins, 4.

5 See, for example, Benedicta Ward, 'Julian the Solitary', in *Julian Reconsidered*, ed. Kenneth Leech and Benedicta Ward (Oxford, SLG Press, 1988), 11–35; Liz Herbert McAvoy, *Authority and the Female Body in the Writings of Julian of Norwich and Margery Kempe* (Cambridge, D. S. Brewer, 2004), 64–95.

6 *Middle English Dictionary*, s.v. 'travail' n. 3(f).

7 Felicity Riddy, '"Women Talking about the Things of God": A Late Medieval Sub-Culture', in *Women and Literature in Britain, 1150–1500*, ed. Carol M. Meale (Cambridge, Cambridge University Press, 1993), 111.

8 In-text page references are to *The Book of Margery Kempe*, ed. Sanford Brown Meech and Hope Emily Allen, Early English Text Society original series 212 (Oxford, Oxford University Press, 1940). Translations from the Middle English are my own.

9 *Middle English Dictionary*, s.v. 'barain(e' adj. 1(a) and (b).

10 For a discussion of Julian's universalism, see, for example, Nicholas Watson, 'Visions of Inclusion: Universal Salvation and Vernacular Theology in Pre-Reformation England', *Journal of Medieval and Early Modern Studies* 27 (1997), 145–87.

11 Felicity Riddy, 'Julian of Norwich and Self-Textualization', in *Editing Women*, ed. Ann M. Hutchison (Cardiff, University of Wales Press, 1998) 111–12.

12 *Writings*, ed. Watson and Jenkins, 387 n.

13 *Bede's Ecclesiastical History of the English People*, ed. Bertram Colgrave and R. A. B. Mynors (Oxford, Clarendon Press, 1969), 457–69.

14 *A Book of Showings*, ed. Colledge and Walsh, 447 n.

15 Alan Deighton, 'Julian of Norwich's Knowledge of the Life of St John of Beverley', *Notes and Queries* 40 (December 1993), 440–3.

16 *Middle English Dictionary*, s.v. 'performen' v. 1 (a), 1 (c), 2 (a).

17 Sarah McNamer, 'The Exploratory Image: God as Mother in Julian of Norwich's *Revelations of Divine Love*', *Mystics Quarterly* 15 (1989), 27.

18 See the extracts from Aristotle, *The Generation of Animals*, in *Woman Defamed and Woman Defended: An Anthology of Medieval Texts*, ed. Alcuin Blamires (Oxford, Clarendon Press, 1992), 39–41.

19 The classic study is Caroline Walker Bynum, *Jesus as Mother: Studies in the Spirituality of the High Middle Ages* (Berkeley, University of California Press, 1982).

20 The Sloane manuscript mentions Julian's 'service' only once: *Writings*, ed. Watson and Jenkins, 394 n.

21 *The Pricke of Conscience (Stimulus Conscientiae): A Northumbrian Poem*, ed. Richard Morris (Berlin, A. Asher, 1863), ll. 456–61. The translation from Middle English is my own.

22 Nicholas Watson, 'Julian of Norwich', in *The Cambridge Companion to Medieval Women's Writing*, ed. Carolyn Dinshaw and David Wallace (Cambridge, Cambridge University Press, 2003), 218.

23 *The Chastising of God's Children and the Treatise of Perfection of the Sons of God*, ed. Joyce Bazire and Eric Colledge (Oxford, Blackwell, 1957), esp. 173–7; Watson, 'Julian of Norwich', 218–19.

24 See *The Booke of Gostlye Grace of Mechtild of Hackeborn*, ed. Theresa A. Halligan (Toronto, Pontifical Institute of Mediæval Studies, 1979), 67.

25 Watson, 'Julian of Norwich', 213.
26 *Writings*, ed. Watson and Jenkins, 415 n.
27 Riddy, 'Self-Textualization', 101–24; see also Lynn Staley Johnson, 'The Trope of the Scribe and the Question of Literary Authority in the Works of Julian of Norwich and Margery Kempe', *Speculum* 66 (1991), 820–38.
28 *Writings*, ed. Watson and Jenkins, 414.
29 Riddy, 'Self-Textualization', 118.
30 *Writings*, ed. Watson and Jenkins, 410 n.
31 Riddy, 'Self-Texualization', 118.
32 Marguerite Porete, *The Mirror of Simple Souls: A Middle English Translation*, ed. Marilyn Doiron, with an appendix 'The Glosses by "M.N." and Richard Methley to *The Mirror of Simple Souls*', by Edmund Colledge and Romana Guarnieri, *Archivio Italiano per la Storia della Pietà* 5 (1967), 243–382; Marleen Cré, 'Women in the Charterhouse? Julian of Norwich's *Revelations of Divine Love* and Marguerite Porete's *Mirror of Simple Souls* in British Library, MS Additional 37790', in *Writing Religious Women: Female Spiritual and Textual Practices in Late Medieval England*, ed. Denis Renevey and Christiana Whitehead (Cardiff, University of Wales Press, 2000), 43–62.
33 *Writings*, ed. Watson and Jenkins, 400 n.
34 *Writings*, ed. Watson and Jenkins, appendix A, 417–31; Hugh Kempster, 'A Question of Audience: The Westminster Text and Fifteenth-Century Reception of Julian of Norwich', in *Julian of Norwich: A Book of Essays*, ed. Sandra J. McEntire (New York, Garland, 1998), 257–89.
35 *Writings*, ed. Watson and Jenkins, 5 and appendix B, 431–5, esp. 435 n. 74.
36 Riddy, 'Self-Textualization', 122 n. 33.
37 Cré, 'Women in the Charterhouse?' 47.
38 See *Writings*, ed. Watson and Jenkins, 12–17 and appendix D, 437–48.
39 *A Book of Showings*, ed. Colledge and Walsh, 734 n. As my modernized version is very close to the original I have only provided the text of the former.
40 Riddy, ' "Women Talking" ', 115.

5   Margery Kempe (*c*.1373–after 1439)

1 All in-text page references are to *The Book of Margery Kempe*, ed. Sanford Brown Meech and Hope Emily Allen, Early English Text Society original series 212 (Oxford, Oxford University Press, 1940). Throughout this chapter, quotations are from this edition and translations from the Middle English are my own.
2 The most important recent study of this is Nicholas Watson, 'The Making of *The Book of Margery Kempe*', in *Voices in Dialogue: Reading Women in the Middle Ages*, ed. Linda Olson and Kathryn Kerby-Fulton (Notre Dame, Ind., University of Notre Dame Press, 2005), 395–434; but see also A. C. Spearing, 'Margery Kempe', in *A Companion to Middle English Prose*, ed. A. S. G. Edwards (Cambridge, D. S. Brewer, 2004), 83–97; and Ruth Evans, 'The Book of Margery Kempe', in *A Companion to Medieval English Literature and Culture c.1350– c.1500*, ed. Peter Brown (Oxford, Blackwell, 2007), 507–21. I am grateful to Professor Evans for providing me with a copy of this essay prior to publication.
3 For a sensible reconsideration of Kempe's engagement with literary culture, see Jacqueline Jenkins, 'Reading and *The Book of Margery Kempe*', in *A Companion to* The Book of Margery Kempe, ed. John H. Arnold and Katherine J. Lewis (Cambridge, D. S. Brewer, 2004), 113–28.
4 Douglas Gray, 'Popular Religion and Late Medieval English Literature', in *Religion in the Poetry and Drama of the Late Middle Ages in England*, ed. Piero Boitani and Anna Torti (Cambridge, D. S. Brewer, 1990), 1–28, 23. Gail McMurray Gibson makes a similar claim in *The Theater of Devotion: East Anglian Drama and Society in the Late Middle Ages* (Chicago,

University of Chicago Press, 1989), 65. For the counter-argument, see Katherine J. Lewis, 'Margery Kempe and Saint Making in Later Medieval England', in *A Companion*, ed. Arnold and Lewis, 195–215.

5 For an overview, see John H. Arnold, 'Margery's Trials: Heresy, Lollardy and Dissent', in *A Companion*, ed. Arnold and Lewis, 75–93.

6 Middle English Dictionary, s.v. 'secretari(e)' n. 1 (*b*).

7 Jennifer Summit, 'Women and Authorship', in *The Cambridge Companion to Medieval Women's Writing*, ed. Carolyn Dinshaw and David Wallace (Cambridge, Cambridge University Press, 2003), 99.

8 Middle English Dictionary, s.v. 'secretari(e)' n. 1 (*a*). Here I develop an argument first put forward in my study *Secretaries of God: Women Prophets in Late Medieval and Early Modern England* (Cambridge, D. S. Brewer, 1997), 1. Some sentences in this chapter have been borrowed and adapted from that book. I am grateful to the publisher for permission to reuse this material.

9 Summit, 'Women and Authorship', 92–3.

10 J. A. Burrow, *Medieval Writers and their Works: Middle English Literature and its Background, 1100–1500* (Oxford, Oxford University Press, 1982), 29–30; A. J. Minnis, *Medieval Theory of Authorship: Scholastic Literary Attitudes in the Later Middle Ages*, 2nd edn (Aldershot, Hants, Scholar Press, 1988), 94–5.

11 *Guide for Anchoresses*, parts 7 and 8, in *Medieval English Prose for Women: From the Katherine Group and* Ancrene Wisse, ed. Bella Millett and Jocelyn Wogan-Browne (Oxford, Clarendon Press, 1990), 129.

12 Burrow, *Medieval Writers*, 30.

13 *The Book of Margery Kempe*, ed. Meech and Allen, pp. vii–viii.

14 Watson, 'The Making', 399.

15 Here I disagree, crucially, with Watson, who argues that the two were not 'friends' and that their relationship was primarily professional: Watson, 'The Making', 408.

16 See Robert C. Ross, 'Oral Life, Written Text: The Genesis of *The Book of Margery Kempe*', *Yearbook of English Studies* 22 (1992), 226–37.

17 Gray, 'Popular Religion', 10. For a recent rearticulation of the idea of clerical authorship, see Spearing, 'Margery Kempe', 92–4.

18 Lynn Staley Johnson, 'The Trope of the Scribe and the Question of Literary Authority in the Works of Julian of Norwich and Margery Kempe', *Speculum* 66 (1991), 820–38.

19 For a lively debate about genre, language (or voice) and other issues, see Watson, 'The Making'; Felicity Riddy, 'Text and Self in *The Book of Margery Kempe*', in *Voices in Dialogue*, ed. Olson and Kerby-Fulton, 435–53; and Riddy and Watson, 'Afterwords', in *Voices in Dialogue*, ed. Olson and Kerby-Fulton, 454–7. See also Spearing, 'Margery Kempe', 92–4, and Evans, 'The Book of Margery Kempe'.

20 Gibson, *Theater of Devotion*, 47.

21 See Katherine J. Lewis, *The Cult of St Katherine of Alexandria in Late Medieval England* (Woodbridge, Suffolk, Boydell Press, 2000), 242–56.

22 *The Writings of Julian of Norwich*: A Vision Showed to a Devout Woman *and* A Revelation of Love, ed. Nicholas Watson and Jacqueline Jenkins (Turnhout, Brepols, 2006), 237–9.

23 Anthony Goodman, *Margery Kempe and her World* (London, Longman, 2002), 87.

24 Jonathan Hughes, *Pastors and Visionaries: Religion and Secular Life in Late Medieval Yorkshire* (Woodbridge, Suffolk, Boydell Press, 1988), 305.

25 Norman P. Tanner, *The Church in Late Medieval Norwich, 1370–1532* (Toronto, Pontifical Institute of Mediæval Studies, 1984), 231–3.

26 For the suggestion that Sleightholme served as private confessor to Joan Beaufort, see Hughes, *Pastors and Visionaries*, 109. For the view that Kempe's influence over Joan Beaufort and her daughter may have been understood as politically subversive by her enemies,

see Nancy Bradley Warren, *Spiritual Economies: Female Monasticism in Late Medieval England* (Philadelphia: University of Pennsylvania Press, 2001), 166–8.

27 *The Book of Margery Kempe*, ed. Meech and Allen, 267–8 n. 22/9 sq.

28 *The Book of Margery Kempe*, ed. Meech and Allen, 267–8 n. 22/9 sq.

29 Hughes, *Pastors and Visionaries*, 324.

30 *The Book of Margery Kempe*, ed. Meech and Allen, 259 n. 6/9.

31 Lynn Staley, *Margery Kempe's Dissenting Fictions* (Philadelphia, Pennsylvania State University Press, 1994), 3.

32 See also the discussion of the naming of Margery Kempe in Evans, 'The Book of Margery Kempe'.

33 Nicholas Watson, 'The Making', 402.

34 Paul Strohm, 'Chaucer's Audience(s): Fictional, Implied, Actual', *Chaucer Review* 18 (1983), 137–45, 138.

35 Strohm, 'Chaucer's Audience(s)', 140.

36 Sarah Rees Jones, ' "A Peler of Holy Cherch": Margery Kempe and the Bishops', in *Medieval Women: Texts and Contexts in Late Medieval Britain: Essays for Felicity Riddy*, ed. Jocelyn Wogan-Browne, Rosalynn Voaden, Arlyn Diamond, Ann Hutchison, Carol M. Meale and Lesley Johnson (Turnhout, Brepols, 2000), 391.

37 See further A. J. Minnis, *Medieval Theory of Authorship: Scholastic Literary Attitudes in the Later Middle Ages*, 2nd edn (Aldershot, Herts, Scholar Press, 1988).

38 Watson, 'The Making', 424.

39 Goodman, *Margery Kempe*, 13, 78 and *passim*. For an excellent analysis of the geography and politics of Margery Kempe's Lynn, see Kate Parker, 'Lynn and the Making of a Mystic', in *A Companion*, ed. Arnold and Lewis, 55–73.

40 Strohm, 'Chaucer's Audience(s)', 142.

41 See *The Book of Margery Kempe* ed. Meech and Allen, pp. xxxii–xxxv.

42 *The Book of Margery Kempe*, ed. Meech and Allen, pp. xxxvi–xxxvii, xl.

43 The extracts are reproduced in *The Book of Margery Kempe*, ed. Meech and Allen, 353–7. The printing history is outlined at pp. xlvi–xlviii. Important reassessments of the printed extracts are Jennifer Summit, *Lost Property: The Woman Writer and English Literary History, 1380–1589* (Chicago, University of Chicago Press, 2000), 126–38; and Allyson Foster, 'A Shorte Treatyse of Contemplacyon: The Book of Margery Kempe', in *A Companion*, ed. Arnold and Lewis, 95–112.

44 For important discussions of the difficulties of locating Margery Kempe's voice, see Evans, 'The Book of Margery Kempe'; and also Spearing, 'Margery Kempe', 92–4.

6   The Paston Letters (1440–1489)

1 See *The Paston Women: Selected Letters*, ed. and trans. Diane Watt (Cambridge, D. S. Brewer, 2004), especially the introduction, 'Three Generations of Women', and the interpretative essay ' "In the Absence of a Good Secretary": The Letters, Lives, and Loves of the Paston Women Reconsidered'; and my earlier essay, ' "No Writing for Writing's Sake": The Language of Service and Household Rhetoric in the Letters of the Paston Women', in *Dear Sister: Medieval Women and the Epistolary Genre*, ed. Karen Cherewatuk and Ulrike Wiethaus (Philadelphia, University of Pennsylvania Press, 1993), 122–38.

2 For a key study of collaboration and medieval women's letters, see Joan M. Ferrante, *To the Glory of her Sex: Women's Roles in the Composition of Medieval Texts* (Bloomington, Indiana University Press, 1997), 11–35.

3 Here I revise my argument in ' "In the Absence of a Good Secretary" '.

4 *The Paston Letters and Papers of the Fifteenth Century*, ed. Norman Davis, 2 vols. (Oxford, Clarendon Press, 1971, 1976), no. 332. Letters from this edition are identified by number (letters and documents in this edition are numbered consecutively through the two

volumes). All quotations in the original Middle English are from this edition. For a modernized version of this letter, see *The Paston Letters: A Selection in Modern Spelling*, ed. Norman Davis (Oxford, Oxford University Press, 1983), no. 84. Throughout this chapter, translations from the Middle English are my own. The practice of distinguishing the three John Pastons (the father and his two eldest sons) is a modern convention.

5 I am grateful to P. J. Field for pointing this out to me.

6 All in-text references to the letters in modernized form are to *The Paston Women: Selected Letters*, ed. and trans. Watt. I am grateful to the publishers for permission to cite my own translations of the letters and documents in this volume.

7 *Paston Letters and Papers*, ed. Davis, no. 203.

8 *Paston Letters and Papers*, ed. Davis, no. 203.

9 *Paston Letters and Papers*, ed. Davis, no. 208.

10 *Paston Letters and Papers*, ed. Davis, no. 861. For a modernized version of part of this letter, see *Paston Letters: A Selection in Modern Spelling*, ed. Davis, no. 85.

11 *Paston Letters and Papers*, ed. Davis, no. 84; see *Paston Letters: A Selection in Modern Spelling*, ed. Davis, no. 22.

12 See Norman Davis, 'The *Litera Troili* and English Letters', *Review of English Studies* n.s. 16 (1965), 233–44, 236–7.

13 For an overview of the range of scholarly approaches applied to letters, see the editor's introduction to *Early Modern Women's Letter Writing, 1450–1700*, ed. James Daybell (Basingstoke, Palgrave, 2001), 1–15, 3.

14 Jennifer Summit, 'Women and Authorship', in *The Cambridge Companion to Medieval Women's Writing*, ed. Carolyn Dinshaw and David Wallace (Cambridge, Cambridge University Press, 2003), 105.

15 Two important recent studies of the letters of Margaret Paston are: Rebecca Krug, *Reading Families: Women's Literate Practice in Late Medieval England* (Ithaca, NY, Cornell University Press, 2002), 17–64; and Joel T. Rosenthal, *Telling Tales: Sources and Narration in Late Medieval England* (University Park, Pennsylvania State University Press, 2003), 95–147.

16 For a discussion of the literacy of the Paston women, see my essay, ' "In the Absence of a Good Secretary" '.

17 See Rosenthal, *Telling Tales*, 104–14.

18 *Paston Letters and Papers*, ed. Davis, no. 388.

19 *Paston Letters and Papers*, ed. Davis, no. 198.

20 The most important recent account of the family's history and historical context is Helen Castor, *Blood and Roses: The Paston Family in the Fifteenth Century* (London, Faber & Faber, 2004).

21 *Paston Letters and Papers*, ed. Davis, no. 426.

22 *Paston Letters and Papers*, ed. Davis, no. 657.

23 *Paston Letters and Papers*, ed. Davis, nos 929, 930.

24 *Paston Letters and Papers*, ed. Davis, no. 711.

25 *Paston Letters and Papers*, ed. Davis, no. 524.

26 *Paston Letters and Papers*, ed. Davis, no. 656.

27 *Paston Letters and Papers*, ed. Davis, no. 209, A and B; see *The Paston Women: Selected Letters*, trans. and ed. Watt, no. 64, for part of the second version of this letter.

28 *Paston Letters and Papers*, ed. Davis, no. 323; see *Paston Letters: A Selection in Modern Spelling*, no. 65; see also no. 66.

29 *Paston Letters and Papers*, ed. Davis, no. 77.

30 *Paston Letters and Papers*, ed. Davis, no. 193.

31 For the annotations, see *Paston Letters and Papers*, ed. Davis, nos 192, 193.

32 *Paston Letters and Papers*, ed. Davis, no. 773; see *Paston Letters: A Selection in Modern Spelling*, no. 124.

33 See also Krug, *Reading Families*, 39–42.

34 Colin Richmond has put the case that the more intimate of the two, which ends with the invocation, 'I beg you that you will not let anyone on earth see this letter, except yourself', was written by Margery herself. Scrutiny of the manuscript does not support his case, although he is probably correct to claim that the initials at the end are in her hand: Colin Richmond, *The Paston Family in the Fifteenth Century: Endings* (Manchester, Manchester University Press, 2000), 52 and n. 135.
35 See *Paston Letters and Papers*, ed. Davis, headnote to no. 820.
36 *Paston Letters and Papers*, ed. Davis, no. 791.
37 *Paston Letters and Papers*, ed. Davis, no. 378.

Afterword

1 See, for example, *The Cambridge History of Medieval English Literature*, ed. David Wallace (Cambridge, Cambridge University Press, 1999); and my review, 'The Manly Middle Ages,' *English* 49 (2000), 177–81.
2 Margaret J. M. Ezell, *Writing Women's Literary History* (Baltimore, Johns Hopkins University Press, 1993), 163–4.

Suggestions for Further Reading

1   Christina of Markyate (c.1096–after 1155)

Editions and translations

Geddes, Jane, *The St Albans Psalter: A Book for Christina of Markyate* (London, British Library, 2005).
A detailed study of the Psalter, with full-colour illustrations, that reads it in the context of Christina's life and argues for its importance in terms of what it reveals about Anglo-Saxon and Norman integration.

St Albans Psalter website at <http://www.abdn.ac.uk/stalbanspsalter> [accessed 31 August 2006].
The digitized manuscript of the St Albans Psalter with a full transcription, translation and commentary, critical essays and bibliography. The website includes a good assessment of the evidence concerning the possible date of the Psalter.

Talbot, C. H., ed. and trans., *The Life of Christina of Markyate: A Twelfth Century Recluse* (Oxford, Clarendon Press, 1959; reprinted Toronto, Toronto University Press/Medieval Academy of America, 1998).
The only edition of the sole surviving and badly damaged manuscript text of the Latin Life with facing-page English translation, and a useful but now outdated and sometimes inaccurate introduction.

Secondary reading

Carrasco, Magdalena Elizabeth, 'The Imagery of the Magdalen in Christina of Markyate's Psalter (The St Albans Psalter)', *Gesta* 38 (1999), 67–80.
An innovative essay that examines two illustrations featuring Mary Magdalen in the St Albans Psalter in relation to Christina's spirituality and the emergent cult of the Magdalen in the period and its association with affective piety.

Cartlidge, Neil, *Medieval Marriage: Literary Approaches, 1100–1300* (Cambridge, D. S. Brewer, 1997).
A useful study that includes a chapter on the St Albans Psalter, with a full analysis of the history of and the depiction of marriage in the Chanson of St Alexis *and its relationship to* The Life of Christina of Markyate.

Caviness, Madeline H., 'Anchoress, Abbess, Queen: Donors and Patrons or Intercessors and Matrons?' in *The Cultural Patronage of Medieval Women,*

ed. June Hall McCash (Athens, Ga., University of Georgia Press, 1996), 105–54.
A wide-ranging exploration of the relationship between medieval women and their books that argues that in the context of Christina of Markyate's ownership of the St Albans Psalter, the categories of patron, donor, recipient and reader are inherently unstable.

Elkins, Sharon K., *Holy Women of Twelfth-Century England* (Chapel Hill, NC, University of North Carolina Press, 1988).
A very detailed analysis of feminine piety in the post-Conquest period, which includes discussions of Christina, her associates, virginity and spiritual friendship in a chapter on the eremitic life, and of the transformations of her hermitage into a priory in a chapter on female monasticism in southern England.

Elliott, Dyan, 'Alternative Intimacies: Men, Women and Spiritual Direction in the Twelfth Century', in *Christina of Markyate*, ed. Fanous and Leyser, 160–83.
An essay that examines Christina's friendships with her male religious advisers by exploring models of spiritual direction.

Fanous, Samuel and Henrietta Leyser, eds, *Christina of Markyate: A Twelfth-Century Holy Woman* (London, Routledge, 2005).
An invaluable collection of largely original essays by important scholars in the field, which locates Christina of Markyate within her literary, cultural, social, religious and historical context.

Geddes, Jane, 'The St Albans Psalter: The Abbot and the Anchoress', in *Christina of Markyate*, ed. Fanous and Leyser, 197–216.
An invaluable section-by-section commentary on the St Albans Psalter, focusing on the questions of the extent to which the Psalter was produced for Christina by Geoffrey of St Albans, and of its reception. The essay includes a brief account of the date of the Psalter.

Gray, Douglas, 'Christina of Markyate: The Literary Background', in *Christina of Markyate*, ed. Fanous and Leyser, 12–24.
An essay that argues that The Life of Christina of Markyate *is, like* The Book of Margery Kempe, *the product of collaborative authorship.*

Hanning, Robert W., *The Individual in Twelfth-Century Romance* (New Haven, Yale University Press, 1977).
A study of the emergence of the individual in the literature of the twelfth-century renaissance that includes a chapter comparing the autobiographical writing of Abelard to The Life of Christina of Markyate, *focusing on the conflicts between individual conscience and social and religious environment.*

Head, Thomas, 'The Marriages of Christina of Markyate', *Viator* 21 (1990), 75–101.
This essay examines Christina's role as bride of Christ, and examines the social context and contemporary theological context. This essay is also reproduced in Christina of Markyate, *ed. Fanous and Leyser, 116–37.*

Holdsworth, Christopher J., 'Christina of Markyate', in *Medieval Women: Dedicated and Presented to Professor Rosalind M. T. Hill on the Occasion of her Seventieth Birthday*, ed. Derek Baker (Oxford, Basil Blackwell, 1978), 185–204.
A broad-ranging and widely cited introductory essay.

Hollis, Stephanie and Jocelyn Wogan-Browne, 'St Albans and Women's Monasticism: Lives and their Foundations in Christina's World', in *Christina of Markyate*, ed. Fanous and Leyser, 25–52.
Responding in part to Rachel Koopman's essay published in 2000, this study counters the apparently unique nature of The Life of Christina of Markyate *first, by examining the history of St Albans Abbey's associations with women, and second, by placing it in the context of other writings concerning medieval holy women, such as lives of Anglo-Saxon and Anglo-Norman female saints.*

Jaeger, C. Stephen, *Ennobling Love: In Search of a Lost Sensibility* (Philadelphia, University of Pennsylvania Press, 1999).
A ground-breaking study that includes a discussion of Christina of Markyate, foregrounding the significance of love and of her relationships with men (and Christ) within her narrative, and arguing that the writer of her Life *both dramatizes and romanticizes events. This material is also reproduced in* Christina of Markyate, *ed. Fanous and Leyser, 99–116.*

Jones, E. A., 'Christina of Markyate and *The Hermits and Anchorites of England*', in *Christina of Markyate*, ed. Fanous and Leyser, 229–53.
This essay contributes to a larger project concerned with revising Rotha Mary Clay's seminal work, Hermits and Anchorites of England *(1914), and provides a survey of solitaries in the vicinity of Markyate, providing a fuller eremitic context for understanding Christina's own religious vocation.*

Karras, Ruth Mazo, 'Friendship and Love in the Lives of Two Twelfth-Century English Saints', *Journal of Medieval History* 14 (1988), 305–20.
A thoughtful comparison of the depiction of spiritual love in the Lives *of Aelred of Rievaulx and Christina of Markyate.*

Koopmans, Rachel M., 'The Conclusion of Christina of Markyate's *Vita*', *Journal of Ecclesiastical History* 51 (2000), 663–98.
An extremely important essay that argues that the abrupt conclusion to Christina's Life *is linked to factionalism within St Albans Abbey and the suppression of her cult. Koopmans provides a clear account of the textual evidence concerning Christina and makes a convincing case for the dating of the* Life.

Koopmans, Rachel M., 'Dining at Markyate with Lady Christina', in *Christina of Markyate*, ed. Fanous and Leyser, 143–59.
A detailed examination of the relationship between the writer of The Life of Christina of Markyate *and his subject that emphasizes the extent to which the text is the creation of the former. This essay also explores Christina's links with other religious communities beyond St Albans Abbey.*

McLaughlin, Eleanor, 'Women, Power and the Pursuit of Holiness in Medieval Christianity', in *Women of Spirit: Female Leadership in the Jewish and Christian Traditions*, ed. Rosemary Ruether and Eleanor McLaughlin (New York, Simon & Schuster, 1979), 99–130.
An early feminist defence of female piety in the Middle Ages that includes a brief account of Christina's resistance to her family and the Church, of her relationships with her male religious guides and of her spirituality (especially her visions of the Blessed Virgin Mary).

Millett Bella, 'Women in No Man's Land: English Recluses and the Development of Vernacular Literature in the Twelfth and Thirteenth Centuries', in *Women and Literature in Britain, 1150–1500*, ed. Carol M. Meale (Cambridge, Cambridge University Press, 1993), 86–103.
An essay that includes a very sensible discussion of Christina's literacy.

Petroff, Elizabeth Alvilda, *Body and Soul: Essays on Medieval Women and Mysticism* (Oxford, Oxford University Press, 1994).
An account of female visionaries and mystics in the Middle Ages with a useful discussion of Christina of Markyate.

Renna, Thomas, 'Virginity in the *Life* of Christina of Markyate and Aelred of Rievaulx's *Rule*', *American Benedictine Review* 36 (1985), 79–92.
An essay that argues that the writer of Christina's Life *and Aelred of Rievaulx articulate their respective support of Benedictine and Cistercian reforms through their discussions of virginity.*

Staples, Kathryn Kelsey and Ruth Mazo Karras, 'Christina's Tempting: Sexual Desire and Women's Sanctity', in *Christina of Markyate*, ed. Fanous and Leyser, 184–96.
An examination of sexual temptation in The Life of Christina of Markyate *in the context of early Christian and medieval writings on the topic.*

Wogan-Browne, Jocelyn, 'Saints' Lives and the Female Reader', *Forum for Modern Language Studies* 27 (1991), 314–32.
An essay that examines the representation of female saints in twelfth- and thirteenth-century hagiography, and includes a comparison between The Life of Christina of Markyate *and the Middle English* Life of St Juliana.

2   Marie de France (*fl.* 1180)

Editions and translations

Lais

Burgess, Glyn S. and Keith Busby, trans., *The Lais of Marie de France*, 2nd edn (Harmondsworth, Penguin, 1999).
An easily available translation that includes the French text of three lais and a useful introduction.

Ewert, Alfred, ed., *Marie de France: Lais*, with an introduction and bibliography by Glyn S. Burgess (Oxford, Basil Blackwell, 1944; republished London, Bristol Classics, 1995).
A republication of Ewert's 1944 edition, on which Burgess and Busby based their translation, that includes a good bibliography.

Hanning, Robert and Joan Ferrante, trans., *The Lais of Marie de France* (New York, E. P. Dutton, 1978).
A useful but quite free translation.

Fables
Ewert, A., and R. C. Johnston, eds, *Marie de France: Fables* (Oxford, Basil Blackwell, 1942).
A teaching edition, with introduction, notes and a good glossary.

Martin, Mary Lou, *The Fables of Marie de France: An English Translation* (Birmingham, Ala., Summa, 1984).
A translation with contextual introduction and select bibliography.

Spiegel, Harriet, ed. and trans., *Fables* (Toronto, University of Toronto Press, 1994; reprinted Toronto, University of Toronto Press/Medieval Academy of America, 2000).
An edition of the French text with a facing-page translation and helpful introduction.

Saint Patrick's Purgatory
Curley, Michael J., trans., *Saint Patrick's Purgatory: A Poem by Marie de France* (Binghamton, NY, Medieval and Renaissance Texts and Studies, 1993).
An edition of the French text with a facing-page translation and an intelligent, informative introduction.

Warnke, Karl, ed., *Das Buch vom Espurgatoire S. Patrice der Marie de France und seine Quelle* (Halle, Max Niemeyer, 1938).
An edition of Marie de France's translation and her source text.

Secondary reading

Bloch, Howard R., *The Anonymous Marie de France* (Chicago, University of Chicago Press, 2003).
A fascinating book-length study that gives equal attention to each of Marie de France's three works and examines common themes linking them together and historical and political context. Bloch suggests that Marie de France's 'anonymity' (in other words, the way she gives little away about her identity even as she reflects on her authorial role) may have been consciously constructed.

Bruckner, Matilda Tomaryn, 'Of Men and Beasts in *Bisclavret'*, *Romanic Review* 82 (1991), 251–69.
A subtle reading of the ambiguities in and gender politics of 'Bisclavret' that contends that it may not be as antifeminist as it first appears.

Bruckner, Matilda Tomaryn, *Shaping Romance: Interpretation, Truth, and Closure in Twelfth-Century French Fictions* (Philadelphia, University of Pennsylvania Press, 1993).
A detailed study that includes a useful chapter on Marie de France's Lais, examining their relationship to romance, and issues of identity and naming, orality and writing, and closure. The chapter offers close readings of 'Guigemar' and 'Eliduc' and pays particular attention to narrative structure.

Burgess, Glyn S., *The Lais of Marie de France: Text and Context* (Manchester, Manchester University Press, 1987).
An examination, focusing on idealization of love and the representation of the courtly knight and lady within the poems, that argues that the order of composition is crucial to the meaning of the Lais.

Burgwinkle, William E., *Sodomy, Masculinity, and Law in Medieval England: France and England, 1050–1230* (Cambridge: Cambridge University Press, 2004).
An innovative approach to Anglo-Norman literature and society that includes a chapter offering a queer reading of Marie de France's Lais, reading 'Guigemar' alongside the Ovidian myth of Narcissus and its medieval transmissions, and also discussing 'Lanval' and 'Bisclavret' in some detail.

Bynum, Caroline Walker, *Metamorphosis and Identity* (New York, Zone Books, 2001).
An important study that discusses Marie de France's 'Bisclavret' alongside Ovid and Angela Carter.

Cohen, Jeffrey Jerome, *Of Giants: Sex, Monsters, and the Middle Ages* (Minneapolis, University of Minnesota Press, 1999).
A key study of medieval monstrosity that includes a short discussion of 'Bisclavret' in a chapter on dog–men hybrids.

Faust, Diana M., 'Women Narrators in the *Lais* of Marie de France', *Stanford French and Italian Studies* 58 (1988), 17–27.
A somewhat simplistic reading of Marie de France's self-representation as a woman writer and narrator, and of the female protagonists of the Lais who are also narrators, in some sense, and who are interpreted as mirroring Marie de France herself.

Finke, Laurie A. and Martin B. Shichtman, 'Magical Mistress Tour: Patronage, Intellectual Property, and the Dissemination of Wealth in the *Lais* of Marie de France', *Signs* 25 (2000), 479–503.
An exploration of the marginalization of women and younger sons in Norman aristocratic society that considers the related questions of the patronage systems and gender and class-based identity.

Freeman, Michelle A., 'Marie de France's Poetics of Silence: The Implications for a Feminine *Translatio*', *PMLA* 99 (1984), 860–83.
A useful argument that argues that the Lais *are characterized by ambiguity, omissions and evasiveness that Freeman views as specificially feminine. The article includes detailed analyses of 'Laüstic' and 'Chievrefoil'.*

Freeman, Michelle A., 'Dual Natures and Subverted Glosses: Marie de France's "Bisclavret"', *Romance Notes* 25 (1985), 288–301.
A defence of the apparent antifeminism of 'Bisclavret'.

Griffin, Miranda, 'Gender and Authority in the Medieval French Lai', *Forum for Modern Language Studies* 35 (1999), 42–56.
An intelligent discussion of the critical problems surrounding the identification of Marie de France's authorship of and feminine voice within the Lais. *The article also acknowledges the antifeminism of some of the narratives.*

Jambeck, Karen K., 'The *Fables* of Marie de France: A Mirror of Princes', in *In Quest of Marie de France*, ed. Maréchal, 59–106.
An important article that argues that the Fables *are indebted to the genre of the advice to princes (and thus can be usefully read alongside the* Policraticus *of John of Salisbury) and aimed at an aristocratic audience.*

Jambeck, Karen K., 'Truth and Deception in the *Fables* of Marie de France', in *Literary Aspects of Courtly Culture: Selected Papers from the Seventh Triennial Congress of the Courtly Literature Society*, ed. Donald Maddox and Sarah Sturm-Maddox (Cambridge, D. S. Brewer, 1994), 221–29.
A concise article that stresses the coherence of the moral vision of the Fables.

Kinoshita, Sharon, 'Cherchez La Femme: Feminist Criticism and Marie de France's *Lai de Lanval*', *Romance Notes* 34 (1994), 263–73.
Another exploration of the question of the female narrative voice of the Lais, *making the strong case that 'Lanval' serves to critique patriarchal feudalism.*

Krueger, Roberta L., 'Transforming Maidens: Singlewomen's Stories in Marie de France's *Lais* and Later French Courtly Narratives', in *Singlewomen in the European Past, 1250–1800*, ed. Judith M. Bennett and Amy M. Froide (Philadelphia, University of Pennsylvania Press, 1999), 146–91.
A detailed study of the figure of the unmarried young woman that argues that Marie de France's narratives focus on the maidens' transitions into maturity, and that they grant them some power to transform their social worlds.

Krueger, Roberta L., 'Beyond Debate: Gender in Play in Old French Courtly Fiction', in *Gender in Debate from the Early Middle Ages to the Renaissance*, ed. Thelma S. Fenster and Clare A. Lees (London, Palgrave, 2002), 79–95.
An exploration of the challenge to established gender roles in 'Guigemar' and two mid-thirteenth-century French texts.

Krueger, Roberta L., 'Marie de France', in *The Cambridge Companion to Medieval Women's Writing*, ed. Carolyn Dinshaw and David Wallace (Cambridge, Cambridge University Press, 2003), 172–83.

An invaluable and up-to-date overview of Marie de France's three works that stresses the importance of the role of the reader as interpreter.

McCash, June Hall, '*La vie seinte Audree*: A Fourth Text by Marie de France?' *Speculum* 77 (2002), 744–77.
A detailed reconsideration of the evidence supporting the contention that Marie de France was the author of a vernacular hagiography.

Maréchal, Chantal A., ed., *In Quest of Marie de France: A Twelfth-Century Poet* (Lewiston, Edwin Mellen Press, 1992).
A valuable collection of essays, including some by key scholars in the field.

Pickens, Rupert T., 'The Poetics of Androgyny in the *Lais* of Marie de France: *Yonec, Milun*, and the General Prologue', in *Literary Aspects of Courtly Culture: Selected Papers from the Seventh Triennial Congress of the International Courtly Literature Society*, ed. Donald Maddox and Sara Sturm-Maddox (Cambridge, D. S. Brewer, 1994), 211–19.
An article that contends that Marie de France focuses in her Lais on the ambiguous sexuality of the body and on the theme of reproduction in order to take upon herself the traditionally male role of writer.

Rothschild, Judith Rice, *Narrative Technique in the Lais of Marie de France: Themes and Variations* (Chapel Hill, North Carolina Studies in Romance Languages and Literatures, 1974).
A study offering close readings of six of the Lais.

Spence, Sarah, *Texts and the Self in the Twelfth Century* (Cambridge, Cambridge University Press, 1996).
A theorized approach to the articulation of the self and of agency in Latin and vernacular texts that includes a chapter focusing on the visual in Marie de France's Lais.

Spiegel, Harriet, 'The Woman's Voice in the *Fables* of Marie de France', in *In Quest of Marie de France*, ed. Maréchal, 45–58.
An article that focuses on the often positive or sympathetic representation of the female in the Fables, comparing the narratives to their sources, and arguing for a female audience or readership.

Spiegel, Harriet, 'The Male Animal in the *Fables* of Marie de France', in *Medieval Masculinities: Regarding Men in the Middle Ages*, ed. Clare A. Lees (Minneapolis, University of Minnesota Press, 1994), 111–26.
An article that demonstrates that within the Fables masculinity is often associated with public power and political authority and femininity with the domestic sphere.

Sturges, Robert, 'Texts and Readers in Marie de France's Lais', *Romanic Review* 71 (1980), 244–64.
An insightful study of reading and interpretation in the Lais, which includes convincing readings of 'Yonec', 'Chievrefoil', 'Guigemar', 'Eliduc' and 'Lanval'.

3   Legends and Lives of Women Saints (Late Tenth to Mid-Fifteenth Centuries)

Editions and translations

Old English lives of women saints

Donovan, Leslie A., ed. and trans., *Women Saints' Lives in Old English Prose* (Cambridge, D. S. Brewer, 1999).
A very readable translation of most of the lives of the Old English women saints found in London, British Library, MS Cotton, Julius E.vii, with a useful contextual introduction and an interpretative essay focusing on issues of gender, plus a bibliography.

Skeat, Walter W., ed., *Ælfric's Lives of Saints*, Early English Text Society 76, 82, 94, 114, 2 vols (London and Oxford, Trübner and Kegan Paul, Trench and Trübner, 1881–1900).
The standard edition of the Lives *with literal facing-page translations.*

Clemence of Barking, *Life of St Catherine*

MacBain, William, ed., *The Life of St Catherine*, Anglo-Norman Text Society 18 (Oxford, Blackwell, 1964).
An edition of the Anglo-Norman text, with contextual introduction, annotations and glossary.

Wogan-Browne, Jocelyn and Glyn S. Burgess, trans., *Virgin Lives and Holy Deaths: Two Exemplary Biographies for Anglo-Norman Women* (London, Everyman, 1996).
Excellent prose translations of Clemence of Barking's Life of St Catherine *and the Anglo-Norman* St Lawrence, *with an informative contextual introduction and annotations.*

Middle English saints' lives: the Katherine Group

d'Ardenne, S. R. T. O. and E. J. Dobson, eds, *Seinte Katerine*, Early English Text Society supplementary series 7 (Oxford, Oxford University Press, 1981).
A scholarly edition of the Middle English life, based on the Bodley manuscript, with diplomatic texts of the Lives found in the Royal and Titus manuscripts, followed by the Latin text, with introduction, notes on the various text, and commentary on and glossary to the English text.

Millett, Bella and Jocelyn Wogan-Browne, eds and trans., *Medieval English Prose for Women: From the Katherine Group and Ancrene Wisse* (Oxford, Clarendon Press, 1990).
A scholarly edition of selections from Ancrene Wisse *and the early- thirteenth-century 'Katherine Group', including the life of St Margaret, with facing-page translations, contextual introduction, textual commentary and glossary.*

Savage, Anne and Nicholas Watson, trans., *Anchoritic Spirituality: Ancrene Wisse and Associated Works* (New York, Paulist Press, 1991).

An excellent, annotated translation of a range of works, including the early-thirteenth-century Middle English life of St Katherine.

Osbern Bokenham, *Legends of Holy Women*

Delaney, Sheila, trans., *A Legend of Holy Women: A Translation of Osbern Bokenham's* Legends of Holy Women (Notre Dame, Ind., University of Notre Dame Press, 1992).
A literal prose translation with a critical introduction, notes and select bibliography.

Reames, Sherry L., ed., *Legends of St. Anne, Mother of the Virgin Mary* (Kalamazoo, Mich., Medieval Institute Publications, 2003).
A TEAMS student edition that includes Bokenham's version of the life of St Anne, with introduction, bibliography, textual notes and glossary. Available on-line at <http://www.lib.rochester.edu/camelot/TEAMS/44sr.htm> [accessed 5 October 2006].

Serjeantson, Mary S., ed., *Legendys of Hooly Wummen by Osbern Bokenham*, Early English Text Society original series 206 (London, Oxford University Press, 1938).
The standard edition of the Middle English text, with glossary.

Other

Ryan, William Granger, trans., *Jacobus de Voragine: The Golden Legend: Readings on the Saints*, 2 vols (Princeton, Princeton University Press, 1993).
A fluent, accessible translation.

Secondary reading

Batt, Catherine, 'Clemence of Barking's Transformations of *Courtoisie* in *La Vie de Sainte Catherine d'Alexandrie*', *New Comparison* 12 (1991), 102–23.
A key account of the literary and devotional contexts of Clemence of Barking's work (including lyrics, Marian poetry, sermon literature and narrative romance) and of her representation of God's love.

Bridges, Margaret, 'Uncertain Peregrinations of the Living and the Dead: Writing (Hagiography) as Translating (Relics) in Osbern Bokenham's Legend of St Margaret', in *Chaucer and the Challenges of Medievalism: Studies in Honor of H. A. Kelly*, ed. Donka Minkova and Theresa Tinkle (Frankfurt am Main, Peter Lang, 2003), 275–87.
An essay that examines the analogy between the translation of the relics of Saint Margaret in Bokenham's version of her life, and Bokenham's own representation of his role as translator.

Cubitt, Catherine, 'Virginity and Misogyny in Tenth- and Eleventh-Century England', *Gender and History* 12 (2000), 1–32.
A key essay that argues for the centrality of virginity in Ælfric's writing.

Delaney, Sheila, *Impolitic Bodies: Poetry, Saints and Society in Fifteenth-Century England: The Work of Osbern Bokenham* (Oxford, Oxford University Press, 1998).

An extended feminist and historicist study of Bokenham that pays particular attention to gender issues and places his work within its social and political context.

Delaney, Sheila, ' "Matronage or Patronage?" The Case of Osbern Bokenham's Women Patrons', *Florilegium* 16 (1999), 97–105.
A short examination of the patronage and political networks that lie behind Bokenham's collection of legends.

Edwards, A. S. G., 'The Transmission and Audience of Osbern Bokenham's *Legendys of Hooly Wummen*', in *Late-Medieval Religious Texts and their Transmission: Essays in Honour of A. I. Doyle*, ed. A. J. Minnis (Cambridge, D. S. Brewer, 1994), 157–67.
An influential study of the textual history of Bokenham's Legends.

Elliott, Dyan, *Spiritual Marriage: Sexual Abstinence in Medieval Wedlock* (Princeton, Princeton University Press, 1993).
A detailed and nuanced account of early Christian and medieval women, sexuality and spirituality, focusing on the practice of chaste marriage.

Foster, Tara, 'Clemence of Barking: Reshaping the Legend of Saint Catherine of Alexandria', *Women's Writing* 12 (2005), 13–27.
A study that focuses on the ways in which Clemence of Barking establishes parallels between herself and her protagonist in order to authorize her writing.

Gaunt, Simon, *Gender and Genre in Medieval French Literature* (Cambridge, Cambridge University Press, 1995).
A study of French vernacular genres, focusing on issues of gender, that includes a chapter on hagiography which looks at male and female virgin saints. It includes a discussion of Clemence of Barking.

Gulley, Alison, ' "Seo fæmne þa lærde swa lange þone cniht oðþæt he ge-lyfde on þone lifigendan god": The Christian Wife as Converter and Ælfric's Anglo-Saxon Audience', *Parergon* 19 (2002), 39–51.
An article that argues that Ælfric's Life of Cecilia would have had a particular didactic function for an audience of Anglo-Saxon nuns.

Hill, Joyce, 'The Dissemination of Ælfric's *Lives of Saints*: A Preliminary Survey', in *Holy Men and Holy Women: Old English Prose Saints' Lives and their Contexts*, ed. Paul E. Szarmach (Albany, NY, SUNY Press, 1996), 235–59.
A survey of the textual history of Ælfric's Lives of Saints.

Horner, Shari, 'The Violence of Exegesis: Reading the Bodies of Ælfric's Female Saints', in *Violence against Women in Medieval Texts*, ed. Anna Roberts (Gainesville, Fla., University Press of Florida, 1998), 22–43.
An examination of torture and martyrdom in the Old English lives of women saints.

Horner, Shari, *The Discourse of Enclosure: Representing Women in Old English Literature* (Albany, NY, SUNY Press, 2001).
A study that includes chapters on the female saints in Ælfric's Lives and on their influence on Christina of Markyate.

Jenkins, Jacqueline and Katharine J. Lewis, eds, *St Katherine of Alexandria: Texts and Contexts in Western Medieval Europe* (Turnhout, Brepols, 2003).
A collection of essays that examines the literary, devotional and visual evidence of the cult of St Katherine in a variety of European countries.

Johnson, Ian, 'Tales of a True Translator: Medieval Literary Theory, Anecdote and Autobiography in Osbern Bokenham's *Legendys of Hooly Wummen*', in *The Medieval Translator 4*, ed. Roger Ellis and Ruth Evans (Binghamton, NY, Medieval and Renaissance Texts and Studies, 1994), 104–24.
A study of Bokenham's utilization of medieval theories of authorship and authority.

Lees, Clare A., *Tradition and Belief: Religious Writing in Late Anglo-Saxon England* (Minneapolis, University of Minnesota Press, 1999).
A ground-breaking study of Old English religious texts, analysed in terms of the culture that produced them, that includes a key chapter on Ælfric and the women saints.

Lees, Clare A. and Gillian R. Overing, *Double Agents: Women and Clerical Culture in Anglo-Saxon England* (Philadelphia, University of Pennsylvania Press, 2001).
A key account of women and agency in the Anglo-Saxon period, focusing on historical as well as literary texts, which includes a chapter on gender and hagiography that speculates about how women readers might have responded to the Old English saints' lives.

MacBain, William, 'Anglo-Norman Women Hagiographers', in *Anglo-Norman Anniversary Essays*, ed. Ian Short (London, Anglo-Norman Text Society, 1993), 235–50.
A study of the three Anglo-Norman saints' lives by women alongside Marie de France's St Patrick's Purgatory, *that suggests that the life of Edward the Confessor was also by Clemence of Barking.*

Price, Paul, 'Trumping Chaucer: Osbern Bokenham's *Katherine*', *Chaucer Review* 36 (2001), 158–83.
An examination of the innovations in Bokenham's treatment of the legend of St Katherine of Alexandria, explained in terms of the work's literary and historical context.

Robertson, Duncan, *The Medieval Saints' Lives: Spiritual Renewal and Old French Literature* (Lexington, French Forum, 1995).
A detailed study of French hagiography that includes a chapter on the passions of the martyrs in which Clemence of Barking is discussed.

Robertson, Duncan, 'Writing in the Textual Community: Clemence of Barking's Life of St Catherine', *French Forum* 21 (1996), 5–28.
An analysis of Clemence of Barking's Life *that pays particular attention to matters of intertextuality (both other saints' lives and romances) and to the literary and linguistic community for which it was produced.*

Rossi-Reder, Andrea, 'Embodying Christ, Embodying Nation: Ælfric's Accounts of Saints Agatha and Lucy', in *Sex and Sexuality in Anglo-Saxon England: Essays*

in *Memory of Daniel Gillmore Calder*, ed. Carol Braun Pasternack and Lisa M. C. Weston (Tempe, Ariz., Arizona Center for Medieval and Renaissance Studies, 2004), 183–202.
An essay that applies postcolonialist and gender theory to two of Ælfric's lives of women saints, interpreting them in the context of the Danish attacks and Ælfric's nationalism.

Warren, Nancy Bradley, *Spiritual Economies: Female Monasticism in Later Medieval England* (Philadelphia, University of Pennsylvania Press, 2001).
An excellent study of the interaction of medieval politics and religion that includes strong historicist analyses of Osbern Bokenham and The Book of Margery Kempe.

Winstead, Karen A., *Virgin Martyrs: Legends of Sainthood in Late Medieval England* (Ithaca, NY, Cornell University Press, 1997).
An important survey of the subgenre that includes discussion of Osbern Bokenham.

Wogan-Browne, Jocelyn, ' "Clerc u lai, muïne u dame": Women and Anglo-Norman Hagiography in the Twelfth and Thirteenth Centuries', in *Women and Literature in Britain, 1150–1500*, ed. Carol M. Meale (Cambridge, Cambridge University Press, 1993), 61–85.
A study of the three Anglo-Norman saints' lives known to have been written by women, which places them within the context of Anglo-Norman verse hagiography and their social and cultural context, focusing on female monasticism.

Wogan-Browne, Jocelyn, 'Wreaths of Thyme: The Female Translator in Anglo-Norman Hagiography', in *The Medieval Translator 4*, ed. Roger Ellis and Ruth Evans (Binghamton, NY, Medieval and Renaissance Texts and Studies, 1994), 46–65.
A detailed examination of the narrative strategies developed by the Anglo-Norman women hagiographers to justify their adoption of the role of translator.

Wogan-Browne, Jocelyn, *Saints' Lives and Women's Literary Culture, c.1150–1300: Virginity and its Authorizations* (Oxford, Oxford University Press, 2001).
An expansive study of virginity, focusing on vernacular (and especially Anglo-Norman) saints' lives as exemplary biographies for women, which addresses issues of female literacy and authority.

4   Julian of Norwich (1342/3–after 1416)

Editions and translations

Baker, Denise, N., ed., *Julian of Norwich: Showings: Authoritative Text, Contexts, Criticism* (New York, W. W. Norton, 2005).
A Norton teaching edition of the Paris manuscript of the Revelation *with contextual historical, theological and devotional material, and reprints of some classic critical essays.*

Beer, Frances, ed., *Julian of Norwich's Revelations of Divine Love: The Shorter Version, ed. from BL Add. MS 37790* (Heidelburg, Carl Winter, 1978).

A good scholarly edition, with an introduction focusing on the textual history and relationship between the two versions of Julian's work and offering a brief discussion of her mysticism.

Colledge, Edmund and James Walsh, eds, *A Book of Showings to the Anchoress Julian of Norwich*, 2 parts (Toronto, Pontifical Institute of Mediæval Studies, 1978).

An edition of both versions of Julian of Norwich's writings, with detailed descriptions of the surviving witnesses, a contextual and theological introduction (locating possible sources for Julian's ideas), notes and glossary. This edition makes a strong case that Julian was highly educated. The text of the Revelation *is based on the Paris manuscript, collated with the other manuscripts and the early modern printed text.*

Colledge, Edmund and James Walsh, trans., *Julian of Norwich: Showings* (New York, Paulist Press, 1978).

A translation of Colledge and Walsh's critical edition of the Vision *and the* Revelation, *with a preface by Jean Leclerq, and an introduction by the editors offering a commentary on Julian's teaching and spirituality.*

Crampton, Georgia Ronan, ed., *The Shewings of Julian of Norwich* (Kalamazoo, Mich., Medieval Institute Publications, 1993).

A TEAMS student edition of the Revelation *based on the Sloane manuscript, with an introduction, good bibliography, textual notes and glossary. Available on-line at <http://www.lib.rochester.edu/camelot/TEAMS/Crampton.htm> [accessed 8 June 2006].*

Glasscoe, Marion, ed., *Julian of Norwich: A Revelation of Love* (Exeter, University of Exeter Press, 1976).

A good scholarly edition of the Revelation *based on the Sloane manuscript, with an introduction (arguing that Julian of Norwich dictated her showings to a secretary), glossary and bibliography.*

Holloway, Julia Bolton, trans., *Julian of Norwich: Showing of Love* (London, Darton, Longman & Todd, 2003).

A composite translation based on the Sloane manuscript of the Revelation, *collated with the Paris and Westminster manuscripts, and with the manuscript of the* Vision. *The prefatory accounts of Julian's life and history, and of the textual history of her work, often go against accepted opinion.*

Reynolds, Sister Anna Maria and Julia Bolton Holloway, eds and trans., *Julian of Norwich: Showing of Love* (Florence, SISMEL, 2001).

An edition of the Westminster, Paris and Sloane manuscripts of the Revelation *and the Additional manuscript of the* Vision *with facing-page translation, with a speculative commentary of textual history.*

Spearing, Elizabeth, *Julian of Norwich: Revelations of Divine Love*, with introduction and notes by A. C. Spearing (Harmondsworth, Penguin, 1998).

An accessible and widely available translation of the Vision *and of the* Revelation *(based on the Sloane text), with an introduction and notes.*

Watson, Nicholas and Jacqueline Jenkins, eds, *The Writings of Julian of Norwich: A Vision Showed to a Devout Woman and A Revelation of Love* (Turnhout, Brepols, 2006).
An extremely important new edition of both of Julian of Norwich's works, with a very full and reflective introduction, useful editorial supporting material and notes, appendices of medieval and Early Modern records and responses to Julian's writing, and an up-to-date bibliography (by Amy Appleford). The edition of the Revelation *is synthetic and includes an analytic edition of the* Vision *printed beneath the text.*

Wolters, Clifton, trans., *Julian of Norwich: Revelations of Divine Love* (Harmondsworth, Penguin, 1966).
A free translation of the Revelation *based on the Sloane text, now superseded by Salter's translation.*

Secondary reading

Abbott, Christopher, *Julian of Norwich: Autobiography and Theology* (Cambridge, D. S. Brewer, 1999).
A study of the Revelation *that argues for a strong connection between the autobiographical and personal aspects of Julian's work and her religious teaching.*

Aers, David and Lynn Staley, *Powers of the Holy: Religion, Politics, and Gender in Late Medieval English Culture* (University Park, Pennsylvania State University Press, 1996).
An innovative historicist study that includes two complementary chapters on Julian, one by David Aers that challenges Elizabeth Robertson's reading of Julian's feminine affective devotion, and one by Lynn Staley on Julian's uneasy relationship with ecclesiastical authority.

Baker, Denise Nowakowski, *Julian of Norwich's 'Showings': From Vision to Book* (Princeton, Princeton University Press, 1994).
An exploration of Julian of Norwich's development from visionary to theologian in the two versions of her work that stresses her debts to late medieval religious culture and thought and her achievements as a writer.

Barratt, Alexandra, ' "In the Lowest Part of Our Need": Julian and Medieval Gynecological Writing', in *Julian of Norwich: A Book of Essays*, ed. Sandra J. McEntire (New York, Garland, 1998), 239–56.
A reading of Julian's Revelation *and her treatment of the motherhood of God alongside a medieval medical text,* The Knowing of Women's Kind.

Bauerschmidt, Frederick Christian, *Julian of Norwich and the Mystical Body Politic of Christ* (Notre Dame, Ind., Notre Dame University Press, 1999).
An important study that argues against the separation of politics and theology and understands Julian's writing partially in terms of late medieval social theory.

Coiner, Nancy, 'The "Homely" and the Heimliche: The Hidden, Doubled Self in Julian of Norwich's *Showings*', *Exemplaria* 5 (1993), 305–23.

A psychoanalytical reading of Julian's showings.

Cré, Marleen, 'Women in the Charterhouse? Julian of Norwich's *Revelations of Divine Love* and Marguerite Porete's *Mirror of Simple Souls* in British Library, MS Additional 37790', in *Writing Religious Women: Female Spiritual and Textual Practices in Late Medieval England*, ed. Denis Renevey and Christiana Whitehead (Cardiff, University of Wales Press, 2000), 43–62.
An examination of Julian of Norwich's Vision in its manuscript context, paying particular attention to the Carthusian milieu from which it, and Marguerite Porete's text which appears alongside it, emerged.

Deighton, Alan, 'Julian of Norwich's Knowledge of the Life of St John of Beverley', *Notes and Queries* 40 (December 1993), 440–3.
A notice identifying an apocryphal life of St John of Beverley that may, through a lost common source, have indirectly influenced Julian of Norwich's account of that saint.

Jantzen, Grace M., *Julian of Norwich: Mystic and Theologian* (London, SPCK, 1987).
A detailed reading of Julian's work that both contextualizes it in terms of medieval devotional and mystical writing and connects it to issues of contemporary (late twentieth-century) spirituality.

Jantzen, Grace M., *Power, Gender, and Christian Mysticism* (Cambridge, Cambridge University Press, 1995).
An accessible discussion of Julian's spiritual teaching and perception of herself as a woman visionary.

Kempster, Hugh, 'A Question of Audience: The Westminster Text and Fifteenth-Century Reception of Julian of Norwich', in *Julian of Norwich: A Book of Essays*, ed. Sandra J. McEntire (New York, Garland, 1998), 257–89.
A detailed study of an early anthology of extracts from Julian of Norwich's Revelation, arguing for a potential lay audience.

Krantz, M. Diane F., *The Life and Text of Julian of Norwich: The Poetics of Enclosure* (New York, Peter Lang, 1997).
A literary-critical approach to the Revelation, drawing on a range of theoretical positions, including psychoanalysis.

Lochrie, Karma, *Heterosyncracies: Female Sexuality When Normal Wasn't* (Minneapolis, University of Minnesota Press, 2005).
An important historical interrogation of the ideas of 'heterosexuality' and sexual normativity that includes a discussion of Julian of Norwich alongside Chaucer's Prioress.

McAvoy, Liz Herbert, *Authority and the Female Body in the Writings of Julian of Norwich and Margery Kempe* (Cambridge, D. S. Brewer, 2004).
A strong comparative feminist approach to the work of Julian of Norwich and Margery Kempe.

McEntire, Sandra J., ed., *Julian of Norwich: A Book of Essays* (New York, Garland, 1998).

A useful, if somewhat uneven, anthology of critical essays.

McInerney, Maud Burnett, ' "In the Meydens Womb": Julian of Norwich and the Poetics of Enclosure', in *Medieval Mothering*, ed. John Carmi Parsons and Bonnie Wheeler (New York, Garland, 1996), 157–82.
A useful essay that establishes a connection between Julian's anchoritic spirituality and her metaphor of God as mother, focusing on her imagery of gestation and labour.

McNamer, Sarah, 'The Exploratory Image: God as Mother in Julian of Norwich's Revelations of Divine Love', Mystics Quarterly 15 (1989), 21–8.
A good analysis of the connections between the universalism of Julian of Norwich's writings and her representations of God's immanence and a maternal Jesus.

Riddy, Felicity ' "Women Talking about the Things of God": A Late Medieval Sub-Culture', in *Women and Literature in Britain, 1150–1500*, ed. Carol M. Meale (Cambridge, Cambridge University Press, 1993), 104–27.
A lively and original consideration of the intersection of talking, spiritual communities, literary culture and female readership, with a focus on Julian of Norwich.

Riddy, Felicity, 'Julian of Norwich and Self-Textualization', in *Editing Women*, ed. Ann M. Hutchison (Cardiff, University of Wales Press, 1998), 101–24.
A key argument, based on manuscript analysis, supporting the possibility that Julian of Norwich may have used a secretary, and examining the scribal 'voice' in the Sloane manuscript.

Robertson, Elizabeth, 'Medieval Medical Views of Women and Female Spirituality in the *Ancrene Wisse* and Julian of Norwich's *Showings*', in *Feminist Approaches to the Body in Medieval Literature*, ed. Linda Lomperis and Sarah Stanbury (Philadelphia, University of Pennsylvania Press, 1993), 142–67.
A consideration of the impact of medical ideology on late medieval religious texts that argues that Julian celebrates the feminine in her depiction of Christ as mother.

Staley Johnson, Lynn, 'The Trope of the Scribe and the Question of Literary Authority in the Works of Julian of Norwich and Margery Kempe', *Speculum* 66 (1991), 820–38.
A thought-provoking comparative analysis of the 'fiction' of the scribe in the writings of Julian of Norwich and Margery Kempe and of the ways in which these women represent themselves as authors and writers.

Ward, Benedicta, 'Julian the Solitary', in *Julian Reconsidered*, ed. Kenneth Leech and Benedicta Ward (Oxford, SLG Press, 1988), 11–35.
An important study that makes a strong and considered case that Julian of Norwich was a laywoman and widow.

Watson, Nicholas, 'The Composition of Julian of Norwich's *Revelation of Love*', *Speculum* 68 (1993), 637–83.
A ground-breaking article that posits new and later dates for Julian of Norwich's writing, and locates it within contemporary religious and political debates about women and the laity.

Watson, Nicholas, ' "Yf Wommen be Double Naturelly": Remaking "Woman" in Julian of Norwich's *Revelation of Love*', *Exemplaria* 8 (1996), 1–34.
An examination of some of the ways in which Julian of Norwich engages with antifeminist medieval notions of woman in her writing.

Watson, Nicholas, 'Visions of Inclusion: Universal Salvation and Vernacular Theology in Pre-Reformation England', *Journal of Medieval and Early Modern Studies* 27 (1997), 145–87.
A study of universalism in late medieval English writing, with a good discussion of the theology of Julian of Norwich.

Watson, Nicholas, 'Julian of Norwich', in *The Cambridge Companion to Medieval Women's Writing*, ed. Carolyn Dinshaw and David Wallace (Cambridge, Cambridge University Press, 2003), 210–21.
An accessible short introduction to Julian of Norwich's writings.

5   Margery Kempe (*c.*1373–after 1439)

Editions and translations

McAvoy, Liz Herbert, trans., *The Book of Margery Kempe: An Abridged Translation* (Cambridge, D. S. Brewer, 2003).
A good choice of selections with a useful introduction and interpretative essay.

Meech, Sanford Brown and Hope Emily Allen, eds, *The Book of Margery Kempe*, Early English Text Society original series 212 (Oxford, Oxford University Press, 1940).
The standard edition with an excellent introduction, notes and appendices.

Staley, Lynn, ed., *The Book of Margery Kempe* (Kalamazoo, Mich., Medieval Institute Publications, 1996).
A TEAMS student edition of The Book, *with an informative introduction, good bibliography, textual notes and glossary. Available on-line at <http://www.lib.rochester.edu/camelot/TEAMS/kempint.htm> [accessed 5 October 2006].*

Staley, Lynn, trans. and ed., *The Book of Margery Kempe*, Norton Critical Edition (New York and London, W. W. Norton & Co., 2001).
An excellent translation with a selection of contextual material and key critical essays.

Windeatt, Barry, trans., *The Book of Margery Kempe* (Harmondsworth, Penguin, 1985).
An accessible and widely used translation with a good introduction.

Windeatt, Barry, ed., *The Book of Margery Kempe* (Harlow, Longman, 2000).
A useful edition with on-page glossing and glossary.

Secondary reading

Arnold, John H., 'Margery's Trials: Heresy, Lollardy and Dissent', in *A Companion to* The Book of Margery Kempe, ed. John H. Arnold and Katherine J. Lewis (Cambridge: D. S. Brewer, 2004), 75–93.

A sensible reassessment of the extent to which Margery Kempe's piety might be seen as dissenting.

Arnold, John H. and Katherine J. Lewis, eds, *A Companion to* The Book of Margery Kempe (Cambridge: D. S. Brewer, 2004).
A recent collection of essays on Margery Kempe, largely from the perspective of historians.

Atkinson, Clarissa W., *Mystic and Pilgrim: The Book and the World of Margery Kempe* (Ithaca, Cornell, 1983).
The first book-length study of The Book of Margery Kempe. *Atkinson set out to complete the project of historical and religious contextualization originally undertaken by Hope Emily Allen.*

Beckwith, Sarah, 'A Very Material Mysticism: The Medieval Mysticism of Margery Kempe', in *Medieval Literature: Criticism, Ideology and History*, ed. David Aers (Brighton, Harvester, 1986), 34–57.
A key theoretically informed study concerned with ideology and mysticism in relation to women. It offers some extremely perceptive and provocative insights about Margery Kempe.

Beckwith, Sarah, 'Problems of Authority in Late Medieval English Mysticism: Language, Agency and Authority in *The Book of Margery Kempe*', *Exemplaria* 4 (1992), 171–99.
An important essay addressing the question of Margery Kempe's agency.

Delany, Sheila, 'Sexual Economics, Chaucer's *Wife of Bath* and *The Book of Margery Kempe*', in *Feminist Readings in Middle English Literature*, ed. Ruth Evans and Lesley Johnson (London, Routledge, 1994), 72–87.
A reading of The Book of Margery Kempe *alongside the* Wife of Bath, *informed by feminist and Marxist theory.*

Dinshaw, Carolyn, *Getting Medieval: Sexualities and Communities, Pre- and Post-modern* (Durham, NC, Duke University Press, 1999).
A highly innovative and compelling queer approach to history, literature and theory. It includes readings of Margery Kempe's white clothes (seen as a form of cross-dressing) and of her 'queer' spiritual family.

Dinshaw, Carolyn, 'Margery Kempe', in *The Cambridge Companion to Medieval Women's Writing*, ed. Carolyn Dinshaw and David Wallace (Cambridge, Cambridge University Press, 2003), 222–39.
A subtle study of time and history in relation to The Book of Margery Kempe *arguing that Kempe was both of her time and out of it.*

Evans, Ruth, 'The Book of Margery Kempe', in *A Companion to Medieval English Literature and Culture, c.1350–c.1500*, ed. Peter Brown (Oxford, Blackwell, 2007), 507–21.
An innovative and challenging study that proposes a new materialist approach to The Book *and to Margery Kempe's subjectivity, which accepts that writing is collaborative and authorship constructed historically.*

Foster, Allyson, 'A Shorte Treatyse of Contemplacyon: The Book of Margery Kempe', in *A Companion*, ed. Arnold and Lewis, 95–112.
A timely reassessment of the Early Modern printed extracts of The Book *and their readership.*

Gibson, Gail McMurray, *The Theater of Devotion: East Anglian Drama and Society in the Late Middle Ages* (Chicago, University of Chicago Press, 1989).
A fascinating study that includes an interesting chapter on 'Saint Margery'.

Goodman, Anthony, *Margery Kempe and her World* (London, Longman, 2002).
An excellent extended reading that places Margery Kempe in her historical context.

Harding, Wendy, 'Body into Text: The Book of Margery Kempe', in *Feminist Approaches to the Body in Medieval Literature*, ed. Linda Lomperis and Sarah Stanbury (Philadelphia, University of Pennsylvania Press, 1993), 168–87.
A useful study focusing on Margery Kempe's maternal body.

Hirsch, John C., 'Author and Scribe in The Book of Margery Kempe', *Medium Aevum* 44 (1975), 145–50.
A provocative essay that argues for the importance of the scribe in the composition of The Book of Margery Kempe.

Hirsch, John C., *The Revelations of Margery Kempe: Paramystical Practices in Late Medieval England*, Medieval and Renaissance Authors 10 (Leiden, E. J. Brill, 1989).
An account of Margery Kempe's 'paramystical' piety, seen as located on the boundaries of mysticism and affective devotion. Comparisons are drawn with medieval texts and modern charismatic churches.

Jenkins, Jacqueline, 'Reading and The Book of Margery Kempe', in *A Companion*, ed. Arnold and Lewis, 113–28.
An intelligent analysis of Margery Kempe's engagement with literary and literate culture.

Johnson, Lynn Staley, 'The Trope of the Scribe and the Question of Literary Authority in the Works of Julian of Norwich and Margery Kempe', *Speculum* 66 (1991), 820–38.
An influential essay that argues that the scribe is a literary trope functioning to provide authority in The Book of Margery Kempe.

Lavezzo, Kathy, 'Sobs and Sighs between Women: The Homoerotics of Compassion', in *Premodern Sexualities*, ed. Louise Fradenburg and Carla Freccero (New York, Routledge, 1996), 175–98.
A queer reading of Margery Kempe's piety.

Lewis, Katherine J., *The Cult of St Katherine of Alexandria in Late Medieval England* (Woodbridge, Suffolk, Boydell Press, 2000).
A book that includes a fascinating analysis of St Katherine's influence on Margery Kempe.

Lewis, Katherine J., 'Margery Kempe and Saint Making in Later Medieval England', in *A Companion*, ed. Arnold and Lewis, 195–215.
A thoughtful reassessment of The Book of Margery Kempe *in terms of popular cults of the saints.*

Lochrie, Karma, *Margery Kempe and Translations of the Flesh* (Philadelphia, University of Pennsylvania Press, 1991).
A crucially important feminist reading of The Book of Margery Kempe, *focusing on ideas of the body and the flesh.*

McAvoy, Liz Herbert, *Authority and the Female Body in the Writings of Julian of Norwich and Margery Kempe* (Cambridge, D. S. Brewer, 2004).
A strong comparative feminist approach to the work of Julian of Norwich and Margery Kempe.

McEntire, Sandra J., ed. *Margery Kempe: A Book of Essays* (New York, Garland, 1992).
An invaluable collection of essays, mainly from a literary perspective.

Mueller, Janel M., 'Autobiography of a New "Creatur": Female Spirituality, Selfhood, and Authorship in *The Book of Margery Kempe*', *New York Literary Forum* 12–13 (1984), 63–75.
A relatively early feminist essay concerned with Margery Kempe's agency and authority.

Parker, Kate, 'Lynn and the Making of a Mystic', in *A Companion*, ed. Arnold and Lewis, 55–73.
An excellent account of the geography, economy, society and politics of Kempe's Lynn.

Rees Jones, Sarah, ' "A Peler of Holy Cherch": Margery Kempe and the Bishops', in *Medieval Women: Texts and Contexts in Late Medieval Britain: Essays for Felicity Riddy*, ed. Jocelyn Wogan-Browne, Rosalynn Voaden, Arlyn Diamond, Ann Hutchison, Carol M. Meale and Lesley Johnson (Turnhout, Brepols, 2000), 377–91.
An innovative, provocative piece that argues that the real subject of The Book of Margery Kempe *is the Church, and that the text was produced by the clergy for the clergy.*

Renevey, Denis, 'Margery's Performing Body: the Translation of Late Medieval Discursive Religious Practices', in *Writing Religious Women: Female Spiritual and Textual Practices in Late Medieval England* (Cardiff, University of Wales Press, 2000), 197–216.
A useful chapter focusing in particular on the connection between Margery Kempe's devotions and anchoritic piety.

Riddy, Felicity, 'Text and Self in *The Book of Margery Kempe*', in *Voices in Dialogue: Reading Women in the Middle Ages*, ed. Linda Olson and Kathryn Kerby-Fulton (Notre Dame, Ind., University of Notre Dame Press, 2005), 435–53.
A vigorous response to Nicholas Watson's piece on the composition of The Book of Margery Kempe *that disputes the contention that it is possible to identify distinct voices within the text.*

Riddy, Felicity and Nicholas Watson, 'Afterwords', in *Voices in Dialogue*, ed. Olson and Kerby-Fulton, 454–7.
A lively exchange between Riddy and Watson in which they defend their respective approaches in their essays in the volume, and develop further their critiques of each other's work.

Ross, Robert C., 'Oral Life, Written Text: The Genesis of *The Book of Margery Kempe*', *Yearbook of English Studies* 22 (1992), 226–37.
An innovative approach to The Book *that argues that the text should be understood in terms of oral history.*

Spearing, A. C., 'Margery Kempe', in *A Companion to Middle English Prose*, ed. A. S. G. Edwards (Cambridge, D. S. Brewer, 2004), 83–97.
A brief introduction to The Book of Margery Kempe *that includes a contentious argument for Robert Spryngolde's authorship, but makes a strong case for the clerical textuality of* The Book, *and makes valid criticisms of the assumption that it communicates almost unmediated the authentic voice of Margery Kempe.*

Staley, Lynn, *Margery Kempe's Dissenting Fictions* (University Park, Pennsylvania State University Press, 1994).
An extremely important book-length historically and politically informed literary study.

Summit, Jennifer, *Lost Property: The Woman Writer and English Literary History, 1380–1589* (Chicago, University of Chicago Press, 2000).
An important study of women's literary history in the medieval and Early Modern periods. Chapter 3 includes a discussion of Pepwell's edition of extracts of The Book of Margery Kempe *and the text's early sixteenth-century reception.*

Warren, Nancy Bradley, *Spiritual Economies: Female Monasticism in Later Medieval England* (Philadelphia, University of Pennsylvania Press, 2001).
An excellent study of the interaction of medieval politics and religion that includes strong historicist analyses of Osbern Bokenham and The Book of Margery Kempe.

Watson, Nicholas, 'The Making of *The Book of Margery Kempe*', in *Voices in Dialogue*, ed. Olson and Kerby-Fulton, 395–434.
A much needed reassessment of Margery Kempe's role in the writing of her book, and of her theology.

Watt, Diane, *Secretaries of God: Women Prophets in Late Medieval and Early Modern England* (Cambridge, D. S. Brewer, 1997).
A study of the female prophetic tradition that includes a chapter on Margery Kempe, examining her role in this context.

Watt, Diane, 'Critics, Communities and Compassionate Criticism: Learning from *The Book of Margery Kempe*', in *Maistresse of my Wit: Medieval Women, Modern Scholarship*, ed. Louise D'Arcens and Juanita Ruys (Turnhout, Brepols, 2004), 191–210.
A reflection on what The Book of Margery Kempe *can teach the contemporary scholar about the production of meaning and the responsibilities of interpretation.*

Watt, Diane, 'Political Prophecy in *The Book of Margery Kempe*', in *A Companion*, ed. Arnold and Lewis, 145–60.
A study of Margery Kempe's self-representation as a political prophet in the tradition of St Bridget of Sweden.

Watt, Diane, 'Margery Kempe's Overseas Pilgrimages', in *A Place to Believe In: Locating Medieval Landscapes*, ed. Clare A. Lees and Gillian R. Overing (University Park, Penn State University Press, 2006), 170–87.
An examination of the representation of foreign landscapes in The Book of Margery Kempe, *and of the ways in which the environment is depicted as impacting on Kempe's piety and religious certainty.*

Wilson, Janet, 'Communities of Dissent: The Secular and Ecclesiastical Communities of Margery Kempe's *Book*', in *Medieval Women in their Communities*, ed. Diane Watt (Cardiff, University of Wales Press, 1997), 155–85.
An essay locating Margery Kempe within the religious communities of East Anglia.

6   The Paston Letters (1440–1489)

Editions and translations

Barber, Richard, ed., *The Pastons: A Family in the Wars of the Roses* (Woodbridge, Suffolk, Boydell Press, 1993).
A good selection of letters in modern spelling, with contextual material.

Davis, Norman, ed., *The Paston Letters and Papers of the Fifteenth Century*, 2 vols (Oxford, Clarendon Press, 1971, 1976).
The standard edition. Volume 1 is available online at <http://etext.lib.virginia.edu/toc/modeng/public/PasLett.html> [accessed on 19 January 2007].

Davis, Norman, ed., *The Paston Letters: A Selection in Modern Spelling* (Oxford, Oxford University Press, 1983).
A useful sample of the letters.

Gairdner, John, ed., *The Paston Letters, A.D. 1422–1509*, 6 vols (London, Chatto & Windus, 1904).
An incomplete edition, with some errors in dating and attribution.

Virgoe, Roger, ed., *Private Life in the Fifteenth Century: Illustrated Letters of the Paston Family* (London, Macmillan, 1989).
A full-colour illustrated edition of selected letters in translation with useful contextual material. For the general reader.

Watt, Diane, ed. and trans., *The Paston Women: Selected Letters* (Cambridge, D. S. Brewer, 2004).
An edition of a large selection of letters by the Paston women, translated into modern English, with a useful introduction and interpretative essay.

Secondary reading

Bennett, H. S., *The Pastons and their England*, 2nd edn (Cambridge, Cambridge University Press, 1932).
A dated but still useful historical account of the Pastons in the fifteenth century. It includes key chapters on marriage, love, women's life, parents and children, houses and furniture, education and books, letters and letter-writing, and religion.

Bosse, Roberta Bux, 'Female Sexual Behavior in the Late Middle Ages: Ideal and Actual', *Fifteenth-Century Studies* 10 (1984), 15–37.
An article looking at attitudes to female sexuality in Holy Maidenhood, The Book of the Knight of La Tour Landry, the letters of Margaret Paston and The Book of Margery Kempe.

Castor, Helen, *Blood and Roses: The Paston Family in the Fifteenth Century* (London, Faber & Faber, 2004).
A readable yet highly informed account of the Paston family and their political and social struggles by a respected historian.

Dalrymple, Roger, 'Reaction, Consolation and Redress in the Letters of the Paston Women', in *Early Modern Women's Letter Writing, 1450–1700*, ed. James Daybell (Basingstoke, Palgrave, 2001), 16–28.
A chapter concentrating on the letters of Agnes and Margaret Paston. It argues that, in addition to serving practical concerns, they are written to convey news, offer consolation or correct false report.

Davis, Norman, 'That Language of the Pastons', *Proceedings of the British Academy* 40 (1955), 119–44.
A study of language and style.

Davis, Norman, 'The *Litera Troili* and English Letters', *Review of English Studies*, n.s. 16 (1965), 233–44.
A study examining the Paston letters in the light of epistolary conventions.

Davis, Norman, 'Style and Stereotype in Early English Letters', *Leeds Studies in English*, n.s. 1 (1967), 7–17.
A study looking at the stylistic range of the Paston letters, from the proverbial to the literary.

Dockray, Keith, 'Why did Fifteenth-Century English Gentry Marry? The Pastons, Plumptons and Stonors Reconsidered', in *Gentry and Lesser Nobility in Late Medieval Europe*, ed. Michael Jones (Gloucester, Alan Sutton, 1986), 61–80.
An article reviewing the evidence of motivations behind late medieval marriages and arguing that love could be an important factor.

Ferrante, Joan M., *To the Glory of her Sex: Women's Roles in the Composition of Medieval Texts* (Bloomington, Indiana University Press, 1997).
An excellent study, which includes a chapter on women in medieval correspondence.

Finke, Laurie A., *Women's Writing in English: Medieval England* (London, Longman, 1999).
A broad survey of medieval women's writing that includes an excellent account of the epistolary genre, in addition to a section devoted to the Paston women, and dealing with questions of literacy, marriage, children, business, litigation, and style and storytelling.

Gies, Frances and Josephine Gies, *A Medieval Family: The Pastons of Fifteenth-Century England* (New York, Harper Collins, 1998).
A chronological account of the family history. It is illustrated and intended for the general reader.

Harding, Wendy, 'Medieval Women's Unwritten Discourse on Motherhood: A Reading of Two Fifteenth-Century Texts', *Women's Studies* 21 (1992), 197–209.
A comparison of the treatment of the topics of pregnancy and giving birth in the Paston letters (especially those by Margaret Paston) and The Book of Margery Kempe.

Haskell, Ann S., 'The Paston Women on Marriage in Fifteenth-Century England', *Viator* 4 (1973), 459–71.
An article concentrating on the female perspective on marriage in the letters of the Paston women.

Knowles, David, 'The Religion of the Pastons', *Downside Review* 42 (1924), 143–63.
An old-fashioned but interesting account.

Krug, Rebecca, *Reading Families: Women's Literate Practice in Late Medieval England* (Ithaca, NY, Cornell University Press, 2002).
A book-length study examining the interaction between female literate practices, family relationships and social circumstances. It focuses on Margaret Paston, Lady Margaret Beaufort, the Norwich Lollards and the Bridgettine nuns of Syon Abbey.

Maddern, Philippa, 'Honour among the Pastons: Gender and Integrity in Fifteenth-Century English Provincial Society', *Journal of Medieval History* 14 (1988), 357–71.
A key study arguing that the Paston letters provide evidence that definitions of 'honour', in relation to battle, the law courts, the protection of family and friends, and personal integrity were extended to women.

O'Mara, V. A., 'Female Scribal Ability and Scribal Activity in Late Medieval England: The Evidence?' *Leeds Studies in English* 27 (1996), 87–130.
A much needed study that, unfortunately, merely reiterates Norman Davis's assumptions and arguments in relation to the evidence of women's ability to write in the Paston letters.

Richardson, Malcolm, 'Women, Commerce, and Rhetoric in Medieval England', in *Listening to their Voices: The Rhetorical Activities of Historical Women*, ed. Molly Meijer Wertheimer (Columbia, SC, University of South Carolina Press, 1997), 133–49.

A discussion of the style of business letters by a selection of medieval women, including the Pastons, Stonors and Plumptons.

Richmond, Colin, 'The Pastons Revisited: Marriage and Family in Fifteenth-Century England', *Bulletin of the Institute of Historical Research* 58 (1985), 25–36.
A self-explanatory account of love, negotiated alliances, engagements and marriage.

Richmond, Colin, *The Paston Family in the Fifteenth Century: The First Phase* (Cambridge, Cambridge University Press, 1990).
The first volume in a trilogy that as whole comprises an exhaustive but fascinating history of the family. Chapter 4, entitled 'Three Marriages', is of particular interest.

Richmond, Colin, *The Paston Family in the Fifteenth Century: Fastolf's Will* (Cambridge, Cambridge University Press, 1996).
The second volume in the trilogy. Chapter 6 on 'Money Matters' deals with Margaret's financial wrangles with her eldest son.

Richmond, Colin, *The Paston Family in the Fifteenth Century: Endings* (Manchester, Manchester University Press, 2000).
The last volume in the trilogy. Chapter 4 is devoted to Margaret Paston.

Richmond, Colin, 'Elizabeth Clere: Friend of the Pastons', in *Medieval Women: Texts and Contexts in Late Medieval Britain: Essays for Felicity Riddy*, ed. Jocelyn Wogan-Browne, Rosalynn Voaden, Arlyn Diamond, Ann Hutchison, Carol M. Meale and Lesley Johnson (Turnhout, Brepols, 2000), 251–73.
An article providing biographical information about Elizabeth Clere and addressing the topic of female friendships, which has been hitherto overlooked in Paston scholarship.

Rosenthal, Joel T., 'Looking for Grandmother: The Pastons and their Counterparts in Late Medieval England', in *Medieval Mothering*, ed. John Carmi Parsons and Bonnie Wheeler (New York, Garland, 1996), 259–77.
An article addressing the neglected question of relationships between grandmothers and grandchildren, concentrating on Agnes and Margaret Paston.

Rosenthal, Joel T., *Telling Tales: Sources and Narration in Late Medieval England* (University Park, Pennsylvania State University Press, 2003).
A study of narrativity in a range of historical sources. Chapter 3 is on Margaret Paston, and considers her productivity, the production, form (including the use of convention) and content of her letters, modes of delivery, and Margaret's networks and her will.

Stiller, Nancy, *Eve's Orphans: Mothers and Daughters in Medieval English Literature* (Westport, Conn., Greenwood Press, 1980).
A book which includes a short discussion of mother–daughter relationships in the Paston letters.

Tarvers, Josephine Koster, 'In a Woman's Hand? The Question of Medieval Women's Holograph Letters', *Post-Script* 13 (1996), 89–100.
A much needed reassessment of the literacy of the Paston women.

Watt, Diane, ' "No Writing for Writing's Sake": The Language of Service and Household Rhetoric in the Letters of the Paston Women', in *Dear Sister: Medieval Women and the Epistolary Genre*, ed. Karen Cherewatuk and Ulrike Wiethaus (Philadelphia, University of Pennsylvania Press, 1993), 122–38.
A reassessment of the Paston women, their literacy, education, epistolary style and role in the household, focusing particularly on Margaret Paston.

Whitaker, Elaine E., 'Reading the Paston Letters Medically', *English Language Notes* 31 (1993), 19–27.
An article that discusses the roles of women as healers in the Paston letters in the context of changing attitudes to medicine.

Woolf, Virginia, 'The Pastons and Chaucer', in *The Common Reader*, 1st series (London, Hogarth Press, 1925), 13–38.
A romanticized, early feminist response to the Paston letters.

Index

Adrian IV, Pope 21
Ælfric: *see Lives of Saints*
Æthelthryth (Audrey or Etheldreda)
 of Ely 6, 27, 64, 68, 72
Aesop 51–2
Alan of Lynn 129
St Albans Psalter 1, 16, 17, 19–23
 Alexis quire 22–6
 Chanson of St Alexis 22–3, 36
 'Discourse on Good and Evil' 23–6,
  34, 37–8
 letter of Pope Gregory 22, 23
 liturgical calendar 27, 30
 Psalms 24
 see also Life of Christina of Markyate
Alfred the Great 52
Alfwen, anchoress 37
Allen, Hope Emily 134
Ancrene Wisse ('Guide for Anchoresses')
 7, 119–20
Anselm of Canterbury 81
audiences and reception 2, 15, 159
authorship
 anonymous texts and 4, 5
 author-function and 8–10
 categories of 158
 collaboration and 13–16
 defining women authors 4–7
 divine 9–10
 gender and 14–15
 medieval notions of 2, 9–13
 modern idea of 9
 oral texts and 15
 originality criteria and 9
 single 159

see also secretaries, translation and
 compilation

Barratt, Alexandra 5
Barthes, Roland 8–9
Batt, Catherine 74
Beatrix, mother of Christina of Markyate
 27, 28–9, 37, 96
Beaufort, Joan, Lady Westmoreland 127
Beaufort, Lady Margaret 6–7
Bede, the Venerable 20, 27–31, 63, 102
Bloch, Howard J. 58
Boffey, Julia 5
Bokenham, Osbern 1, 10, 11
 see also Legends of Holy Women
Bonaventure, St 119
Book of Margery Kempe 17, 61
 as saint's life 124–9, 133
 audience for 16, 129–34
 authorship and secretaries of 7–8,
  12–14, 112, 117–24, 134–5
 the Church and 131
 divine authorship of 9–10
Bourchier, Isabel, Countess of Eu 83, 86,
 88
Breguswith, mother of St Hild 28, 29
Brews, Dame Elizabeth 13, 148, 151–3,
 154
Brews, Margery (Paston) 13, 147, 151–4
Brews, Sir Thomas 151–3, 154
Bridget of Sweden 108, 113, 125, 128
Bruckner, Matilda Tomaryn 49, 50
Burgess, Glyn S. 75, 79
Burgh, Thomas 82–3, 83–4
Burrow, John 120